Praise for
Teens on Trial

"Fascinating.
Here is a thought-provoking book
that will guide teens and adults to a deeper
understanding of our country and its laws.
Superior."—*KLIATT*

"Excellent."—*Booklist*

A "Book for the Teen Age"—New York Public Library System

A "Quick Pick" nominee—American Library
Association/YALSA

Teens on Trial

Young People Who Challenged the Law — and Changed Your Life

Thomas A. Jacobs, J.D.

free spirit
PUBLISHING®
Works for kids®

Library of Congress Cataloging-in-Publication Data

Jacobs, Thomas A.
    Teens on Trial : young people who challenged the law—and changed your life / by Thomas A. Jacobs.
        p. cm.
    Includes bibliographical references and index.
    Summary: Examines legal cases about privacy, visitation and divorce, search and seizure, dress code, drug testing, free speech in school newspapers and yearbooks, sexual harassment at work, transfer to adult court, and the death penalty.
    ISBN 1-57542-081-3 (pbk.)
    1. Teenagers—Legal status, laws, etc.—United States—Juvenile literature. 2. Minors—United States—Juvenile literature. 3. Children's rights—United States—Juvenile literature. [1. Teenagers—Legal status, laws, etc. 2. Children's rights. 3. Law.] I. Title.
KF479.Z9 J328 2000
346.7301'35—dc21   00-027347

At the time of this book's publication, all facts and figures cited are the most current available; all telephone numbers, addresses, and Web site URLs are accurate and active; all publications, organizations, Web sites, and other resources exist as described in this book; and all have been verified. The author and Free Spirit Publishing make no warranty or guarantee concerning the information and materials given out by organizations or content found at Web sites, and we are not responsible for any changes that occur after this book's publication. If you find an error or believe that a resource listed here is not as described, please contact Free Spirit Publishing. Parents, teachers, and other adults: We strongly urge you to monitor children's use of the Internet.

Edited by Cathy Broberg and Elizabeth Verdick
Cover and interior design by Percolator
Index prepared by Randl Ockey

10 9 8 7 6 5 4 3 2
Printed in the United States of America

Free Spirit Publishing Inc.
217 Fifth Avenue North, Suite 200
Minneapolis, MN 55401-1299
(612) 338-2068
help4kids@freespirit.com
www.freespirit.com

The following are registered trademarks of Free Spirit Publishing Inc.:

FREE SPIRIT®
FREE SPIRIT PUBLISHING®
SELF-HELP FOR TEENS®
SELF-HELP FOR KIDS®
WORKS FOR KIDS®
THE FREE SPIRITED CLASSROOM®

free spirit
PUBLISHING®
Works for kids®

*This book is dedicated to our nation's teenagers—
those profiled in this book who have already made a
difference, and those willing to take a stand on issues
of freedom and individual rights. It is also dedicated to
the next generation of teens, including Chase, Austin,
Taylor, Kali, Pauly, Cody, Netaya, Shasheena, Kylie,
Alexandra, Aaron, Ryan, Sandy, and Shelby.*

Acknowledgments

One of the challenges of writing this book was locating the people involved in the cases. Thanks to all who helped in the effort and particularly to those who granted me interviews. Your willingness to discuss the issues in your case was an invaluable contribution to this project.

Thanks also to Judy Galbraith, and her great staff at Free Spirit Publishing, for the opportunity to write this book. The experience, guidance, and wisdom of editors Cathy Broberg and Elizabeth Verdick are appreciated beyond these few words. Appreciation is also extended to Judge Maurice Portley, who somehow found time to review the manuscript and write a thoughtful opener for the book, and to Justice Ruth Bader Ginsburg for her words of inspiration on the cover. In the spirit of saving the best for last, I must also acknowledge my judicial assistant, Jami Taylor. Without her skills, personality, and patience, life at court would be very trying.

Contents

Preface

"All rise. This court is now in session," intoned my bailiff.

I thanked the participants, invited them to sit down, and settled into my chair.

This was my first juvenile court trial. I was nervous, in spite of four years of experience handling adult criminal trials, including death penalty cases. I was in a new courtroom, with new rules and lawyers. I knew that the *Gault*[1] case guaranteed constitutional due process protections for juveniles (meaning young people have the right to fair treatment under the law). I also was aware that the overarching philosophy of the juvenile court was "the best interests of the child." I wanted to make sure that I handled the matter properly—giving the State of Arizona fair opportunity to prove its case, while ensuring the teenage participant's rights. I wanted to try the case the right way, and only one time (meaning that if the case was appealed, my decision would be affirmed).

The teen girl in front of me was charged with possession of marijuana at school; the drugs had been found in her locker and her backpack. My first order of business was to determine whether the marijuana was lawfully seized. The State's lawyer and the teen's lawyer had filed their factual and legal research in writing. According to the teen's lawyer, the evidence (the marijuana) should be ruled as inadmissible because the search of the girl's belongings wasn't lawful. I had reviewed their cases and conducted my own research to make sure I knew the current law about school searches.

Fortunately, during my research, Judge Tom Jacobs had referred me to *New Jersey v. T. L. O.*,[2] the U.S. Supreme Court decision that clearly resolved the issue of the case I was currently hearing. The U.S. Supreme Court had ruled that school searches are legal if there's a reasonable suspicion of guilt. Suspicion existed in the case of the teen girl before me, because another student had reported her to school officials for drug possession. As a result, I ruled that: "Based on the

---

1 See *In re Gault* (1967) on pages 148–155.
2 See *New Jersey v. T. L. O.* (1985) on pages 63–70.

law from the U.S. Supreme Court, the evidence from the school search can be admitted, subject to proof that it is in fact marijuana."

The trial continued. The police officer who had seized the marijuana testified that the teen girl admitted to possessing the drugs after being read her juvenile Miranda warning (her rights). I found the teen guilty beyond a reasonable doubt. It was clear that she had broken the law and would need to face the consequences.

My goal for her was reform, not punishment, in the tradition of "the best interests of the child." The girl was placed on probation, which included a period of drug testing and counseling. Her mom, who sat through all the proceedings, later notified me that her daughter had completed her sentence, had graduated from high school, and was doing well in college.

My ruling was based on a case by a New Jersey teen and a trial judge who had blazed the legal trail to the U.S. Supreme Court years earlier. *Teens on Trial* is about legal trailblazers—young people who questioned the fairness of the courts, police, schools, and sometimes even their parents. Some cases, like *Gault,* proved that the juvenile justice system ignored due process—and eventually forced the system to reform. Others, like *New Jersey v. T. L. O.,* highlighted a problem (school searches) and convinced the courts to establish limits on schools in order to protect students.

As you read the cases in this book, whether from start to finish or for research purposes, think about:

- the courage it took the teens to see the unfairness of a system
- the courage to challenge the unfairness
- how the choices and behavior of these teens affected their futures and yours
- how these teens made a difference in our democracy

In spite of the old adage "Children should be seen and not heard," teens *can* and *do* make a difference. They continually ensure that the U.S. Constitution protects Americans of all ages.

Maurice Portley
Presiding Judge, Maricopa County Juvenile Court
Mesa, Arizona

Introduction

Do you remember the first time somebody told you that life isn't fair? Maybe you were shocked and didn't want to accept it as true. Fairness, after all, is something we've been taught to work for in life. Parents strive to treat all of their children equally, to not give one more than another. Schools promote the idea of fairness, to provide every student with an opportunity to succeed. And we learn that we should treat other people as we want to be treated ourselves—in other words, to be fair. So when we learn that life isn't fair, either through words or personal experiences, we're often very disappointed.

The good news is that our country's judicial system is designed to provide "justice for all." Justice means following the laws, setting things right, or correcting a wrong.

As a juvenile court judge for the past fifteen years, I've had the honor of working with thousands of teenagers and their families to bring about justice. Courts are called on to answer questions and resolve problems about all aspects of life, including crime, individual rights, and relationships at home, work, and school. This means going to court isn't limited to kids who get into trouble. Young people also come into the courtroom to challenge rules in their school, to file claims of sexual harassment, to participate in custody hearings, and more.

Through my experience with families in the court system, I've learned that many people think this part of the government is mysterious and confusing. That's unfortunate, because the law is for you— *the people*—and isn't the exclusive property of lawyers and judges.

Looking at cases that are brought before the U.S. Supreme Court is a good way to learn more about the law and the judicial system. And because the Court hears cases involving our constitutional rights, its decisions affect everyone—including you.

> When you understand how the courts work, you have the knowledge that can help you achieve fairness in your own life and in the lives of others.

This book is divided into two parts. Part 1 contains questions and answers you may have about the U.S. Supreme Court and the U.S. Constitution. Whether this information is new to you or you read it as a refresher, it will help you understand the significance of the cases that follow. Part 2 presents twenty-one cases about teenagers and a few children who were involved in important court cases. Most of the cases were reviewed by the U.S. Supreme Court. In some cases, the teens challenged a law they didn't agree with; other cases focus on the rights of teens and children who are charged with a crime; and still other cases concern the protections that young people have under the law.

Not all of the teens featured in this book are role models. In fact, some committed crimes. Yet, the results of all the cases affect the rights and responsibilities that all American teens have today.

You may notice the following about some of the U.S. Supreme Court cases and the related cases in this book: (1) some include more details than others, (2) some use the full names of the participants, while others contain abbreviated names, and (3) the final decisions in several cases aren't given. This is because each state has different confidentiality laws (laws that restrict how much juvenile court information is made public). For example, some states require that only a juvenile's initials be used, while other states allow the first name and the initial of the last name. Also, when cases before an appeals court are sent back to the lower court, the final results sometimes aren't made public.

The cases you read may spur further questions in your mind. If you want to learn more about the cases and why they were decided a certain way, check out the section in Part 1 called "How to Do Legal Research." You'll find lots of tips for doing in-depth research on the decisions of the U.S. Supreme Court.

In reviewing the cases contained in this book, you'll come across certain legal terms that may be new to you. Terms in **bold** are included in the glossary at the end of the book (see pages 177–182). Other terms are explained within the cases. However, the legalese, or legal language, is kept to a minimum. This is consistent with today's legal profession, which is attempting to speak more English and less Latin.

Teens on Trial allows you to participate in the U.S. Supreme Court cases under discussion. Each case begins with an outline of the facts—this is the information that a judge

As you read these cases, you'll discover that the law is flexible; it sometimes has to change to meet the needs of a nation that's constantly changing and growing. However, you'll also see that the common thread is fairness, in the proceedings and to the participants.

or a jury would hear. Next, you're given a set of questions to help you consider the issues. (You can think about how you'd decide the case.) The ruling, or decision, is then revealed, including the Court's reasoning. Related cases, which illustrate the ongoing debate over these issues in courtrooms across the nation, are presented next. In a few cases in the book, the issues remain unsettled, with U.S. Supreme Court decisions yet to come. At the end of each case, you'll find discussion-starters or activities to help you get more involved in the issues that interest you.

I'm always interested in hearing from teens about their experiences and questions. If you'd like to get in touch with me, you can contact me in care of:

Free Spirit Publishing Inc.
217 Fifth Avenue North, Suite 200
Minneapolis, MN 55401-1299

Or email me at: help4kids@freespirit.com

I look forward to hearing from you!

Tom Jacobs, J.D.

Part 1:
Understanding the Law

The Supreme Court
and How It Works

Q. What exactly is the United States Supreme Court and how does it differ from other courts in our country?

A. The United States Supreme Court was created by federal law in 1789. It's the highest court in the nation, and its decisions affect all of our lives. The Court's job is to settle lawsuits and interpret the U.S. Constitution. It has the final say in cases brought before it. (For more on the Constitution, see "Facts About the U.S. Constitution" on pages 17–20.)

Q. What type of cases does the U.S. Supreme Court hear?

A. As the nation's highest court, the U.S. Supreme Court hears specific types of cases—for example, ones that involve disputes between states. It also interprets federal laws and treaties. The most common type of case before the U.S. Supreme Court involves constitutional questions— requiring the Court to interpret the U.S. Constitution. The Court reviews both civil and criminal cases, as long as a federal issue exists.

Q. What is the difference between a civil and a criminal case? Do the cases go to different courts?

A. A criminal case is brought about by a government prosecutor, when a person is suspected of breaking a law. If found guilty by the court, this person receives punishment. The crime committed may be against a local law (city, municipality, or county, for example) or a state or federal law. The possible penalties range from **probation,** to community service or fines, to jail or prison time.

A civil case usually involves private individuals or businesses—one person or group sues another. In this type of case, the verdict may result in a loss of property or money, but not freedom—no one found guilty goes to jail or prison.

In larger cities, criminal and civil cases are tried by separate courts, where the judges specialize in either criminal or civil proceedings. In smaller locales, judges may hear both civil and criminal cases.

Q. How many different types of courts are there?

A. There are two main judicial systems—state and federal. State courts are responsible for settling disputes among their residents. These courts also interpret their state's constitution, as well as state and local laws. In the federal judicial system, the courts preside over lawsuits based on federal laws and the U.S. Constitution. Each judicial system has three levels of courts—one trial court level and two appellate court levels.

Every court has what's called **jurisdiction,** or the responsibility to hear specific types of cases in a certain geographical area. This means that your lawsuit must be filed in the right county or district court. The money at stake in the case also dictates where it may be filed. In other words, a $500 lawsuit may belong in one court, but a $1 million lawsuit belongs in another.

Within the state court system are other courts with specific functions. These include justice courts, police courts, municipal courts, or city courts. Sometimes referred to as lower courts, or courts of limited jurisdiction, they generally handle lesser offenses (**misdemeanors, petty offenses,** and civil cases under a specified dollar amount).

Q. How does the juvenile justice system fit into the justice system as a whole?

A. The juvenile justice system is one of several components of America's justice system. State courts have jurisdiction over civil and criminal cases, as well as the more specialized areas of probate, mental health, domestic relations, tax, and juvenile matters.

Cases handled in the juvenile justice system include **delinquency** matters, dependent children (abused, abandoned, and neglected children),

termination of parental rights, and adoption. Sometimes an individual or a family may be involved with several divisions of the court at the same time. For example, a child in a foster home may break the law and end up on probation. At the same time, his or her parents may be in domestic relations court for divorce, custody, or visitation.

Q. What happens in a trial court?

A. In trial courts, juries and judges decide the cases. Most of the court news you hear and read about comes from trials. That's because this is where the excitement and drama of courtroom battles occur. At a trial, the evidence in the case is presented—through witnesses testifying or by use of physical evidence (such as weapons, X-rays, or charts). Either the judge or jury will decide the case, following the presentation of all of the evidence and the closing statements of the attorneys.

Q. What happens in an appellate court?

A. Depending on the type of case, the losing party in trial court may have a right to **appeal.** This means that if you lose your case, you may ask a higher court (an appellate court) to review what happened in the trial. Basically, you're asking for a different decision, because of some error made during the trial.

Local rules of court govern whether an appeal is available and to which appellate court it may go. In some jurisdictions, for example, traffic cases may proceed only one level up on an appeal, and go no further. Consequently, your state's highest court may never see a traffic appeal. Most states have two levels of appellate courts, due to the volume of cases. Certain cases are heard by the first level of the court of appeals, with the more significant issues going to the highest state court. These generally review **felony** cases or constitutional issues—which affect all residents of the state.

A case that has gone up to an appellate court is "on appeal." The appellate court doesn't consider new evidence. No witnesses are called to testify, and no jury is involved. Rather, the attorneys make their arguments to the court in writing, called a **brief.** (The lawyers may be allowed to present oral arguments if the court thinks this would be useful in deciding the issues.)

The U.S. Supreme Court is the highest appellate court.

Q. How are cases sent to an appellate court decided? How does this differ from a trial court?

A. The appellate court decides the case by issuing a written statement called an opinion. The cases discussed in this book are the opinions of the state supreme courts and the U.S. Supreme Court. The appellate court may do a number of things in deciding a case. It may reverse the decision of the trial court and send the case back for a new trial. It may also affirm the trial court's decision or modify the decision, as it sees fit.

Q. Why do courts rule differently on the same law?

A. It's important to keep in mind that courts consist of people—and people often have differing opinions. One judge or a panel of judges may be involved. The job of a judge is to consider both the facts of the case and the applicable law. Judges often disagree on the *interpretation* of a law, however. Consequently, appellate courts may review and decide the issue. The U.S. Supreme Court is empowered to make the *final* decision—the one that decides the issue once and for all.

Q. Who determines whether a judge or a jury will decide a case? What factors are involved in this decision?

A. State and federal laws dictate whether you may request a jury trial. In civil cases, the dollar amount of the case may determine whether a jury trial is allowed. For example, if somebody sues for an amount under $5,000, the case may be tried before a judge, without a jury (sometimes called a bench trial). In criminal cases, the maximum jail sentence may determine whether a jury is allowed. Generally, if the maximum sentence is less than six months in jail, a jury trial isn't available.

Q. How does a case get to the U.S. Supreme Court?

A. The U.S. Constitution gives the U.S. Supreme Court the authority to hear cases. This authority is referred to as the Court's jurisdiction. The cases before the Court fall under two categories—original jurisdiction and appellate jurisdiction.

Original jurisdiction includes cases that go directly to the U.S. Supreme Court, bypassing all other courts. This includes: (1) disputes between states—about boundaries, for example, (2) arguments between the federal government and a state, (3) quarrels among citizens of different states. Cases involving ambassadors to other countries also go directly to the U.S. Supreme Court.

The majority of cases filed with the U.S. Supreme Court each year actually fall under appellate jurisdiction. These are cases from lower federal courts and state courts where a federal law or the Constitution is involved. A case that's handled in a state trial court proceeds up through the state's court of appeals. Most cases stop at the state's highest court, with that decision being final. However, if there's a federal issue in the case involving a constitutional right, the case may then go to the federal courts for resolution. For example, if the case involves freedom of speech and you lose in the state courts, you may file a **petition** asking the U.S. Supreme Court to review the case. This is because the First Amendment to the Constitution guarantees speech as a protected right. (See the **Bill of Rights** on pages 19–20.)

As you'll see in Part 2, it may take three to five years for a case to make its way through the state and federal systems and then, if accepted for review by the U.S. Supreme Court, to obtain a final decision.

Q. Who's responsible for seeing that a case gets to the U.S. Supreme Court? The individuals involved or their attorneys?

A. A case that's appealed to a higher court involves writing and arguing about legal issues. The litigants (parties to the lawsuit), including the juveniles and parents, decide with the advice of their attorney whether to appeal a case. But once the decision is made to pursue an appeal through the legal system, the attorneys are responsible for seeing that all of the rules of court are met. The parties in the case take a backseat and let the lawyers handle the appeal.

Q. Who pays the legal fees in U.S. Supreme Court cases, especially if they take years to be resolved?

A. In criminal cases, the public defender's office usually pays expenses, or in the rare case, a private lawyer does. In civil cases, either the family retains a lawyer or the American Civil Liberties Union (ACLU) becomes

Q. Where is the U.S. Supreme Court located? Can anyone visit and watch the Court?

A. The U.S. Supreme Court is located in Washington, D.C., at 1 First Street S.E. It's open year-round, Monday through Friday from 9:00 A.M. to 4:30 P.M. Tours and lectures are available when the Court isn't in session.

Oral arguments, when scheduled, begin at 10:00 A.M. and 1:00 P.M. They're open to the public, but seating in the Court is limited to 188 seats for the public, on a first-come, first-serve basis.

For further information on the Court and its justices, check out the following resources:

- The U.S. Supreme Court's public information office: (202) 479-3211
- The U.S. Supreme Court's Web site: *www.supremecourtus.gov*
- The FindLaw Web site: *www.findlaw.com*
- U.S. Supreme Court Multimedia Database: *oyez.nwu.edu/*

Facts About the
U.S. Constitution

Q. Who wrote the Constitution? At what point in our country's history did it come about?

A. After the first thirteen states won their independence from England in 1783, a convention met in Philadelphia in 1787 to draft a plan for the government. It was intended to define the powers of the national government and establish protection for the rights of the states and each of its citizens.

Following four months of discussion and debate, the Constitution was signed on September 17, 1787, at Independence Hall in Philadelphia. There were fifty-five state delegates at the convention who contributed to the content of the Constitution. Among the delegates were George Washington, Benjamin Franklin, Alexander Hamilton, and James Madison, who received the title Father of the Constitution because of his leadership and participation at the convention.

Q. How and where does the Constitution fit into the structure of our government?

A. The United States Constitution defines the rights and liberties of the American people and establishes a national government. Federal and state judges apply the Constitution in many court cases. The U.S. Supreme Court has the final authority in explaining and interpreting the meaning of the Constitution. It has the power of judicial review, which means that it may declare a law as unconstitutional.

Q. Why is this document so important?

A. Our country is based on laws. The U.S. Constitution has been described as a "living" document, even though it was written more than 200 years ago. This is because the Constitution continues to be debated in classrooms and courtrooms across the nation.

Q. Why is it still debated today if it's more than 200 years old? So much has changed since it was written, how can it still be relevant today?

A. The delegates to the Constitutional Convention were writing for the nation's future. They recognized the need for a document that would expand and develop as the United States grew. James Madison said, "In framing a system which we wish to last for ages, we should not lose sight of the changes which ages will produce."

Americans in the 1780s weren't concerned about drugs at school, student protests, abortion rights, or due process for minors. Yet, the Constitution has grown to now address these and other issues that face Americans today.

Q. Which courts debate what the Constitution means? Only the U.S. Supreme Court?

A. Both state and federal courts often face constitutional issues. A court's decision in a case may be based on its interpretation of the U.S. Constitution, and if one of the parties in the lawsuit disagrees with the court's ruling, an appeal may be made. Depending on the nature of the case and its constitutional issue, the U.S. Supreme Court may hear the case and make the final decision.

Q. What about the Bill of Rights and other amendments? How and why did these come into being?

A. During the American Revolution (1775–1783), the states adopted their own constitutions, which guaranteed individual rights of the people. Following the Constitutional Convention in 1787, ten amendments, or additions, to the Constitution were written; by 1791, they were ratified (approved) by the states. These became known as the **Bill of Rights.** A total of twenty-seven amendments have been passed since 1791.

Bill of Rights—Amendments I to X

I Congress shall make no law respecting an establishment of religion, or prohibiting the free exercise thereof; or abridging the freedom of speech, or of the press; or the right of the people peaceably to assemble, and to petition the Government for a redress of grievances.

II A well regulated Militia, being necessary to the security of a free State, the right of the people to keep and bear Arms, shall not be infringed.

III No soldier shall, in time of peace be quartered in any house, without the consent of the Owner, nor in time of war, but in a manner to be prescribed by law.

IV The right of the people to be secure in their persons, houses, papers and effects, against unreasonable searches and seizures, shall not be violated, and no Warrants shall issue, but upon probable cause, supported by Oath or affirmation, and particularly describing the place to be searched, and the persons or things to be seized.

V No person shall be held to answer for a capital, or otherwise infamous crime, unless on a presentment or indictment of a Grand Jury, except in cases arising in the land or naval forces, or in the Militia, when in actual service in time of War or in public danger; nor shall any person be subject for the same offence to be twice put in jeopardy of life or limb; nor shall be compelled in any Criminal Case to be a witness against himself; nor be deprived of life, liberty, or property, without due process of law; nor shall private property be taken for public use, without just compensation.

VI In all criminal prosecutions, the accused shall enjoy the right to a speedy and public trial, by an impartial jury of the State and district wherein the crime shall have been committed, which district shall have been previously ascertained by law, and to be informed of the nature and cause of the accusation to be confronted with the Witnesses against him; to have compulsory process for obtaining Witnesses in his favor, and to have the Assistance of Counsel for his defence.

VII In suits at common law, where the value in controversy shall exceed twenty dollars, the right of trial by jury shall be preserved, and no fact tried by a jury shall be otherwise re-examined in any Court of the United States, than according to the rules of the common law.

VIII Excessive bail shall not be required, nor excessive fines imposed, nor cruel and unusual punishments inflicted.

IX The enumeration in the Constitution, of certain rights, shall not be construed to deny or disparage others retained by the people.

X The powers not delegated to the United States by the Constitution, nor prohibited by it to the States, are reserved to the States respectively, or to the people.

Q. Who writes amendments to the Constitution and who votes on them?

A. Amendments to the Constitution may be written and proposed by either the U.S. Senate or the House of Representatives. In order to become a permanent addition to the Constitution, the amendment must be ratified by three-fourths of the nation's states.

How to Do
Legal Research

Interested in the law? Legal research? Public libraries and law libraries aren't to be feared—only tackled. Finding a particular law or legal article isn't difficult. Can you imagine adding to your term paper one of these easy-to-find resources in support of your position? Follow the simple instructions offered here, and you'll be ready to present your case.

The published opinions of all of the country's appellate courts are found in a series of books called *Reporters.* The series is divided into regions—for example, California decisions are found in the *Pacific Reporter,* and Vermont decisions are located in the *Atlantic Reporter.* Each state also maintains its own set of reports. This means that each decision may be found in both a regional and a state report. The decisions of the U.S. Supreme Court can be found in at least four different *Reporters.* All of the Supreme Court cases cited in this book are also located in either the *U.S. Supreme Court Reports* or the *Supreme Court Reporter.*

Each published opinion is assigned a citation number. For example, if you want to read the full opinion of the U.S. Supreme Court in *Vernonia School District v. Jimmy Acton* (1995), you start with the case citation, which is 515 U.S. 646 (1995). This means you can find the opinion in volume 515 of the *U.S. Supreme Court Reports,* on page 646; 1995 refers to the year of the decision.

Take the case of *Rachel Kingsley v. Gregory Kingsley* (1993) as another example. Its citation is 623 So.2d 780 (1993). This isn't a U.S. Supreme Court case; its published opinion may be found in volume 623 of the *Southern Reports* (abbreviated So.), 2nd series, on page 780. Legal articles are located in the same way. Their citations usually list

Case 5:

Vernonia School District v. Jimmy Acton, 515 U.S. 646 (Oregon, 1995)

Todd v. Rush County Schools, 133 F.3d 984 (Indiana, 1998)

Anderson Community School Corps. v. Willis, 119 S.Ct. 1254 (Indiana, 1999)

Trinidad School District v. Lopez, 963 P.2d 1095 (Colorado, 1998)

Miller v. Wilkes, 172 F.3d. 514 (Arkansas, 1999)

M. C. English v. Talledega County Board of Education, 938 F.Supp. 775 (Alabama, 1996)

Chandler v. Miller, 520 U.S. 305 (Georgia, 1997)

New Jersey Local 304 v. New Jersey Transit, 701 A.2d 1243 (New Jersey, 1997)

Rebel v. Unemployment Compensation Board, 692 A.2d 304 (Pennsylvania, 1997)

Case 6:

New Jersey v. T. L. O., 469 U.S. 325 (New Jersey, 1985)

State v. Washington, 94 Wash.App. 1055 (Washington, 1999)

DesRoches v. Caprio, 156 F.3d 571 (Virginia, 1998)

Commonwealth v. Cass, 666 A.2d 313 (Pennsylvania, 1995)

Doe v. Renfrow, 631 F.2d 91 (Indiana, 1980)

People v. Parker, 672 N.E.2d 813 (Illinois, 1996)

Cornfield v. School District No. 230, 991 F.2d 1316 (Illinois, 1993)

Oliver v. McClung, 919 F.Supp. 1206 (Indiana, 1995)

Case 7:

Tariq A-R Y v. Maryland, 118 S.Ct. 1105 (Maryland,1998)

Florida v. J. L., 120 S.Ct. 1375 (Florida, 2000)

State v. Lowrimore, 841 P.2d 779 (Washington, 1992)

In re Bounmy V., 17 Cal.Rptr.2d 557 (California, 1993)

Wyoming v. Houghton, 526 U.S. 295 (Wyoming, 1999)

State v. Hauser, 464 S.E.2d 443 (North Carolina, 1995)

State v. Summers, 764 P.2d 250 (Washington, 1988)

State v. Carsey, 664 P.2d 1085 (Oregon, 1983)

In the Interest of Salyer, 358 N.E.2d 1333 (Illinois, 1977)

Case 8:

Kent v. United States, 383 U.S. 541 (District of Columbia, 1966)

State v. Terry, 569 N.W.2d 364 (Iowa, 1997)

Appling v. State, 470 S.E.2d 761 (Georgia, 1996)

Case 9:

Bellotti v. Baird, 443 U.S. 622 (Massachusetts, 1979)

Roe v. Wade, 410 U.S. 113 (Texas, 1973)

In re Jane Doe, 645 N.E.2d 134 (Ohio, 1994)

Lambert v. Wicklund, 520 U.S. 292 (Montana, 1997)

Parents United for Better Schools v. Philadelphia Board of Education, 978 F.Supp. 197 (Pennsylvania, 1997)

Curtis v. School Committee of Falmouth, 652 N.E.2d 580 (Massachusetts, 1995)

Doe v. Irwin, 615 F.2d 1162 (Michigan, 1980)

In re T. A. J., 73 Cal.Rptr.2d 331 (California, 1998)

Case 10:

Tinker v. Des Moines Independent School District, 393 U.S. 503 (Iowa, 1969)

Bethel School District v. Fraser, 478 U.S. 675 (Washington, 1986)

Cecilia Lacks v. Ferguson School District, 154 F.3d 904 (Missouri, 1999)

Broussard v. School Board of City of Norfolk, 801 F.Supp. 1526 (Virginia, 1992)

Pyle v. School Commission, 667 N.E.2d 869 (Massachusetts, 1996)

Denno v. School Board of Volusia County, 959 F.Supp. 1481 (Florida, 1997)

City of Harvard v. Todd Gaut, 660 N.E.2d 259 (Illinois, 1996)

Crouse v. Crouse, 552 N.W.2d 413 (South Dakota, 1996)

E. N. O. v. L. M. M., 711 N.E.2d 886 (Massachusetts, 1999)

In the Interest of Baron, 670 So.2d 357 (Louisiana, 1996)

D. F. S. v. Ellis, 870 S.W.2d 463 (Missouri, 1994)

W. G. T. v. B. C., 675 So.2d 1023 (Florida, 1996)

State v. Waters, 951 P.2d 317 (Washington, 1998)

Case 18:

In re Gault, 387 U.S. 1 (Arizona, 1967)

In the Matter of B. M. B., 955 P.2d 1302 (Kansas, 1998)

State v. Calvin Jones, 566 N.W.2d 317 (Minnesota, 1997)

In the Interest of D. F. L., 931 P.2d 448 (Colorado, 1997)

People v. T. C., 898 P.2d 20 (Colorado, 1995)

People v. Montanez, 652 N.E.2d 1271 (Illinois, 1995)

In re V. L. T., 686 N.E.2d 49 (Illinois, 1997)

Case 19:

Josh Davis v. Alaska, 415 U.S. 308 (Alaska, 1974)

State in the Interest of N. P., 544 So.2d 51 (Louisiana, 1989)

State v. LaMunyon, 911 P.2d 151 (Kansas, 1996)

Appeal in Maricopa County Juvenile No. JV-512600, 930 P.2d 496 (Arizona, 1997)

Wideman v. Garbarino, 770 P.2d 320 (Arizona, 1989)

United States v. Three Juveniles, 61 F.3d 86 (Massachusetts, 1995)

Case 20:

McKeiver v. Pennsylvania, 403 U.S. 528 (Pennsylvania, 1971)

Welfare of J. K. B., 552 N.W.2d 732 (Minnesota, 1996)

State v. Reynolds, 857 P.2d 842 (Oregon, 1993)

U.S. v. Nachtigal, 507 U.S. 1 (California, 1993)

Case 21:

Thompson v. Oklahoma, 487 U.S. 815 (Oklahoma, 1988)

Stanford v. Kentucky, 492 U.S. 361 (Kentucky, 1989)

Penry v. Lynaugh, 109 U.S. 2934 (Texas, 1989)

People v. Launsburry, 551 N.W.2d 460 (Michigan, 1996)

Naovarath v. State, 779 P.2d 944 (Nevada, 1989)

State v. Eric Mitchell, 577 N.W.2d 481 (Minnesota, 1998)

State v. Pilcher, 655 So.2d 636 (Louisiana, 1995)

Check out the bibliography on pages 183–190 for more sources that may be of help.

Part 2:
The Cases

ISSUE:

Can you go to court on your own to protect your rights?

Case: *Rachel Kingsley v. Gregory Kingsley* (1993)

The Constitution and the laws of our country protect **minors** and adults alike. It only makes sense then that teens can go to court to make sure these rights are enforced and protected. When teens challenge a law or a policy, however, they're usually joined in the lawsuit by a parent or a guardian, who files the lawsuit on the minor's behalf. This case, which was initiated by a minor, challenges this custom.

The Facts:

In a Florida case that gained national attention, eleven-year-old Gregory Kingsley asked a court to "divorce" his parents. Although the case wasn't really a divorce case, it had a similar effect. Gregory had lived in the same foster home for three years, after being abandoned by his parents. Now he wanted a new mom and dad, and he filed his own **petition** with the court to legally end his relationship with his biological parents. He also requested to be adopted by his foster family.

Gregory's birth father was an alcoholic and was physically abusive. He didn't fight the lawsuit. Gregory's mother, though, refused to give up her parental rights and asked for custody of Gregory. She also argued that, as a child, Gregory couldn't file a lawsuit. The evidence showed that she was a neglectful parent and that she abused alcohol, used drugs, and hadn't made contact with Gregory for almost two years.

YOU BE THE JUDGE

- **Did Gregory have a right to bring his case to court by himself? What do you think?**

- **Should the case have been dismissed because Gregory was a minor? Why or why not?**

The Ruling:

The Florida Court of Appeals stood by tradition and held that Gregory couldn't sue on his own behalf. The court discussed the concept of **capacity to sue** as the ability of a person to come into court under his own name—a right that's generally limited to adults and minors who have **emancipation.**

The Florida court explained that minors are required to appear in court with an attorney, so the proceeding can move forward with the least amount of confusion and delay. The court also said that it's in the minor's best interests to have the guidance of someone familiar

Some states allow minors to appear in court with their parents or a guardian, and no attorney, on certain types of cases: truancy, name changes, adoptions, minor traffic citations. It's a state-by-state or even county-by-county policy.

the child needed to be represented in the proceedings. The court said the best interests of the child dictate whether he or she should have an attorney or a guardian in an adoption case.

This case points out the discrepancies in legal reasoning. Some courts rule one way, while other courts rule the opposite—all on the same set of facts, and all justified on the basis of what's in the child's best interests. This is why appellate courts exist: to review the decision of lower courts and make a final decision.

Adoption of J. (1996)

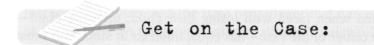

Get on the Case:

- Although, as a teen, you aren't allowed to go to court on your own, there are plenty of other ways to resolve conflicts or to ensure that you're being treated properly. Make a list of the methods that you currently use to solve problems and conflicts with others. Then write down why these methods do or don't work for you. Now commit to discovering new ways to solve problems and to improve your conflict-resolution skills.

- Find out if your school has a peer mediation program to help resolve conflicts. If not, ask your principal or dean if you can work on developing one. If your school does have a peer mediation program, find out how you can get involved. Conflict-resolution skills are also taught through many community service organizations.

ISSUE:

Do your parents have the right to control your education?

Teens on Trial

Case: *Meyer v. Nebraska* (1923)

Almost every U.S. Supreme Court decision on teen rights and family law has relied in part on the decision of this 1923 case. Although the case is about a single issue—parents' rights to make decisions about their children's education—the ruling can be applied to many other types of cases in our changing society.

The next time you hear about a law concerning the rights and responsibilities of parents, or the rights and responsibilities of children to their parents, you can try to find a connection to this case.

The Facts:

Ten-year-old Raymond Parpart attended Zion Parochial School in Hamilton County, Nebraska. Raymond's teacher, Robert T. Meyer, taught a Bible study class for a half hour each day. The class was taught in German, the native language of most of the community members. (Raymond spoke English as a first language.) Although students weren't required to attend Meyer's class, it was full. The purpose of the class was both to teach students German and to familiarize them with Bible stories.

A 1919 Nebraska law forbade teaching anyone in a foreign language, unless that person had finished eighth grade (which Raymond hadn't). The law was intended to encourage people to speak in the English language, so it would become the mother tongue of the state of Nebraska. Raymond's parents, however, wanted their son to learn a second language while he was young. The state of Nebraska charged the teacher with breaking the law.

YOU BE THE JUDGE

- **Do you think Mr. Meyer was breaking the law if the students weren't required to attend the class? Why or why not?**

- **Who should decide what's best for each student in the classroom? Parents, teachers, or the government? Why?**

- **What role should parents play in their child's education? How much authority should they have?**

The Ruling:

The Nebraska trial court and the Nebraska Supreme Court found that Mr. Meyer was guilty of breaking the law. The penalty included a fine of $25 to $100, or thirty days in jail. He **appealed** his conviction, and the U.S. Supreme Court ruled in Mr. Meyer's favor several years later.

This "English only" debate has come full circle. Raymond's case took place in the 1920s. Nearly eight decades later, the debate continues in legislatures and in voting booths across the country. Several states have attempted to pass legislation requiring that English be the official language of the state. This would restrict speech and written documents in the public sector to English. Courts have been asked to decide the constitutionality of English-only laws, and so far have ruled against them. You may have the chance to vote on this issue in your own state.

In making its decision, the U.S. Supreme Court balanced the right of individual freedom with the legitimate interest of a state to protect its citizens. The Court found no harm to anyone in teaching elementary schoolchildren a foreign language. In fact, the Court emphasized the right, duty, and obligation of parents to be involved with the education of their children. It wrote: "Corresponding to the right of control, it is the natural duty of the parent to give his children education suitable to their station in life. . . . The protection of the Constitution extends to all, to those who speak other languages as well as to those born with English on the tongue." The Court also spoke of a student's right to acquire knowledge, a teacher's right to teach, and the parents' power to control their child's education.

The principles outlined in the *Meyer* decision have been applied for nearly eighty years, and with good reason. First, parents have both rights and responsibilities toward their children. Second, children and teens also have certain rights and responsibilities toward each other, their parents, and others. Schools aren't obligated to instill values in students. The laws and courts of this country recognize the family as the primary source of shaping and developing values in children.

Clarifying its limited role in family matters, a New York court ruled: "The court cannot regulate . . . the internal affairs of the home. Dispute between parents when it does not involve anything immoral or harmful to the welfare of the child is beyond the reach of the law. The vast majority of matters concerning the upbringing of children must be left to the conscience, patience, and self-restraint of father and mother. No end of difficulties would arise should judges try to tell parents how to bring up their children." *People v. Sisson* (1936)

Related Cases:

You're probably aware that your parents have obligations and responsibilities when raising you. But did you know that your behavior reflects on your parents—and that they can be held legally accountable for what you do?

■ How responsible are your parents for your actions?

In 1998, Carol Rust and Stephen Tarantino (both **minors**) went to a keg party at the house of seventeen-year-old Heidi Reyer in Merrick, New York. Heidi's parents were out of town for the weekend, and she agreed to allow a local fraternity to sell beer at a party in the Reyer home, in exchange for a cut of the money earned. Approximately 150 underage kids showed up and paid a fee to get in and drink as much beer as they wanted. The neighbors complained, and the police broke up the party.

Stephen had consumed quite a bit of beer and, while in the street in front of Heidi's house, punched Carol in the face and injured her. Carol sued Stephen, Heidi, and Heidi's parents. Because Heidi was a minor, her parents were named in the lawsuit—parents are liable under the law for the acts of their children. Heidi's parents argued that they weren't responsible, because their daughter hadn't supplied the beer or caused anyone at the party to become intoxicated. Under laws that make parents responsible for the unlawful acts of minors, the court ruled that liability exists for "those who knowingly furnish alcoholic beverages to underage persons at graduation parties, church socials, wedding receptions, office parties, and college campuses." Although Heidi's parents didn't furnish the alcohol, they could be held responsible because the party was held in their home, hosted by their underage daughter.

In July 1999, forty-four-year-old Tena Henkel of Midland, Texas, was sentenced to three years in prison for charges of intoxication manslaughter. She was found guilty because she'd served alcohol at her daughter's high school graduation party. While driving home from the party, one of the underage partygoers crashed his truck, killing two eighteen-year-olds and injuring two other people.

Rust v. Reyer (1998)

▪ Can your parents be sentenced as part of your sentence?

E. W. R., a Wyoming resident, was found guilty of a **delinquent** act in 1993. His mother, his stepfather, and his father all attended his sentencing hearing, where he was given **probation** and counseling. In an effort to help the family work through some of the problems that had contributed to E. W. R.'s running away several times, the court ordered his parents to attend parenting classes. Held once a week over an eight-week period, these classes were designed to be flexible, so that people could attend around their work schedules and family commitments. E. W. R.'s father, E. L. R., didn't go to any of the classes. After several attempts to persuade him to attend, the court found him in **contempt of court** and sentenced him to thirty days in jail.

E. W. R. v. State of Wyoming (1995)

▪ Can your parents be held criminally responsible for your actions?

Sixteen-year-old Alex Provenzino and his parents, Anthony and Susan, lived in St. Clair Shores, Michigan. In 1995, Alex was arrested for robbery, assault of his father, and a string of home burglaries. When the police searched Alex's room, they found a stolen handgun and marijuana on his nightstand. Alex was found guilty and sentenced to one year in a **detention** home.

The case didn't close here, however. Alex's parents were charged with violating the city's parent-responsibility law—specifically failing to prevent Alex from committing the burglaries. Anthony and Susan were found guilty by a jury and were ordered to pay $2,200 in fines and court costs, plus approximately $13,000 for Alex's care in the detention home.

Note: Alex's parents appealed their conviction and eventually were acquitted. The appeals court found that the parent-responsibility law was constitutional but that the charges against the Provenzinos—particularly the charge that they failed to get their son into counseling—weren't proven beyond a reasonable doubt.

City of St. Clair Shores v. Provenzino (1997)

A number of states have recently passed parent-responsibility laws, including Arizona, Arkansas, California, Colorado, Kentucky, New Mexico, New York, and Oregon. The increase in juvenile crime has caused state legislatures not only to study the problem but also to pass laws placing greater accountability on parents. Consequences for parents violating these laws include community service work, fines, parent-training classes, counseling, and, in some states, jail time.

The Facts:

In the spring of 1991, thirteen-year-old Alida Star Gebser was an eighth-grade honor student in Lago Vista, Texas. Her teacher, Trudy Waldrop, recommended that she join a book discussion group at the local high school that was led by her husband, Frank Waldrop (a teacher of advanced social studies). During some of the sessions, Mr. Waldrop made sexually suggestive comments to the book group. In the fall, Alida started high school and had Mr. Waldrop for classes both semesters that year. He continued to make inappropriate remarks to Alida in class, when alone with her in the classroom,

> Sexual harassment at school refers to any unwelcome sexual advances, requests for sexual favors, or other verbal or physical contact of a sexual nature. To be unlawful, it must be so offensive and severe that the conduct affects or disrupts the victim's education.

and at her home, where he was mentoring her. (Alida later testified that she knew Mr. Waldrop's behavior was improper, but she didn't know what to do. His class was the school's only advanced program, and she wanted to stay in it.)

Over the next year, this student-teacher relationship progressed to kissing, fondling, and eventually sexual intercourse. Alida didn't report Mr. Waldrop's behavior. The parents of two other students complained to the school principal about the comments the teacher made in class. Then in early 1993, a police officer discovered Alida and Mr. Waldrop having sex in a parked car. Mr. Waldrop was fired and his teaching license was revoked.

Alida and her mother sued Mr. Waldrop and the school district, claiming **negligence** and **discrimination** based on sex. In other words, Alida argued that she was treated differently by Mr. Waldrop because she was a girl. Alida and her mother also held the school district responsible for failing to prevent the teacher's misconduct.

YOU BE THE JUDGE

- **Should the school district be held responsible for Mr. Waldrop's behavior? Why or why not?**

- **Does it matter whether the school knew about the teacher's behavior?**

The Ruling:

The federal court of appeals dismissed the lawsuit against the school district and sent the case back to the trial court for a decision against Mr. Waldrop. Alida **appealed** to the U.S. Supreme Court which, in a five to four decision, agreed with the lower court.

This was a close decision that, at first glance, may surprise you. How could a school district not be held responsible for the behavior of one of its teachers? (Especially over a lengthy period of misconduct, affecting not just one, but a number of students.) Whose responsibility is it to protect students from adult predators? These are good questions, without easy answers.

The U.S. Supreme Court based its decision on a narrow, limited interpretation of what Congress intended when it passed Title 9 of the Education Amendments in 1972. This is a federal law aimed at protecting individuals from discrimination on the basis of sex. The law specifically prohibits discrimination in any educational program or activity that receives federal money. This includes all public schools.

The Court didn't rule that school districts were responsible for every discriminatory act of its employees (teachers, administrators, etc.). School districts can't be held accountable for sexual harassment by a teacher against a student if the incident isn't reported or known by the school district. Although sexual harassment may be discrimination on the basis of sex, the school district must know about the misconduct and have an opportunity to remedy it. If the district knows about the behavior and does nothing, *then* it may be held responsible.

Otherwise, if action is taken—as in this case, where Mr. Waldrop was fired and his license revoked—the school district isn't liable for damages to Alida. (Liability, in this instance, means being legally responsible for any expenses Alida had as a result of the teacher's harassment, such as counseling or medication.) The Court pointed out that the school district wasn't informed of the sexual harassment incidents during the months of misconduct. The principal was only told about the inappropriate comments made by Mr. Waldrop in class and, once the teacher was caught with Alida, immediate action was taken.

The Court said its decision wasn't meant to prevent Alida and her mother from suing Mr. Waldrop as an *individual*. The family just couldn't sue the school district under the federal Education Law or in federal court.

His harassment of Christine started with sexually oriented conversations and progressed to forcibly kissing her and calling her at home. On three occasions, he coerced her into intercourse in a private office at school. Christine reported Mr. Hill to the administration. He resigned from his job, with an understanding that the matter would be dropped.

Christine took her case to court, claiming intentional gender-based discrimination. Although she was no longer a student at the school and Mr. Hill no longer taught there, the U.S. Supreme Court ruled that her sexual harassment claim was valid and the suit would proceed. The Court indicated its unanimous position that schools have a responsibility to protect students.

Franklin v. Gwinnett County Public Schools (1992)

▪ If school officials know of possible abuse and don't take action, are they liable?

Eleven-year-old Oona R. was in the sixth grade at J. C. Fremont Elementary School in Santa Rosa, California. During the 1992–1993 school year, student-teacher Drew Ibach inappropriately touched Oona and other female students. The principal and other teachers ignored reports of the man's behavior, as well as complaints of ongoing verbal and physical abuse of the girls by male students at the school. Oona received lower grades that semester, which she insisted was retaliation by one of her teachers for reporting these incidents.

Oona and her parents sued the school district, the student-teacher, and the principal for failing to prevent a hostile environment for female students. The school officials asked the court for immunity (protection from being sued), based on their positions with the school.

The court denied immunity, stating that a person who doesn't take any action after receiving reports of sexual harassment isn't entitled to protection.

Oona R. v. Santa Rosa City Schools (1995)

▪ What if your teacher is emotionally abusive? Is this a violation of your civil rights?

Twelve-year-old Stephanie Abeyta, a New Mexico student, wrote a note to fifth-grader Dominic saying, "You're cute . . . I like you." Stephanie's teacher found the note and read it to the class. He then asked the class if they thought Stephanie was a prostitute. Over the next three months, Stephanie's teacher and classmates continued to taunt her, until Stephanie changed schools. She and her parents filed a federal lawsuit against the teacher and the school district, alleging psychological abuse. Because Stephanie and her parents claimed that the teacher's actions violated her civil rights—the charges were sexual abuse and harassment, and psychological abuse—they brought their case to a federal court rather than starting out in state court. The Tenth Circuit Court of Appeals ruled that, although Stephanie's teacher emotionally abused her, his actions didn't amount to torture or severe psychological abuse. The court condemned the teacher's behavior but left the matter to be pursued in state court—not federal.

Abeyta v. Chama Valley Ind. School District (1996)

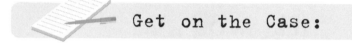

Get on the Case:

- Have you experienced harassment similar to what was described in these cases? What did you do about it? Did you tell anyone or let it go? Would you do anything different now?

- Do you think schools have a duty to protect students from sexual harassment? If so, how can schools do this? What new precautions could your school take to protect students? What role should teachers, school administrators, parents, students, and security officers play in this matter?

- Read the daily newspaper closely for a month, clipping articles about sexual harassment. At the end of this period, sort through the clippings and see if you spot any trends. How many articles did you find on this subject? Compare how many articles were about harassment in the workplace versus in schools. How many involved minors versus adults? What do you learn from the trends you see? What might you do to address problems or unfair situations you discover?

- Does your school have a written sexual harassment policy? Check your school rules or school handbook for the section on sexual harassment and how to report it. (You could also ask an administrator or a school counselor for the policy.) If no handbook exists, most likely one is in the works, as a result of the 1998 *Gebser* decision.

ISSUE:

What if you're sexually harassed at work?

Case: *Beth Ann Faragher v. City of Boca Raton* (1998)

Although teasing, flirting, and cracking jokes are okay in many job situations, at other times they're definitely inappropriate—and even illegal, as you'll see in this case. If you're ever a victim of **sexual harassment** at school, at work, or in the community, you're not alone or without recourse. It's important to understand what your rights are and what action you can take to protect yourself. The laws in this area have been expanded in recent years. Above all, know that you don't have to put up with such behavior by anyone, male or female.

50

The Facts:

After graduating from high school, Beth decided to work her way through college as a lifeguard at the city beach in Boca Raton, Florida. She worked full time during the summers and part time during the school year. Throughout her five years as a lifeguard, she had several male supervisors. She worked with three to five other women; forty to fifty of the lifeguards were men. After finishing college, Beth quit her job and went on to graduate school.

Throughout her time as a lifeguard, Beth experienced "uninvited and offensive touching," and heard sexual comments from her supervisors. One of the supervisors threatened to make her clean the toilets for a year if she didn't date him. She refused. Although she didn't complain to anyone about what was going on, she filed a sexual harassment lawsuit against the city and the offending supervisors after leaving her job. Beth claimed that their acts created a hostile work environment, which amounted to employment **discrimination.** She also argued that the city failed to prevent the harassment.

YOU BE THE JUDGE

- **Do you think that the behavior of Beth's supervisors was sexual harassment?**

- **Is the city responsible for what happened among its employees? Why or why not?**

The Ruling:

While deciding whether to consider Beth's case, the U.S. Supreme Court reviewed the history of civil rights law and how it applies to the workplace. The Court determined that the Civil Rights Act of 1964 provides protection from sexual harassment at work. The Act reads, in part: "It shall be an unlawful employment practice for an employer . . . to discriminate against any individual . . . because of . . . race, color, religion, sex, or national origin."

The Court, in a seven to two decision written by Justice David H. Souter, held that sexual harassment so severe as to create an abusive working environment is prohibited. The Court recognized that human behavior oftentimes leads to simple teasing, offhand comments, and even isolated incidents of abusive language or gender-related jokes. These, by themselves, aren't usually sufficient to claim sexual harassment. *Extreme* conduct, however, is what people are protected against.

The Court requires that all of the circumstances of the work environment be studied in determining whether harassment occurred. This includes (1) the frequency of the discriminating conduct, (2) its severity, (3) whether it's physically threatening or humiliating, and (4) whether it interferes with an employee's work performance. All of these factors are considered in a sexual harassment case—as well as whether the employer knew or should have known about the harassment.

Not every act of harassment is held against the owner of a business or company. The court considers whether the company has a specific policy against harassment and whether all employees are made aware of it. For example, when you start a job, you should be told about your right to raise an issue of harassment if one occurs. On the other hand, it's your duty as an employee to take reasonable care to avoid any harm from a harasser—for example, by reporting all incidents when they occur. (A victim isn't required to confront the abuser but needs to report the abuse to someone in authority, such as a supervisor.)

An earlier sexual discrimination case regarding a young bank teller and the bank manager in Washington, D.C., went to the U.S. Supreme Court in 1986. In a decision written by Justice William H. Rehnquist, it was decided that when a supervisor sexually harasses an employee because of the employee's sex, discrimination has occurred. The key to a sexual harassment claim isn't whether the victim voluntarily participated in sexual incidents with the offender, but whether the superior's advances were unwelcome. *Meritor Savings Bank v. Mechelle Vinson* (1986)

In Beth's case, the Court created a balancing test in sexual harassment incidents: between the reasonableness of the employer's conduct in seeking to prevent and correct harassing behavior, and the reasonableness of the employee's behavior in seeking to avoid harm. Because the city in Beth's case didn't make its lifeguards aware of its anti-harassment policy, the city was liable for the supervisors' acts. Beth was awarded $10,000 against her two supervisors, an additional $500 against one of the supervisors for punitive damages (money awarded to a victim, intended to punish the defendant), and $1 against the city of Boca Raton, which was found least liable for the supervisors' behavior. In addition, the city was told to make sure that all city employees are aware of its anti-harassment policy and to develop a sensible complaint procedure for victims of sexual harassment.

In discussing the responsibility of supervisors at work, the Court stated that a "supervisor is clearly charged with maintaining a productive, safe work environment. . . . A pervasively hostile work environment of sexual harassment is never (one would hope) authorized."

This case is significant because it establishes a standard for determining if certain conduct in the workplace is against the law. It helps employees and employers understand the limits of sexual comments and behavior at work—and helps make it clear that monetary damages are available against the offender *and* the place of employment.

Regardless of your age, you have rights at work. Offensive sexual language or gestures that create a hostile or abusive work environment don't have to be tolerated. As you enter the workforce, be aware that if you're harassed by someone on the job, you can do something about it. Putting up with the abuse allows it to continue—and spread to other victims.

Related Cases:

Incidents of sexual harassment were ignored for many years, but today people are much more aware of the laws surrounding this issue. As a result, we're witnessing many changes and expansions in the protections against sexual harassment, including same-sex harassment.

■ If you're harassed at work, do you need to take action right away?

At age fifteen, Sunny was hired as a hostess at a restaurant in Denver, Colorado. During her first month on the job, the restaurant manager allegedly sexually harassed and assaulted her. Sunny didn't report his behavior until after she voluntarily transferred to another restaurant the next month. Sunny was eventually fired for missing work and arriving late.

Sunny later sued the first restaurant and its manager for sexual harassment. The Colorado District Court dismissed the case in part because Sunny hadn't acted fast enough. The court considered the fact that she hadn't told anyone at the time of the incidents, that the restaurant hadn't taken action against her (by demoting or transferring her, for example), and that her eventual termination wasn't related to the sexual harassment claim.

Sunny Kim Smith v. Flagstar Corporation (1998)

The lesson here is to act promptly if you're harassed at work, instead of letting a lot of time go by before reporting the incident; be sure to talk to someone in authority, too. You can go over your supervisor's head, if he or she is the harasser. Inform a higher-level manager or the owner of the establishment you work for. Here's a recommended plan of action:

1. Discuss the situation with your mom or dad.
2. Report the problem to an authority at work.
3. Contact the Equal Employment Opportunity Commission (EEOC) or state civil rights office.
4. Find out if the employer is willing to remedy the situation.
5. If the employer doesn't fix the problem, you may want to contact a lawyer and file a lawsuit.

▪ Is it sexual harassment if the person is the same sex as you are?

Joseph Oncale, twenty-one, worked as a member of an eight-man crew on an oil derrick (tower) in the Gulf of Mexico. Three of his coworkers sexually harassed and threatened him. Joseph complained to the company's superiors, but no action was taken. He eventually quit due to "sexual harassment and verbal abuse." He sued the company, his supervisors, and his coworkers, claiming that harassment between members of the same sex is no different than discrimination among members of the opposite sex. The U.S. Supreme Court reviewed this Louisiana case and agreed, saying the law "protects men as well as women" in the workplace. The Court also said that sexual harassment laws provide protection only in cases where the behavior in question is so severe that it prevents the victim from doing his or her job. The Court, in a unanimous decision, indicated that common sense would help courts and juries distinguish between simple teasing or roughhousing and behavior that's severe enough to be called sexual harassment.

Joseph Oncale v. Sundowner Offshore Services (1998)

Get on the Case:

- Consider the following situations and with your classmates or parents discuss what you think about each.

  Julie works at a fast-food restaurant after school and on weekends. Her boss promises her a raise—if she'll go out with him. Is this sexual harassment? What can Julie do in this situation?

  Maya works as a cashier at a gas station. Some of the mechanics make sexual comments to her during the day, and their work area is covered with pictures of nude women. Maya's boss tells her to ignore these issues—that she's working in a "man's world" and she can either get used to it or find another job. Does Maya have any recourse? Can she, as the youngest person and the only female on the job, change her work environment without losing her source of employment? What would you recommend that she do?

  Seventeen-year-old Craig is spending the summer working in his father's accounting office. The office manager is interested in him and asks him to meet her after work. She's also Craig's supervisor. Is this sexual harassment? Craig doesn't want to jeopardize his job or ruin his father's trust in him. How should he respond?

- What about when people who work together date each other? Do you think this has the potential to cause problems, or is it okay? Why? Does it matter whether the two people are on the same job level, or whether one is in a higher position than the other? Do you think employers can create rules about dating among employees?

- Create a poster or flyer to spread the word about sexual harassment in the workplace. Start by coming up with a list of behaviors that are inappropriate, and then cross them out or write "no" beside them. Be creative, using paints, markers, or other materials to make the poster eye-catching. Ask your teacher or principal if you can display the poster at school as a way to inform others; if you have a job, ask your boss to display the poster at work.

Do you have to be tested for drugs to try out for school sports?

Case: *Vernonia School District v. Jimmy Acton* (1995)

Underage drinking and drug use is a growing concern for schools—public and private—across the country. School districts are trying to combat this problem in many ways, including drug testing. Although such tests are yet to be required of an entire public school population, they're more frequently required of students who wish to participate in sports and other activities. The question is, does this rule violate a student's right to privacy? And is it fair to demand such a test for students in some school activities but not in others?

The Facts:

James (Jimmy) Acton was a seventh-grader in Vernonia, Oregon. During the 1980s, this logging community of approximately 3,000 people witnessed a sharp increase in drug and alcohol use by students. Class disruptions and sports-related injuries due to the influence of drugs frequently occurred. Consequently, the school district developed a drug policy requiring student athletes to take a drug test. Following a parent-input meeting, where unanimous approval was given, the policy went into effect in 1989.

This same year, twelve-year-old Jimmy wanted to try out for the football team. Under the new policy, he was given consent forms for drug testing, which he and his parents needed to sign. After talking about the issue at home, the family decided not to sign the forms. They explained to the principal, Randall Aultman, that they objected to the testing because there was no evidence that Jimmy used drugs or alcohol. Following the new policy, the school suspended Jimmy from sports for the season. He and his parents filed a lawsuit against the school district, challenging the urinalysis requirement for sports participation. They argued that mandated, suspicionless drug testing is a search that violates the Fourth Amendment protection (see the **Bill of Rights** on pages 19–20) against unreasonable searches.

YOU BE THE JUDGE

- **Do you think the school district's policy violated the Fourth Amendment—was it unreasonable to require all student athletes to be tested for drug use?**

- **The policy didn't call for drug testing of students who weren't active in sports. Do student athletes have fewer privacy rights than other students?**

The Ruling:

The question put to the U.S. Supreme Court was whether mandatory drug tests violated students' Fourth Amendment protection against unreasonable **search and seizure.** There's no question that drug testing, which is done by analyzing a blood or urine sample, is a personal search. So the issue is whether a student's right to privacy is more important than the school's job of keeping its campus safe and drug-free for all students.

Drugs are more easily traced in urine than in blood. And because giving a urine sample is less "invasive" than having blood drawn, it's the more frequent method of drug testing.

The U.S. Supreme Court ruled that the school district policy was reasonable and constitutional based on (1) a student athlete's decreased expectation of privacy, (2) the limited invasion of privacy in obtaining a urine sample, and (3) the importance of the need met by the search, which was to reduce drug use by athletes. In a six to three decision, the Court said that any intrusion of a student's privacy by submitting to a drug test is minimal.

The Court also ruled that the protections provided in the testing procedures further supported their use. The tests were only for drugs—not, for example, to detect pregnancy or disease. In addition, the test results would be shared only with certain school employees; the results wouldn't be turned over to the police or be used for school disciplinary action. The school district had outlined very specific procedures: If a student tested positive, a second test would be conducted; if the second test was negative, the matter would be considered closed; if the second test came back positive, the parents and student would be notified. The student would then be required to complete a six-week outpatient drug-counseling program and be tested for drugs each week. After meeting these requirements, the student could return to sports. If the student refused the counseling or further drug tests, he or she would be suspended from all sports for the season.

In making its decision, the U.S. Supreme Court considered a student's expectation of privacy. You surrender some privacy when you go to school. Your parents turn over temporary custody to the school, for educational and disciplinary purposes when necessary. The school, in turn, is responsible for following laws that are intended to protect you. For example, they must conduct physical examinations, such as vision, hearing, and scoliosis tests. Schools also need to make sure that students have had all of their immunizations. These requirements mean that, in the eyes of the law, you can expect less privacy in school.

If you're a student athlete, you have even fewer privacy rights. By trying out for a team, you agree to follow a number of rules that aren't imposed on other students—you must have a physical exam, insurance coverage, and a minimum grade point average, for example. Getting dressed in locker rooms, with open shower areas and toilet stalls, reduces your privacy level as well. After reviewing these facts, the U.S. Supreme Court decided that it was reasonable for schools to test student athletes for drug use.

Related Cases:

In addition to the formal opinion in the *Vernonia* case, written by Justice Antonin Scalia, Justice Ruth Bader Ginsburg wrote a separate opinion agreeing with the decision (a **concurring opinion**). In it she raised the possibility of schools requiring routine drug testing of all students. This opens the door for future discussion and, possibly, another case for the U.S. Supreme Court to decide. For now, the debate continues, in classrooms and courtrooms across the country.

▪ Should students who want to participate in any extracurricular activity be forced to undergo drug tests?

William Matthew Todd, a freshman at Rushville High School in Indiana, was a volunteer who wanted to videotape the football team. The school required all students interested in extracurricular activities to be randomly tested for drugs, alcohol, and nicotine (the school had a no-smoking policy). This rule applied not only to athletes but also to members of the student council, foreign language clubs, fellowship groups, Future Farmers of America, and even the library club.

William and his parents refused to consent to the testing, and he was barred from videotaping the team; he took the case to court. The federal court of appeals ruled that because these school activities were voluntary, the rule was justified and not unconstitutional. "Successful extracurricular activities require healthy students" the court said. The

court also determined that the benefits and status attached to participating in school activities carry with them an obligation to undergo
drug testing. William and his parents **appealed** this decision and in
1998 asked the U.S. Supreme Court to consider the case. It refused, so
the decision of the lower court remains.

Todd v. Rush County Schools (1998)

■ Can schools require students who are suspended to be tested for drugs before returning to school?

Highland High School in Anderson, Indiana, required suspended students to undergo drug testing as a requirement for readmission. This
policy applied to all suspended students—it didn't matter whether they
were suspected of using drugs. James R. Willis was a freshman who
faced a five-day suspension for fighting. The school had no evidence
that James had been using drugs or alcohol but still required him to be
tested for drug use. He refused the test and went to court. The court
agreed with James; he was allowed to return to school without taking
the drug test. In 1999, the U.S. Supreme Court let this ruling stand.

Anderson Community School Corps. v. Willis (1999)

■ Should marching band members be held to the same standard as student athletes?

Trinidad High School senior Carlos Lopez played in the marching
band. His Colorado school district required random drug testing of all
students in grades six through twelve who were involved in extracurricular activities. Carlos refused the test and was therefore suspended
from the band and his two band classes. He and his parents filed a
lawsuit against the school district, the school board members, and the
principal, asking the court to invalidate (declare as unacceptable) the
drug-testing policy. The Colorado Supreme Court found the policy to
be unconstitutional. The court held that band members can expect
more privacy than student athletes and that applying the policy to band
members wasn't the best way to address the school's drug problem.

Trinidad School District v. Lopez (1998)

■ Do any courts allow policies that require drug testing of students in all extracurricular activities?

Pathe Miller, an Arkansas resident, was interested in joining Cave City
High School's radio club and the prom committee, and participating in

the quiz bowl. In order to do so, he'd have to sign a consent form to be tested for drugs, and then submit to the test when directed. This was the school district's policy for students involved in extracurricular activities. Pathe and his father refused to consent, and they challenged the policy in court. The Arkansas court ruled that the invasion of Pathe's privacy was minimal and that the policy was legal. The school district's interest in preventing drug and alcohol use outweighed Pathe's right to privacy. Pathe changed schools before the case was decided. *Miller v. Wilkes* (1999)

Get on the Case:

- Are you surprised by any of the decisions about drug tests? What's next—do you think all students, regardless of whether they're involved in clubs or activities outside of class, will be subject to random, suspicionless drug testing? Will this keep drugs off school grounds? Or will students continue using drugs and take a chance that on any given day, for example, they won't be picked for a drug test? What about testing for cigarette use? Do you think this is going too far, or is there a good reason for such a school rule?

- You may have heard about drug testing of professional and Olympic athletes. But did you know that drug tests are being required more frequently of adults in other fields? Often, such policies are being challenged in court. Review the following cases and then consider the questions below.

School bus drivers: M. C. English worked for an Alabama school district as a mechanic who also drove school buses occasionally. In January 1995, he was fired from his job after testing positive for marijuana use. (This drug test was required under the federal Transportation Employee Testing Act of 1991.) M. C. sued the school district and lost. The federal district court found that the test was a minimal intrusion into M. C.'s privacy and was justified in order to guard the safety of children. *M. C. English v. Talledega County Board of Education* (1996)

Political candidates: In 1997, the U.S. Supreme Court declared a Georgia law requiring drug testing of all political candidates unconstitutional. The Court reviewed the recent history of drug testing in

America and decided that drug tests are a search under the Fourth Amendment and must be reasonable—based on a suspicion that a person is breaking the law. People whose jobs affect public safety, such as airline pilots and railroad employees, may be required to submit to suspicionless tests. Because politicians and candidates for office don't usually perform high-risk or safety-sensitive tasks, this test was considered unlawful. *Chandler v. Miller* (1997)

Transit officers: In New Jersey, the transit (train) authority's police officers carry weapons and may use deadly force in certain circumstances. Their job includes promoting the safety of all employees and customers by creating a drug- and alcohol-free workplace. Requiring these officers to submit to random testing was found to be reasonable under the law. *New Jersey Local 304 v. New Jersey Transit* (1997)

Electrical engineers: David Rebel was an electrical engineer at a nuclear power plant in Pennsylvania. All employees were subject to random drug testing, and David was selected to test in 1995. He refused, claiming he didn't believe in the program. He considered the test to be an insult and an invasion of his privacy. David was fired and also denied unemployment benefits, on the grounds that his loss of employment was his own doing. He appealed his case and lost. The Commonwealth Court of Pennsylvania upheld the drug-testing policy. *Rebel v. Unemployment Compensation Board* (1997)

- What do you think about each of these cases? Do you agree that candidates for public office shouldn't be required to undergo drug tests? If you think they should submit to random testing, what about student-body officers? Is there any difference in responsibility here? Why or why not? Or should all who hold office, regardless of level, be expected to live drug- and alcohol-free?

- Can you think of any jobs or activities where drug testing should *absolutely* be done? Do you believe that some workers should *never* be required to take such tests? Why?

- Research the history of drug testing—at the library or online. When were drug tests first given and why? What group of people was first required to take these tests? Were such requirements immediately met with objections? Are the tests themselves always accurate?

ISSUE:

Do you have privacy rights at school?

Case: *New Jersey v. T. L. O.* (1985)

Schools today are faced with the difficult task of protecting students in an age where violent outbursts and underage drug use seem common. Yet, as new measures are introduced to ensure the safety of students, teachers, and school personnel—metal detectors, video cameras, and security officers, to name a few—questions about students' rights to privacy invariably crop up. Likewise, as school administrators strive to enforce drug policies—which sometimes means conducting random locker and canine searches, as well as personal searches—they run the risk of sacrificing students' privacy.

Justice Byron White summed up the issue this way: "How, then, should we strike the balance between the schoolchild's legitimate expectation of privacy and the school's equally legitimate need to maintain an environment in which learning can take place?"

The Facts:

In March 1980, Lenore Chen, a teacher at Piscataway High School in New Jersey, caught T. L. O. (Terry), who was a fourteen-year-old freshman, and another girl smoking in the bathroom. She took the two girls to the principal's office, where they were questioned by the assistant principal, Mr. Choplick. Terry's friend admitted to violating the school's no-smoking rule, but Terry denied that she'd been smoking. Mr. Choplick asked Terry for her purse, opened it, and immediately saw a pack of cigarettes. While reaching for the cigarettes, he noticed a pack of rolling papers, which he knew were usually used with marijuana. Mr. Choplick then thoroughly searched Terry's purse. He found a small amount of marijuana and a metal pipe, empty plastic bags, an index card that listed students who owed her money, two letters that suggested drug dealing, and $40, mostly in $1 bills. The school turned the matter over to the police. At the police station, in the presence of her mother, Terry confessed to selling drugs at school. She was charged with possession of marijuana and was later found guilty.

Terry **appealed** her case, claiming that Mr. Choplick had violated her Fourth Amendment protection (see the **Bill of Rights** on pages 19–20) against an unreasonable **search and seizure.** Terry's attorney argued that her confession at the police station should be disregarded because it resulted from the unlawful search of her purse.

YOU BE THE JUDGE

- **Do you think the assistant principal's search of Terry's purse was legal? Why or why not? Did it violate Terry's Fourth Amendment protection against unreasonable searches?**

- **Do constitutional protections apply to students in public schools? Or can schools create and enforce their own set of rules?**

The Ruling:

In a six to three decision, written by Justice Byron White, the U.S. Supreme Court ruled that the initial search of Terry's purse for cigarettes was reasonable based on the teacher's report that she'd been smoking in the bathroom. Then, the assistant principal's discovery of the rolling papers created a reasonable suspicion that Terry possessed marijuana, which justified further exploration. Terry was sentenced to one year of **probation** and ordered to receive counseling and to enter a drug program.

T. L. O. is the landmark case on the issue of search and seizure at school. In this case, the Court needed to determine how to balance a student's right to privacy and the school's need to maintain an environment of learning. The Court decided that a "reasonableness" test could settle such questions.

First, it's clear that you're protected against unreasonable searches at school—your constitutional rights aren't left behind once you "enter the schoolhouse." As a student, you have a reasonable expectation of privacy that's balanced with the school's duty to do its job—to ensure the security and safety of students, to maintain order, and to promote an environment where education thrives.

The rules of this case apply only to public schools, not private and parochial schools. Because public schools receive government money, school officials are viewed as acting on behalf of the government and must follow the rules of the Constitution. People who work in private schools, on the other hand, aren't viewed as government employees and may conduct searches whenever they see fit.

This means school officials may search you and your property if they have a "reasonable suspicion" that you've broken a school rule or have committed, or are in the process of committing, a crime. The U.S. Supreme Court said the decision to search a student must be based on the "totality of circumstances"— including the student's age, history, and school records; the seriousness of the problem in the school (for example, weapons, drugs, or stolen property); and the source of information. These are called "suspicion-based" searches. There are also "suspicionless searches," in which everyone in a certain group or classification is subject to a search.

In order for a suspicion-based search to be legal, it must be justified at the beginning—reasonable grounds must exist to believe that the search will turn up evidence that a person violated a rule or law.

The search must also be conducted within reasonable limits. The age and gender of the student must be considered, as well as the importance of the object of the search.

Related Cases:

The *T. L. O.* case didn't ultimately settle what protection the Fourth Amendment offers students. Since this U.S. Supreme Court decision, courts around the country have reviewed hundreds of cases involving student searches. The increase of weapons and drugs in schools has become a "compelling circumstance" justifying more searches. However, the issue of reasonableness isn't always clear. Courts have accepted some searches as reasonable under certain circumstances, while deeming similar ones as unreasonable.

▪ Under what circumstances can school officials legally search you?

At Ingraham High School in Seattle, Washington, a security officer stopped two students, Eric and Adrian, who were entering the school after classes had begun. Both smelled of marijuana and had red, droopy eyes. They were questioned separately, and each admitted that he'd smoked marijuana with another student, John Washington, that morning before school. A marijuana pipe was found in their possession, but no marijuana. The security officer knew that John Washington had been involved in a previous drug-related incident. John was taken out of his gym class and escorted to the principal's office. The officer searched John, who at first protested but later consented when told the police would be called. The officer found a plastic bag containing twelve pieces of crack cocaine in John's shirt pocket. John was charged with drug possession and found guilty. He challenged the search, claiming it was illegal. The Washington Court of Appeals ruled that the amount of suspicion against John justified the warrantless search by the school official.

State v. Washington (1999)

▪ If they suspect you of wrongdoing, can school officials search your belongings?

Ninth-grader James DesRoches attended Granby High School in Norfolk, Virginia. He took an art class that met before and after lunch. In May 1997, his classmate Shamra Hursey went to lunch, leaving her tennis shoes on top of her desk. When she returned, her shoes were gone. The dean ordered a search of the belongings of the nineteen students in the class. James wouldn't let school personnel search his backpack, so he was sent to the principal's office. He called his parents and continued to refuse the search. James was suspended for ten days. He and his father sued the principal, the school superintendent, and the school board. They claimed that the search would violate James's protection against unreasonable searches. The federal court who heard the case upheld the school suspension. It stated that, although James wasn't a suspect at the beginning of the incident, he became one after the other eighteen students were searched and nothing was found. By the process of elimination, James became a suspect in the question of the missing shoes, which justified a search of his backpack.

DesRoches v. Caprio (1998)

▪ Does an "alert" by a drug-sniffing dog justify a locker search?

At Harborcreek High School in Erie County, Pennsylvania, an unannounced canine search of all 2,000 student lockers was conducted. Rudy, the dog, "hit" on eighteen of the lockers, which were then opened and searched. Marijuana and drug paraphernalia were found in a student named Vincent's jacket, which was hanging in his locker. Vincent admitted the marijuana and related items were his but argued that the search was conducted illegally. The school contended that the purpose of the search was to maintain a drug-free campus and was therefore legal. The Superior Court of Pennsylvania disagreed with the school, ruling that the alert by a drug-trained dog didn't alone justify a locker search. The court said Vincent had a reasonable expectation of privacy in his locker. Because the school had no evidence that Vincent was using or dealing drugs, reasonable suspicion of illegal activity didn't exist. The charges were dropped because the results of the search couldn't be used as evidence against him.

Commonwealth v. Cass (1995)

▪ Is a strip-search acceptable if a drug-sniffing dog calls an "alert" to a student?

Diane Doe was thirteen years old when a school-wide drug inspection at Highland Junior High in Indiana was performed. All 2,700 students were sniffed by police dogs. Depending on the dogs' behavior, some students had their pockets searched for drugs; others were told to remove their clothing for a visual examination. The dog reacted to Diane, who was told to empty her pockets. She was also instructed to undress, which she did in front of two women in the nurse's office. Nothing was found. Diane and her parents sued the school district, the principal, the police chief, and the dog trainer for violating Diane's civil rights by conducting the search. The federal court agreed with Diane and her parents that the search was unreasonable, stating: "[I]t does not require a constitutional scholar to conclude that a nude search of a thirteen-year-old child is an invasion of some magnitude. More than that: it is a violation of any known principle of human decency."

Doe v. Renfrow (1980)

▪ Does a police officer's hunch justify a search?

Sixteen-year-old Demond, a student in Illinois, arrived at school one morning to discover police officers and a metal detector. Students were lined up to go through the detector. Demond turned around to leave but was stopped by the police and told to proceed through the detector. In response, Demond raised his shirt and said, "Someone put this gun on me." He was arrested and charged with possession of a weapon at school. Demond argued that the search was illegal.

The Illinois Court of Appeals found that Demond's act of turning around and leaving didn't create reasonable suspicion that he possessed anything illegal. A "hunch" isn't enough to justify a search, according to the court. The police were wrong to stop Demond, so the gun was ruled as inadmissible evidence. The case against Demond was dismissed.

People v. Parker (1996)

▪ Is a strip-search justified if you're suspected of possessing illegal drugs?

School officials at Carl Sandburg High School in Orland Park, Illinois, noticed an unusual bulge in sixteen-year-old Brian Cornfield's clothing. A teacher thought he was hiding drugs, but Brian denied this when confronted by the teacher and the school dean. Brian was told to call his mother and ask for her permission to search him, which she refused. Because of recent reports by teachers and school aides of drug-related activity on campus, and because of the suspicions raised by Brian's appearance, school officials decided a strip-search of Brian was justified. The teacher and the dean escorted him to the boys' locker room, locked the door, and told him to remove his clothes and put on a gym suit. They visually inspected him while naked and searched his clothes. Nothing was found, and Brian was sent home. Brian and his mother sued the teacher, the dean, and the school district for violating his civil rights. Because the strip-search was based on a reasonable suspicion of drug activity and conducted in private, it was approved by the federal court.

Cornfield v. School District No. 230 (1993)

▪ Is a strip-search unreasonable if the school is searching for something of little value?

After gym class in West Jay County Middle School in Dunkirk, Indiana, two seventh-grade students told their teacher that $4.50 was missing from the locker room. The principal was notified and decided to search the girls in the gym class and their lockers. Thirteen-year-old Amanda and five of her friends were interviewed by the principal. The girls were then told to take off their shoes and socks; their lockers and book bags were also searched. Then, in front of a female school official, they were told to loosen or remove their bras and shirts. Amanda, her five friends, and their parents all filed a lawsuit after this incident. Based on the object of the search ($4.50), the court ruled that a strip-search was unreasonable.

Oliver v. McClung (1995)

Get on the Case:

- How much authority should school officials have over you while you're at school? Where do you draw the line, and based on what—age, gender, the extent of the search?

- Considering recent incidents of school violence in the United States, what do you think schools could do to provide a safer environment for learning? Put yourself in the shoes of a teacher or principal—is your opinion on these issues the same from this standpoint? Why or why not?

- What rules or policies does your school have on searches of lockers or students? Check your student handbook or ask your principal for a copy of this written policy. Then talk to other students and your parents about the policy. Do you agree or disagree with it? Why? How do you think the policy works or doesn't work? How would you change or improve it if you could?

ISSUE:

Do you have to wait until you're eighteen to get some privacy?

Case: *Tariq A-R Y v. Maryland* (1998)

As you grow older, it's only natural to want some privacy. After all, you can't become an adult if you don't break away from your parents and develop thoughts and dreams all your own. And all of these changes require space and time to yourself.

While everyone needs privacy, a person's legal right to this freedom isn't always clear. Different people, and different courts, have varying views on what parts of your life deserve to be kept private—and what age you need to be to have privacy rights.

The Facts:

In May 1995, an anonymous tip sent the police to Tariq's home in Frederick County, Maryland. Tariq was a **minor** who lived with his mother. When he answered the door, the police officers saw a bottle of beer on the floor and smelled marijuana in the air and alcohol on Tariq's breath.

Suspecting that Tariq was drinking alcohol or using illegal drugs, the police officers asked his mother for permission to search the home. She said yes, they could search the house and "anything in it." The officers found a bag of marijuana in a vest that was in the dining room. Tariq admitted the vest belonged to him but argued that, without his permission, the police had no right to search it.

Tariq was arrested for possession of an illegal substance. He punched and kicked the officers when he was arrested, so he was also charged with resisting arrest.

YOU BE THE JUDGE

- **Can a parent of a minor give police permission to search a child's personal belongings—over the child's objection?**

- **The Fourth Amendment (see the Bill of Rights on pages 19–20) protects each of us from unreasonable search and seizure. This right may be waived by the person being searched. The question in this case is who may waive this right—the minor or the minor's parent?**

- **Tariq didn't expect the police to search his vest; he assumed that his privacy would be recognized and honored. Was Tariq's expectation reasonable?**

Legally, you're considered a minor, juvenile, or child until you're eighteen. Then you're emancipated (free) and recognized as an adult. Once you're emancipated, your parents or legal guardians are no longer responsible for you or your actions. They now have no authority over you, and you no longer have the right to be taken care of by them.

You automatically become emancipated when you turn eighteen. Some states, however, allow teenagers to **petition** the courts for **emancipation** before they're eighteen, under special circumstances. The case of *Rachel Kingsley v. Gregory Kingsley* (1993) on pages 32–36 explores this issue in more depth.

The Ruling:

The Maryland Court of Appeals stood by the principle that parents have the authority to make decisions about their homes and everything in them. The state court also reviewed the concept of reasonable expectation of privacy and concluded that it wasn't reasonable for Tariq to expect his belongings left in an open area of his mother's home to be viewed as private. After considering the circumstances of the search, the court ruled that the police didn't need Tariq's permission to search his property: his mother's consent was enough, and Tariq's objection didn't matter.

> *Reasonable* is a key word when it comes to privacy and the law. Courts recognize that everyone needs and deserves a certain amount of privacy—what they call a "reasonable expectation of privacy." But what's reasonable to one person may not be to another.

Tariq was convicted of possession of marijuana and resisting arrest. His case was **appealed** to the U.S. Supreme Court, which turned down the request to hear the case in 1998. The Maryland ruling stayed in place. Tariq was sent to Maryland's department of juvenile services.

This case demonstrates that, legally, parents have authority over their underage children. Besides being in charge of the home, your parents can legally control and make decisions about where you go to school, what place of worship you attend, whether you can get a job, what sports you're allowed to play, and who you can spend your free time with. Does this mean your parents have control over *every* aspect of your life? No, some parts *are* beyond their control. See *Bellotti v. Baird* (1979) on pages 86–92 and *Parham v. J. R.* (1979) on pages 134–140 for more information.

▪ Is your property private when you're a passenger in a vehicle?

In 1999, the U.S. Supreme Court made a decision that reduced a person's zone of privacy. In this case, Sandra Houghton, a legal adult in Wyoming, was riding in a car that was stopped for speeding. The driver had a syringe in his shirt pocket and, when asked, admitted he'd used it to take drugs. Sandra lied about her name, had fresh needle tracks on her arms, and, when the car was searched, told the police the purse on the backseat was hers. During the search, the police found the drug methamphetamine and drug-related items in Sandra's purse. She was arrested and later convicted of drug possession and sentenced to two to three years in prison. The search of Sandra's purse was upheld by the U.S. Supreme Court. The justices determined that, as a passenger in a car, your expectation of privacy is considerably less than in other situations.

Wyoming v. Houghton (1999)

▪ Is your garbage private property?

In July 1992, sanitation worker Nelson Dowd picked up Allen Hauser's garbage as he did every week in Winston-Salem, North Carolina. This time, though, at the direction of the police, Nelson kept it separate from the rest of the trash. (Note: a private citizen wouldn't normally be given such a task, except at the request of the police.) He turned the garbage over to the authorities, who found evidence of cocaine possession. Allen was convicted and sentenced to ten years in prison. He appealed, claiming the **search and seizure** of his garbage was illegal. The court disagreed, holding that any expectation of privacy was lost once the garbage was put out for the public to see and take. This case demonstrates that, regardless of age, a person's right to privacy is limited.

State v. Hauser (1995)

▪ Can adults other than your parents give police permission to search your property?

Dion Summers and a friend were seen walking down the street carrying stereo equipment. A burglary had been reported earlier that day in Dion's neighborhood in Seattle, Washington. His mother was out of town, and Dion's adult sister was staying at the house, caring for the children. She later gave the police permission to search Dion's room, where the stereos were found. Dion was charged with and convicted of burglary. He argued that his sister didn't have the authority to allow a search of his belongings. The court disagreed, ruling that his sister, who was in charge during his mother's absence, did indeed possess this authority.

State v. Summers (1988)

▪ When is an "expectation of privacy" considered reasonable?

In Bend, Oregon, nineteen-year-old Eugene Carsey was on parole and was required to live with his grandparents. He paid them $60 a month to rent a room in their home. His grandparents never entered his room, based on an unspoken agreement that he alone had control over it. He cleaned it himself and did his own laundry. On a tip that Eugene had received stolen stereo equipment, the police conducted a warrantless search of his room and found marijuana. Although Eugene's grand-mother had given her permission to search his room, in this case, the state court determined that her consent was invalid. Under the family's living arrangements, Eugene had a reasonable expectation of privacy.

State v. Carsey (1983)

▪ What if your belongings are under lock and key?

A police officer in Illinois spotted fifteen-year-old Ricky Salyer driving his mother's car, which she had reported missing. When Ricky got home later, his mother found a canvas bag containing marijuana in the car's backseat. She gave the police permission to search Ricky's room, where they found more incriminating evidence. Ricky's room was kept locked on the inside and had a combination lock on the outside. His mother didn't have the combination and, in fact, had only been in the room once or twice in the previous three months. Nevertheless, the court held that Ricky's mother had the final word over the room, because the house was hers and Ricky was a minor. Her consent was ruled valid, and the evidence was allowed in court. Ricky was convicted of theft, drug, and firearm charges and committed to the state department of juvenile corrections.

In the Interest of Salyer (1977)

Get on the Case:

- Do you think everyone deserves privacy? Under what circumstances should a person's right to privacy be taken away? Is it important to you to keep some of your belongings and thoughts private? Why?

- What about when someone keeps a journal? Do you think this should always be kept private, or are there certain circumstances when it should be allowed as court evidence? Why? What about personal mail or email? How private should these items be in the eyes of the law?

- Hold a family meeting to discuss the issue of privacy. Talk about how family members can respect each other's privacy and what is and isn't private in your home.

ISSUE:

Can you be tried as an adult and receive an adult sentence?

Case: *Kent v. United States* (1966)

Although juvenile courts were created to decide cases against **minors**, more and more often teenagers are being tried in adult court. A move into adult court means that juveniles may receive longer sentences for their crimes—instead of being released when they turn eighteen or twenty-one. Their sentence is also focused on punishment and protecting the community, rather than rehabilitation and treatment—the goals of juvenile court.

The Facts:

Morris Allen Kent was arrested in Washington, D.C., on September 5, 1961, for three home burglaries, three robberies, and two counts of rape. The sixteen-year-old had been on **probation** since he was fourteen for burglary and purse snatching.

Morris was held in **detention** for almost a week. (At the time of Morris's arrest, the District of Columbia allowed minors to be held for up to five days before a hearing—now it's a maximum of forty-eight hours.) His mother hired a lawyer who arranged for two psychiatrists and a psychologist to evaluate Morris and determine his mental state. Morris's lawyer wanted to argue that Morris's case should be kept in the juvenile court—not go into adult court. His lawyer asked the juvenile court for a hearing on the question of **waiver** to adult court, and he asked for Morris's **social file,** so he could be better informed about his client's history. The psychiatrist found Morris to be "a victim of severe psychopathology" and recommended hospitalization.

The court didn't respond to these requests or to the psychiatrist's evaluation. No hearing was held, and neither Morris, his parents, nor an attorney were allowed to address the court. The court signed a waiver "after full investigation" that sent Morris to adult court. No reasons for the waiver were given. The jury found Morris guilty of the burglary and robbery charges, but not guilty by reason of insanity of the rape charges. The court sentenced Morris to thirty to ninety years in prison.

Morris and his attorney **appealed,** arguing that the court wasn't given enough information about Morris's mental state or his history. They said that he shouldn't have been charged or tried in adult court.

YOU BE THE JUDGE

- **Do you think Morris should have been waived into adult court under these circumstances? Why or why not?**

- **What factors do you think the court considers when deciding whether to waive a minor into adult court?**

The Ruling:

This is a key case in the law of juvenile rights. Because the U.S. Supreme Court thought that some of the police and juvenile court practices were "disturbing," it examined the juvenile court system for the first time. In particular, it looked at **due process** and fair treatment of juveniles before **transfer** to adult court.

The Court determined that waiving a minor into adult court is a "critically important" issue that requires fair treatment, a thorough investigation, and careful consideration. Courts need to follow the laws of their individual states when making the waiver decision. These state laws outline the factors that courts need to consider, including the seriousness of the crime; how it was committed; the juvenile's age, maturity, and lifestyle; whether the offense is a personal or property crime; and the minor's criminal background and mental state. Community safety is to be considered, as well as the likelihood of rehabilitating the juvenile in the juvenile justice system.

The Court felt strongly about protecting an individual's rights when faced with a criminal charge. It recognized the consequences of sending a juvenile to adult court and wanted to create strict safeguards in the process. In a five to four decision, Justice Abe Fortas wrote: "There is no place in our system of law for reaching a result of such tremendous consequences without ceremony—without hearing, without effective assistance of counsel, without a statement of reasons." The Court ruled that a hearing must be held to decide whether to transfer a juvenile into adult court, the juvenile must be given an opportunity to address the court with the assistance of an attorney, and the court must provide an explanation of its decision.

Courts generally recognize that juveniles lack the experience, judgment, and maturity of adults. Consequently, they are seen as good candidates for rehabilitation. Rehabilitation may include probation, community service, a fine, **restitution** to victims, individual and family counseling, and detention. The majority of juveniles who successfully complete a juvenile court sentence have no further contact with the justice system.

The Court found that the lower court violated Morris's rights. The case was sent back to the trial court for it to determine whether Morris should be transferred into adult court. The federal district court considered the U.S. Supreme Court's position on Morris's rights but again decided that Morris should be tried as an adult. Another court of appeals later reversed this decision, due to Morris's mental condition. It found Morris was mentally ill and needed psychiatric treatment, not prison. The court set aside the conviction and sentence, and ordered that Morris remain hospitalized under the **civil commitment laws.**

An 1843 English case that became known as the M'Naghten Rule of Insanity established the test that a number of states use today in criminal trials. It states that a person isn't criminally responsible for his or her crime if, at the time of committing the act, the person didn't know (1) what he or she was doing and (2) that the act was wrong and violated the rights of another. Those states that don't use M'Naghten have their own test for determining criminal responsibility.

Although the *Kent* decision is more than thirty years old, its principle is continually turned to—that juveniles can be treated as adults in the criminal system, but they must be afforded full due process throughout the proceedings. It's a serious matter for teenagers to face adult consequences for their acts. The responsibility for deciding a teenager's fate weighs heavily on all of the participants.

Related Cases:

In some states, juveniles charged with certain crimes start off in adult court—the juvenile must convince the court that he or she belongs in juvenile court instead. Arkansas, New York, Oklahoma, and Vermont are some states that proceed in this manner. It's a legislative decision, based in part on community protection. Other states have a direct-file policy regarding certain crimes. If the juvenile is a certain age and allegedly commits a specific offense (usually a violent crime), the charges are filed in adult court and *stay* there. Arizona, Florida, Kansas, and Massachusetts are four states with a direct-file procedure.

■ How does the type of crime influence whether a minor will be tried in adult court?

In a case in Iowa, Mario Terry (age sixteen), his girlfriend Jessica Springsteen (fifteen), and another boy, Thomas Hull, went to Harold Mitchell's home, where they beat him with a baseball bat and a crowbar. Mr. Mitchell was Jessica's stepfather, who disapproved of Jessica and Mario's relationship and had banned Mario from his home. The man survived the beating, with minor back injuries. Under Iowa law, juveniles charged with certain crimes start in adult court and argue to be moved to juvenile court. Mario and his lawyers were unable to persuade the state trial court that he should be treated as a juvenile rather than an adult. The age of all three teens, their motivation, and the circumstances of the crime along with all legal requirements were considered in deciding whether to change the **jurisdiction** of Mario's case. A jury convicted him of attempted murder and first-degree burglary (entering the house with the intent to commit a crime). He was sentenced to twenty-five years in prison.

In most states, minors don't have a fundamental right to be prosecuted as juveniles. Instead, it's considered a privilege granted by the legislature. This means that each state may set its own age and other guidelines for which cases go to juvenile court and which ones fall under the jurisdiction of an adult court—as long as the state laws don't treat people in the same class differently. For example, in 1995, Wisconsin lowered the age for adult prosecution to ten for juveniles charged with murder. This applies to all ten-year-olds, whether boys or girls.

State v. Terry (1997)

■ Can you be tried as an adult if you're only eleven years old?

In 1997, eleven-year-old Nathaniel Abraham borrowed a rifle and randomly shot and killed eighteen-year-old Ronnie Greene Jr. in Pontiac, Michigan. Nathaniel was 70 yards away from Ronnie, who was standing outside a convenience store when the incident took place. Under Michigan law, Nathaniel was tried as an adult and convicted in 1999 of second-degree murder. The law allowed the court to sentence him either as a juvenile or an adult, or under a blended sentence that would require him to be under supervision past the age of twenty-one. Nathaniel also could have received a life sentence. The judge stated that although Nathaniel committed a heinous crime, there were eight years left to rehabilitate him; the judge preferred this option over sending the boy to an adult prison, where rehabilitation and treatment wouldn't be available. In January 2000, Nathaniel was sentenced to a juvenile detention facility until the age of twenty-one. At this point, he had already been locked up for two years, and the judge noticed that Nathaniel had made progress during that time.

▪ Do minors have a right to have their parents with them in court?

School was just getting out at Miller Grove Middle School in Georgia. Behind one of the buildings, fourteen-year-old Fabian Appling approached two boys and, at gunpoint, took the shoes and wallet of one of the boys. Fabian was charged with armed robbery and was tried as an adult. During the trial, the prosecution excluded witnesses from the courtroom—all witnesses who were to testify had to stay out of the courtroom until it was their turn to take the stand. (This is done to prevent witnesses from hearing the testimony of others and possibly changing their story; it's a common practice in criminal trials.) In this case, Fabian's mother was listed as a possible witness, because she may have noticed her son's behavior after the incident and heard statements he made about the robbery.

Fabian was found guilty. He and his lawyer appealed the conviction, arguing that his mother should have been allowed in the courtroom to help him understand the trial and make decisions along with his lawyer. The Georgia Court of Appeals decided that a parent's right to be present at trial is not absolute. It did state, however, that trying a juvenile as an adult doesn't *make* a juvenile an adult and said: "Parental guidance in a felony case is a necessary safeguard for a juvenile." In this case, though, no error was found and Fabian's conviction was affirmed.

Appling v. State (1996)

In the 1980s and 1990s, there was an increase in the number of teenagers tried in adult court—due to a new focus on community protection and a move away from treatment and rehabilitation of juveniles. Many states passed laws authorizing automatic waiver to adult court for certain crimes. This means that, depending on the offense and age of the offender, a juvenile bypasses juvenile court and goes straight to adult court. Prosecutors have been given greater discretion in charging juvenile offenders. Those who don't go directly to adult court may still end up there through the waiver process in juvenile court. The juvenile court judge may decide that the juvenile isn't appropriate for juvenile court services and that the community needs protection from this individual. In such a case, the juvenile court may waive, or give up, its jurisdiction and send the case to adult court. A hearing is conducted to determine the appropriateness of treating a minor as an adult.

Get on the Case:

- What do you think about the factors that are considered when deciding whether to waive a minor into adult court—more specifically, the crime and how it was committed; the juvenile's age, maturity, and lifestyle; whether the offense is a personal or property crime; and the minor's criminal background and mental state? What other factors do you think the court should consider?

- What do you think about rehabilitating juveniles? Do you think that most minors who get in trouble with the law can be helped? Why or why not? What do you think it would take to rehabilitate someone?

- What's the law in your state about sending juveniles to adult court? Call or write a local lawyer and ask. The police or your district attorney also may be of help; so may your local and state bar associations. The telephone numbers you need should be in the phone book or on the Internet. You can check the Yellow Pages under Attorneys or Criminal Law for the names of practicing attorneys to contact.

- Identify a local story where a juvenile has been charged with a crime and a waiver hearing is scheduled. Follow it through to the end and see if you agree with the outcome. Keep an open mind until you consider all the facts—from everyone involved, including the juvenile's witnesses as well as the victim's. Call the prosecutor and defense attorney involved with the case; explain that you're studying the process. Ask if you may follow the case to its conclusion. You may even be able to attend court as an observer. (Courts often allow observers from high schools and colleges.) Remember to ask about any confidentiality rules that you may be expected to follow. Look under Attorneys or in the governments section of the phone book, under City Attorney, District Attorney, or Public Defender.

Can you get an abortion without a parent's consent?

Case: *Bellotti v. Baird* (1979)

If you ever broke a bone when you were little, your mom or dad probably brought you to the hospital to have a cast put on. Or if you needed surgery to have your appendix or tonsils removed, a parent was most likely by your side. Legally, your mom or dad needed to give the hospital permission to treat you.

What happens when you're older, but not yet an adult, and you want to see a doctor for something you consider private, such as birth control or an abortion? Does a parent still have to give consent for you to receive medication or have surgery?

The Facts:

Sixteen-year-old Mary Moe was an unmarried teenager, living with her parents in Massachusetts. In October 1974, she discovered that she was eight weeks pregnant. She no longer saw the father of the baby, a sixteen-year-old boy she had dated for three months. Mary decided to have an abortion. However, in Massachusetts it was illegal for a doctor to perform an abortion on an unmarried **minor** without informing and getting the permission of both parents. If the minor's parents refused to consent, then the minor could ask a court to grant permission for the abortion. Either way, parental notice was required.

Mary didn't want to tell her parents that she was pregnant. Her father had become quite upset at an earlier time when he learned that one of her friends was pregnant. Mary remembered that he had said that if she got pregnant, he would kick her out of the house and kill her boyfriend. So, out of fear of what her father might do, dread about letting her parents know she'd had sex, and a desire to spare her parents' feelings, Mary chose not to tell them about her situation. She did confide, however, in her older sister.

In October 1974, Mary and the Parents Aid Society, a nonprofit clinic in Boston that performed abortions, filed a lawsuit challenging the Massachusetts law that prevented underage women from getting abortions without their parents' consent. They argued that the law discriminated against minors—that it violated their **due process** and **equal protection** rights, as outlined in the Fourteenth Amendment (see the **Bill of Rights** on pages 19–20).

Although she was a minor, the Massachusetts court determined that Mary was of average intelligence, that she fully understood the court proceedings, and that she was competent and emotionally capable of making a decision about her pregnancy without her parents' guidance. In fact, before she became pregnant, she decided that if she was faced with such a situation, she'd seek an abortion. Mary testified in court that she contacted the clinic about an abortion "about five minutes after I found out I was pregnant."

Mary received counseling and had the abortion during a time in the lawsuit when the law was suspended. The lawsuit began in 1974 and was settled in 1979.

In 1970, Norma McCorvey, an unmarried woman who lived in Dallas, Texas, learned that she was pregnant. She immediately tried to get an abortion but couldn't because of an 1854 Texas law that allowed abortion only if the woman's life was in danger as a result of the pregnancy. Norma challenged the law, claiming that it violated her right to privacy. Throughout her case, she used the name Jane Roe. The U.S. Supreme Court agreed with Norma, and in 1973 said that the Fourteenth Amendment's protection of liberty is broad enough to include a woman's decision whether to terminate her pregnancy. The landmark case is known as *Roe v. Wade* (1973).

YOU BE THE JUDGE

- **Do parents have a right to prevent their daughter from getting an abortion?**

- **Do parents have a right to know that their daughter is seeking an abortion?**

- **Do you think teenage girls are capable of making this decision without their parents help?**

The Ruling:

In deciding whether a teenager can get an abortion without telling her parents or getting their permission, the U.S. Supreme Court reviewed the history of parent-child relationships in terms of government protection and intervention.

The Court recognized that deeply rooted in our nation's history and traditions is the belief that parents have a great deal of authority over their children. This is basic in the structure of our society. We place certain legal restrictions on minors to protect them and to allow them to grow up in a safe environment. These include safeguards from obscenity, employment restrictions, and due process protections when arrested or charged with a crime.

The Court also noted two considerations regarding teens and abortion:

1. A substantial number of girls under eighteen are capable of forming a valid consent; this means they're mature enough to make an intelligent, well-informed decision regarding their pregnancy, after considering the options available.

2. A mother's right to an abortion in the first trimester (first three months of pregnancy) doesn't depend on her calendar age. Teen and adult mothers alike have this right.

The question then becomes how to balance the parents' right to raise their children against the underage mother's right to get an abortion.

The eight to one Court opinion, written by Justices Lewis F. Powell and John P. Stevens, strongly recommended that states encourage unmarried pregnant teens to ask their parents for help and advice: "[T]he decision whether or not to bear a child . . . is a grave decision, and a girl of tender years, under emotional stress, may be ill-equipped to make it without mature advice and emotional support."

The Court also recognized the need to make the abortion decision quickly—there may be little time between discovering a pregnancy and the end of the first trimester. Unlike other parent-child decisions (such as marriage, driving, and employment), the abortion decision can't be postponed.

Consequently, the Court determined that the Massachusetts law was unconstitutional; a state may not require parental consent for a minor's abortion without also providing another way for an underage woman to get authorization for the abortion. In other words, a state may not give parents an absolute veto over a minor's decision to have an abortion.

A state may set up what's called a **judicial bypass procedure.** In this situation, the minor may show the court that she's mature enough and well-informed enough to make a decision, in consultation with her doctor and independent of her parents' wishes. If not mature enough to make a decision, she may show that the abortion is in her best interests. The Court recognized that some parents hold strong views on abortion and would obstruct their daughter's access to both an abortion and the court. Consequently, a minor may go directly to the court to receive authorization for an abortion.

Justice Byron R. White disagreed with the majority of the Court. He commented on the effect of this decision, which allows a minor to obtain an abortion without parental notice or consent: "Until now, I would have thought inconceivable a holding that the United States Constitution forbids even notice to parents when their minor child who seeks surgery objects to such notice and is able to convince a judge that the parents should be denied participation in the decision."

Related Cases:

Although the U.S. Supreme Court has recognized your right to privacy in sexual matters, it may be in your best interests to keep an open mind and an open line of communication with your mom or dad, who could be an invaluable source of advice and support. Having the ability and the right to do something doesn't mean that you have to act. There may be a better alternative, once you're fully informed and have given the situation some thought. In reading about the teens in the following cases, consider your reaction if you were in their position.

▪ Does your home situation affect the parental notification requirement for abortions?

Days before her eighteenth birthday, Jane Doe asked a juvenile court judge in Franklin County, Ohio, for permission to have an abortion without telling her parents. Jane told the court that she'd been physically abused by her parents and threatened with future abuse. Although the juvenile court denied her request, a higher court granted it. Jane's "horrible home life," the Ohio court ruled, justified concealing her pregnancy from her parents.

In re Jane Doe (1994)

▪ Do you really need to notify both of your parents that you want an abortion?

In 1997, the U.S. Supreme Court decided another challenge to a parent notification law. A Parental Notice of Abortion Act had been passed in Montana in 1995; it allowed an unemancipated minor to have an abortion after one of her parents was notified. The Court had already decided that requiring notice to both parents was unconstitutional.

However, a bypass provision gave Montana minors a right to convince a court that notifying either parent wouldn't be in her best interests. The Court ruled that if clear and convincing evidence exists that any of the following three conditions are met, notice to parents may be **waived:**

1. The minor is mature enough to decide whether to have an abortion.

2. There is evidence of a pattern of physical, sexual, or emotional abuse by one of her parents or a guardian.

3. Notification to the parent isn't in the minor's best interests.

Lambert v. Wicklund (1997)

▪ Do you need to get a parent's permission before getting birth control?

In an attempt to prevent teen pregnancy and the spread of sexually transmitted diseases among students, the Philadelphia Board of Education developed a voluntary, in-school condom distribution and counseling program. Parents could veto their children's participation in the high school program. This meant that before a student would be given condoms, a counselor would check if the student's parent had opted-out. If they had, the request would be denied. If not, and after counseling regarding abstinence and appropriate use, the condoms would be provided.

A parent group asked the court to stop the program, claiming it was illegal and infringed upon students' privacy rights. The court denied this request, stating that a condom program is a legitimate service that helps keep students healthy. The court noted that a "student's education is hindered when they drop out of school because they are pregnant, sick with venereal disease, or dying of AIDS. . . . high schools must teach wellness and fitness, and give instruction regarding the prevention of HIV and AIDS."

Parents United for Better Schools v. Philadelphia Board of Education (1997)

▪ Do school condom programs violate a parent's rights?

A number of students and their parents in Falmouth, Massachusetts, opposed a junior and senior high school condom program. They claimed it violated their right to family privacy, to raise their children as they saw fit, and to control their education. The Massachusetts Supreme Court disagreed and upheld the condom program. The court said, "Parents have no right to tailor public school programs to meet their individual religious or moral preferences."

Curtis v. School Committee of Falmouth (1995)

▪ Do clinics have to get parents' permission before prescribing birth control pills for minors?

A public family planning clinic in Lansing, Michigan, was sued for providing contraceptive devices and medication to minors without parental notice or consent. The clinic required minors to attend a two-hour "rap session" about birth control methods, the responsibilities of being sexually active, and the importance of talking to parents about sexual activity. In each case, a doctor decided whether to give the minor contraceptives. Female patients had to undergo a thorough physical examination and provide a complete medical history. The federal court of appeals found that the clinic's activities didn't interfere with the parents' constitutional rights. Furthermore, the clinic didn't have a duty to notify parents of their child's visit.

Doe v. Irwin (1980)

▪ Do teens have the right to have sex?

Under California law, sixteen-year-old T. A. J. was charged with **statutory rape**—having sexual intercourse with someone under the legal age limit. In this case, T. A. J.'s partner, T. P., was fourteen. The California law on consensual sex with minors set penalties ranging from **probation** to prison and fines up to $25,000. (All states have some form of this law.)

T. A. J. was found guilty by the court and placed on probation. He **appealed,** claiming an invasion of privacy—that minors, closely related in age, have a right to engage in intercourse without breaking the law. The California Court of Appeals disagreed, stating that there's no privacy right among minors to have consensual sex.

In re T. A. J. (1998)

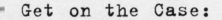 Get on the Case:

- The law gives a woman the right to have an abortion, but what is the definition of a *woman?* Is it any female who becomes pregnant, or a female over the age of eighteen? Do you think a minor who becomes pregnant should have a right to choose an abortion? Why or why not? Do you think the age of the minor plays a role—for example, whether the minor is twelve or seventeen?

- What rights do you think teenagers should have concerning their own bodies? At what age should a juvenile be given more rights? Why? What about birth control? Do you think minors have the right to receive prescriptions for birth control without informing their parents? Why or why not?

- Brainstorm a list of other adult rights that minors are usually restricted from (driving, voting, getting married). Choose one of these rights, and then make a list of the pros and cons of abolishing the age requirement for it. Do the pros outweigh the cons? Why or why not?

Do you have complete freedom of expression at school?

Case: *Tinker v. Des Moines Independent School District* (1969)

High school is often a time when students strive to blend in with the crowd while still being unique individuals. Do you feel comfortable doing something that sets you apart from the rest of your class or might lead to criticism? The teens in this case held strong views about war, particularly the United States involvement in Vietnam. They took a stand, and their case became the benchmark for future free speech issues at school.

The Facts:

In December 1965, a group of students and parents in Des Moines, Iowa, decided to express their objection to the war in Vietnam by wearing black armbands during the holiday season. The school district, fearing that the protest would create a disruption, passed a policy banning armbands at school. Students who wore one would be asked to remove it. Refusal meant suspension until they returned without it.

John Tinker was fifteen and in high school. His sister Mary Beth (age thirteen) was in junior high, while Paul (eight) and Hope (eleven) Tinker attended elementary school. All four kids, along with a friend, Chris Eckhardt (fifteen), wore the two-inch-wide black cloth armbands to school. When John, Mary Beth, and Chris refused to take the bands off, they were suspended and sent home. After the holidays, they returned to school without them.

The Tinkers sued the school district, asking the court to throw out the rule as an unconstitutional violation of their freedom of expression guaranteed in the First Amendment (see the **Bill of Rights** on pages 19–20).

YOU BE THE JUDGE

- **The First Amendment provides for freedom of expression. Do schools have a right to limit a student's freedom? Why or why not?**

- **Do you think that the type of expression affects this decision? If so, how?**

The Ruling:

In this case, the U.S. Supreme Court needed to balance the authority of school officials to maintain order on campus and the First Amendment rights of students, including freedom of speech and expression.

The principles of this case, which remain valid today, start with the premise that students are persons in and out of school, with fundamental rights. The Court stated, in a seven to two decision written by Justice Abe Fortas, that the classroom is a marketplace of ideas and depends on a robust exchange of ideas. Students and teachers don't "shed their constitutional rights to freedom of speech or expression at the schoolhouse gate." Consequently, the school district lost this case.

The Court stated firmly that free speech on campus is the basis of our national strength and of the independence and vigor of Americans. In fact, a student's right to expression goes beyond the classroom to the cafeteria, playing field, or anyplace else on campus. "A subject should never be excluded from the classroom merely because it is controversial," the Court wrote.

Does this mean there are no limits—that you can say or do anything while at school? Where is the line drawn?

The test is one of disturbance or disorder. As long as the act of expression doesn't greatly disrupt classwork or school activities, or invade the rights of others, it's acceptable. (This is decided by a school administrator or district policy.) There's no hard-and-fast rule that applies to every situation. Each case presents its own set of circumstances and must be dealt with accordingly.

It was decided in *Tinker* that there was no evidence of disruption at school or interference with other students' rights. The armbands were a symbolic act—a "silent, passive expression of opinion" unaccompanied by any disorder. In fact, it generated discussion on the subject outside of the classroom.

The Court further stated that school officials must have "more than a mere desire to avoid discomfort and unpleasantness that always accompany an unpopular viewpoint" in order to justify the limitation of student expression. It said: "Undifferentiated fear or apprehension of disturbance is not enough to overcome the right to freedom of expression."

In 1999, the teens who took this case to court commented on how it affected their lives: John Tinker, a systems analyst, said: "Freedoms are not likely to remain, unless we exercise them. If we expect to have a democracy, schools should be a laboratory for ideas and expression."

Mary Beth Tinker, now a nurse practitioner in Missouri, supports the political activities of students who are trying to make a positive impact on the world. "You have more power than you may realize," she said.

Chris Eckhardt, once named the kid with the cleanest locker, was asked by the vice principal if he wanted a "busted nose" after refusing to remove the armband. Now involved with politics in Florida, the *Tinker* case reinforced his belief that one person can make a difference. He said: "Practice democracy daily, and exercise your rights. Stand up not only for your rights, but also for your fellow students' rights."

This case supports your right to express your opinion and to protest. That right, however, isn't without limits. Responsibilities go hand-in-hand with rights. This means that when you act in support of an issue, you still have to respect the rights of others. At school, for example, acts that disrupt classes or the student body may be legally restricted. Off campus, there are also limits when your actions disrupt the public or infringe on the rights of others.

Related Cases:

The following cases demonstrate that courts differ in resolving these thorny First Amendment issues. How the "disturbance" standard is interpreted varies from case to case.

■ Can you be suspended for using foul language?

About twenty years after *Tinker,* the Court considered the issue of indecent or vulgar expression on campus. During an assembly at Bethel High School in Washington state, Matthew Fraser gave a nominating speech for a friend who was running for student office. His speech was filled with "elaborate, graphic, and explicit sexual metaphors," which school officials said violated the school's disruptive conduct rule. Matthew was suspended for three days and forfeited a chance to be a speaker at that year's graduation ceremony. Matthew argued that he shouldn't be punished for expressing his views, even if he used offensive language. The Court upheld the school's decision, stating that public schools have the right to prohibit the use of vulgar and offensive terms in school.

Bethel School District v. Fraser (1986)

■ Can a teacher be fired for allowing students to swear?

After twenty years of teaching, a Missouri high school teacher, Cecilia Lacks, was fired for allowing her students to use profanity in their creative writing assignments and in the performance of their plays. This violated the school's ban on profanity on campus. She **appealed** to the U.S. Supreme Court, which in 1999 let the lower court's decision stand.

Cecilia Lacks v. Ferguson School District (1999)

■ Can schools suspend you for wearing T-shirts with offensive language?

When Kimberly Ann Broussard was twelve years old, she bought a T-shirt at a New Kids on the Block concert. It was black with eight-inch white letters declaring "Drugs Suck!" When she wore the shirt to class at Blair Middle School in Norfolk, Virginia, it caught the attention of a teacher. She was asked to either change her shirt, turn it inside out, or borrow another shirt from a friend. Kimberly refused and was suspended for one day. Kimberly and her parents challenged this decision in court. The federal district court for Virginia ruled that, although the message against drugs was acceptable, the form wasn't. School officials may limit offensive words.

Broussard v. School Board of City of Norfolk (1992)

■ What if school officials think the message on your T-shirt is vulgar? Can they discipline you?

Jeffrey Pyle, a Massachusetts high school senior and band member, received three detentions for wearing offensive T-shirts to school. One of the shirts was a Christmas gift from his mother that read "Coed Naked Band—Do It to the Rhythm." Another shirt pictured a marijuana leaf and said "Legalize It."

The school dress code prohibited wearing apparel that "harassed, intimidated, or demeaned an individual because of sex, color, race, handicap, national origin, or sexual orientation." Jeff's challenge to the school policy was successful. The Massachusetts Supreme Court found that even though some of the shirts could be considered vulgar, they weren't disruptive.

Pyle v. School Commission (1996)

■ Can you be suspended for your "symbolic speech"?

During lunch one day, Wayne Denno, a student in Florida, showed his friends a four-by-four-inch Confederate flag. A teacher saw the flag, told Wayne to put it away, and took him to the principal's office. Although Wayne claimed that he had the flag in school because of its historical significance, he was suspended for nine days for disruptive behavior. School officials argued that Wayne attempted to start a riot, disobeyed school authorities, and encouraged another student who was wearing a T-shirt with a Confederate flag on it to stick to his principles when he was ordered to turn it inside out.

The school's actions were upheld by the federal district court in Florida, due to a history of racial tension associated with the Confederate flag. Symbolic speech (such as T-shirts, buttons, and armbands), as well as pure speech, may be restricted under certain circumstances.

Denno v. School Board of Volusia County (1997)

The law distinguishes between what's called pure speech and symbolic speech. Both are protected by the First Amendment. Pure speech is the spoken word, which is restricted if it constitutes what are known as "fighting words," or words meant to incite a riot. Symbolic speech, as seen in *Tinker,* is expressing yourself through objects, which may also be limited if determined to be disruptive.

■ Should it be illegal to wear gang colors or symbols?

In an effort to control gang activity and crime, the City of Harvard, Illinois, made it illegal to wear gang colors or symbols, or to use hand signals. Thirteen-year-old Todd Gaut was out in public and wore a six-pointed star around his neck. When he saw the police, he tried to hide the star. They questioned him, and he admitted that he knew it was a gang symbol (for the "Action Packed Gangster Disciples"). Todd was found guilty of breaking the law and was placed on **probation.** An Illinois appeals court found the law too broad and threw out Todd's conviction. Wearing certain clothing, even if some find it offensive, is protected symbolic speech, the court said.

City of Harvard v. Todd Gaut (1996)

■ Is burning a U.S. flag a form of free expression and therefore legal?

The U.S. Supreme Court had another opportunity to address the issue of symbolic speech in 1989. Joey Johnson, a young adult, burned an American flag as a political protest during the 1984 Republican National Convention in Dallas, Texas. He was charged and convicted of desecrating (treating disrespectfully) the flag, a violation of Texas law. He was sentenced to one year in jail. The U.S. Supreme Court, in a five to four decision, reversed Joey's conviction, stating: "If there is a bedrock principle underlying the First Amendment, it is that the government may not prohibit the expression of an idea simply because society finds the idea itself offensive or disagreeable."

Texas v. Johnson (1989)

▪ Can you be suspended for wearing a button with a slogan that school officials find disruptive?

During a teachers' strike, the high school in McMinnville, Oregon, hired replacement teachers. David Chandler's and Ethan Depweg's fathers were both teachers who joined the strike. High school students David and Ethan wore pro-strike buttons to school, including one that said: "We want our real teachers back." School officials found the buttons to be disruptive and asked the boys to remove them. When they refused, they were suspended for the rest of the day.

The buttons were determined not to be inherently disruptive. The Ninth Circuit Court of Appeals held that merely expressing a viewpoint by wearing a button wasn't an activity that would distract students or upset classroom order. The court said: "The classroom prepares children for citizenship, and the proper exercise of the First Amendment is a hallmark of citizenship in our country."

Chandler v. McMinnville School District (1992)

▪ Can you be disciplined in school for something that school authorities predict will happen?

Fifty-four students at the high school in Brazil, Indiana, held a walkout in protest of the school's rules on smoking and attendance. The next day, five female students handed out leaflets calling for another walkout on a set date and time. The five girls were suspended for three days.

The girls and their parents appealed, arguing that merely handing out a flyer doesn't merit suspension. The Indiana federal district court determined that, taken by itself, distributing leaflets or flyers is a protected right of students. But applying what's called the forecast rule, which judges the likelihood of disruption based on recent events, it was reasonable to predict that the girls' actions could incite a walkout. The earlier walkout raised a red flag to the administration that could be relied on to predict future disruption. The court ruled that discipline, in this case, was appropriate.

Dodd v. Rambis (1981)

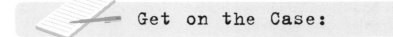

Get on the Case:

- Are there places or circumstances when your freedom of speech or right to express yourself is limited? What are they? Should there be limits at school? Why or why not?

- What do you think about participating in a peaceful demonstration? Is this something you've ever discussed with your friends or parents? What issue would you be willing to take a stand on? What type of demonstration do you think would be effective?

- Develop a campaign at school in support of an issue that's important to you—for example, against smoking or underage drinking. How might you act out your plan, gather support for your views, and bring them to the attention of the administration?

Can you dye your hair or wear a nose-ring to school?

Teens on Trial

Case: *Olff v. East Side Union High School District* (1972)

Suppose you want to get your nose pierced and dye your hair to match your school's colors. Does your school have any say about your personal appearance? Are school dress codes legal?

The Facts:

In 1969, fifteen-year-old Robert Olff was a student at James Lock High School in San Jose, California. He did well in school and had a clean discipline record. At the beginning of the school year, the vice principal told Robert that he couldn't go to class until he cut his hair. The school district had a regulation on personal appearance that stated: "Boys: Hair shall be trim and clean. A boy's hair shall not fall below the eyes in front and shall not cover the ears, and it shall not extend below the collar in back." The rule didn't restrict girls' hairstyles.

Robert and his parents challenged the rule in court, arguing that it prevented him from freely expressing himself—a guarantee of the First Amendment (see the **Bill of Rights** on pages 19–20).

YOU BE THE JUDGE

- **Do you think schools have a right to restrict how students look or dress? Why or why not?**

- **Why do you think a school would be concerned with a student's appearance?**

The Ruling:

As Robert's case made its way through the courts, another lawsuit was filed in California. Lindahl King challenged the hair length regulations at a junior college. He and four other students tried to register at Saddleback Junior College, in Mission Viejo, California, and were denied because of their hair length. Because the issues and arguments were the same, the cases were considered together by the U.S. Supreme Court.

The school district, in Robert's case, argued that long hair on boys interfered with the educational process. Sworn statements from eleven teachers and administrators described the need for a hair regulation for boys. They said that long hair tended to create a less serious atmosphere, more discipline problems and distractions, and "less education" in the classroom.

The first court that Robert went to ruled in his favor. The federal trial court said that the U.S. Constitution protects the freedom to determine your own hairstyle and personal appearance. The court ordered the school to allow Robert to attend without cutting his hair. He was a junior at the time he returned to school. But the school district disagreed with the court's decision and asked a higher court to consider the case. Two years later, the federal court of appeals reversed the trial court's decision. It decided that school authorities have the right to develop a code of dress and conduct, without unconstitutionally infringing on the rights of students.

Robert and his lawyer took the final step and asked the U.S. Supreme Court to review the lower court's decision. The Court denied Robert's request; the decision of the lower court in favor of the school was left standing.

Because the U.S. Supreme Court decided not to get involved with managing schools, the rules regarding dress codes are left to the states and school districts. Private schools may establish their own rules, but public schools must balance individual student rights and the freedom of speech and expression with the school's responsibility to maintain a safe, peaceful campus. Dress code restrictions need to be reasonably related to an educational purpose.

When the U.S. Supreme Court decided not to consider Robert Olff's case, two of the justices disagreed and voted to hear it. Justice William O. Douglas wrote a brief opinion, stating in part: "Hairstyle is highly personal, an idiosyncrasy which I had assumed was left to family or individual control, and was no legitimate concern to the State. . . . One's hairstyle, like one's taste for food, or one's liking for certain kinds of music, art, reading, and recreation, is certainly fundamental in our constitutional scheme—a scheme designed to keep government off the backs of people."

He then concluded with: "The question tendered [by Robert's case] is of great personal concern to many, and of unusual constitutional importance which we should resolve." Justice Douglas, however, was in the minority. The Court hasn't yet considered the issue raised in Robert's case.

Related Cases:

In addition to hair regulations, students have challenged other dress code restrictions. Students have wanted to wear Indian feathers or a kente cloth at graduation, or wear jewelry with religious symbols on it—and so the debate continues. The cases discussed here give you an idea of the discretion courts have in deciding these issues. School authority takes priority over individual rights, if the school rule is reasonably connected to the goal of education.

▪ Can schools restrict how you express your religion?

In 1999, seventeen-year-old Crystal Seifferly sued Lincoln Park High School in Detroit, Michigan. She claimed that the school's ban on wearing white power, gang, and satanic symbols violated her freedom to practice her Wiccan religion. Crystal wanted to wear a five-star pentagram as a religious symbol, but the school forbade it. The school also banned black nail polish, dog collars, and death-style makeup. Crystal and her lawyer reached an agreement with the school after a hearing in federal court. Before the court made its decision, the school agreed to change its policy and allow students to wear religious jewelry or other symbols of their spiritual beliefs.

▪ What about accessories that symbolize your heritage? Can these be restricted under a school's dress code?

In 1998, Aisha Price and Enockina Ocansey were told they couldn't wear a kente cloth during their high school graduation ceremony. The colorful sash symbolized their African heritage, but the dress code at the high school in Arvada, Colorado, prohibited any adornments to the traditional graduation cap and gown. The students were told they could wear the cloth before and after the ceremony.

Aisha, Enockina, and their parents asked the federal district court for an order allowing them to wear the cloth. A federal trial court ruled against Aisha and Enockina, and they agreed to follow the court's ruling.

The courts have upheld similar school dress codes. In 1996, three Oklahoma students were disciplined for the same issue. (They were ordered to serve thirty days in an alternative summer program, in order to receive their high school diploma.) At their graduation, two of the students had worn the kente cloth and a third wore an eagle feather in honor of her American Indian heritage.

▪ Do school dress codes violate your freedom of expression?

A Phoenix, Arizona, middle school required all students to wear a uniform of white shirts with blue pants or shorts; girls could wear skirts. Clothing logos were forbidden. Two students came to school wearing white shirts that weren't plain—one had the U.S. flag on it, and the other had a picture of Jesus on the front. After refusing to follow the dress code, both students were transferred to another school that didn't have dress regulations. The students and their parents asked a court to abolish the dress code, as a violation of their right to free speech. The court refused, stating that although the school cannot restrict the

> Many educators in the United States see uniforms and dress regulations as a simple and inexpensive way to make schools safer. Many educators maintain that baggy clothes make it easier for students to bring weapons or drugs into schools. Uniforms help curb these problems and allow school administrators to spot non-students on campus.

message (speech), it can restrict the way a message is given (on clothes). The interest of the school in providing a uniform student body outweighed the individual freedom of expression.

Phoenix Elementary School District v. Candace L. Green (1997)

▪ Is it gender discrimination if a school places hairstyle restrictions on boys but not girls?

The length of eight-year-old Zachariah Toungate's hair was debated in a Texas case. Mina Elementary School in Bastrop, Texas, had a rule that limited the hair length on boys. Zachariah, a third-grader, was suspended until he cut his ponytail. After three days, he was allowed to return without cutting his hair but was placed in the in-school suspension program. This meant he was separated from other students, received individual lessons from a substitute teacher, and had no physical education, music classes, or extracurricular activities. After four months of this, and following a psychological recommendation, Zachariah began homeschooling with his mother.

Zachariah and his mother sued the school district, claiming gender **discrimination,** because the hair length rule didn't apply to girls. The court of appeals decided that Zachariah had been discriminated against and that the rule had no legitimate basis. There was no evidence that Zachariah's hair had caused any disruption or affected school discipline in any way. The school was unable to show that the rule advanced any educational goal. Two years later, however, the Texas Supreme Court reversed the decision of the lower court, ruling that it was not discriminatory to have a different grooming code for boys and girls.

Bastrop Independent School District v. Zachariah Toungate (1996)

■ Should courts even get involved with school dress and grooming code disputes?

Eighteen-year-old Austin Barber disagreed with his Texas high school's rule that restricted hair length and banned earrings on boys. Austin claimed that although he was a senior at the school, he was eighteen and therefore legally an adult. He argued that the school rules didn't apply to him.

The Texas Supreme Court disagreed, ruling against Austin. It reasoned that such matters should be dealt with by the parents, school boards, principals, and teachers. The court decided that a school grooming code doesn't require judicial intervention, saying: "We refuse to use the Texas Constitution to micro-manage Texas high schools."

Austin Barber v. Colorado Independent School District (1995)

■ What about earrings? Can girls wear them even if they're banned on boys?

Ten-year-old Jimmy Hines, a fourth-grader at Caston Elementary School in Indiana, was asked to remove the earring he wore to school. When he refused, he was suspended. Rather than transfer to another school (an option given to him), Jimmy took the earring out and returned to school. He and his parents asked the Indiana court to set aside the school rule because it discriminated against boys (the policy didn't apply to girls). They also claimed that the rule denied Jimmy the right to express himself through his personal appearance.

The Indiana Court of Appeals upheld the ban, indicating that there was evidence supporting the school's dress code. The court found a rational relationship between the rule and the educational mission of the school. Citing safety, discipline, pride, attitude, attendance, and achievement as underlying

Students aren't the only ones who may be required to follow a dress code. Employers may also restrict the appearance of employees, as long as the policy doesn't discriminate—for example, by placing more demands on women than men. Employers who have dress codes are usually trying to ensure that their employees present a professional image to the public. Today, however, more and more companies are loosening their dress code restrictions, allowing employees to dress in a more casual manner.

reasons for the dress code, the school persuaded the court to let the policy stand.

Hines v. Caston School (1995)

■ Can schools restrict the style of clothing that students wear?

A New Mexico high school freshman, Richard Bivens, wore saggy pants to school which, he was told, violated the school dress code. On many occasions, he was told to follow the rule or face the consequences. Richard insisted that he "sagged" as an expression of his black culture. He was suspended for the rest of the semester for refusing to follow the rule. Richard and his mother asked the court to lift the suspension. The court refused, finding the dress code appropriate. It said: "Not every defiant act by a high school student is constitutionally protected speech."

Richard Bivens v. Albuquerque Public Schools (1995)

Get on the Case:

- Are you surprised that this issue hasn't yet been decided by the U.S. Supreme Court? Why do you think that is? As the Texas Supreme Court said, is personal appearance any concern of the courts or should parents and schools resolve these matters?

- Do you think there should be rules regarding personal appearance at school? Is there a risk to student safety if no rules exist? Why or why not? What about gangs at school? Should bandannas, earrings, and other tokens of identification be restricted? If so, should the restrictions also apply to girls—even if it means not wearing certain colors of lipstick or nail polish? What are the pros and cons of mandatory school uniforms?

- Brainstorm with your classmates or friends about how kids in your school express themselves. For example, through their hairstyles or makeup, by wearing nose-rings, or by having tattoos. Which things on your list are sometimes disruptive in school? Why? Do you think these forms of expression should be banned in your school? Why or why not?

Can your student newspaper be censored?

Case: *Hazelwood School District v. Kuhlmeier* (1988)

You may keep a journal or write letters or email messages to family or friends, and there are no rules or restrictions on what you write—unless your parents have certain expectations of what's appropriate. At school, however, the situation is different. Your expressive activities, whether in writing, art, photography, or other mediums, can be reviewed by the school. They may also be limited if they don't meet the school's standards or if they're determined to be disruptive. This case sets the tone for school **censorship** of student expression.

The Facts:

The school year was ending at Hazelwood School in Missouri. As the layout editor of the school paper, the *Spectrum*, Cathy Kuhlmeier put together the final issue with her staff. Leslie Smart was the movie critic, and Leanne Tippett a reporter and cartoonist. The newspaper was usually four to six pages and sold on campus for twenty-five cents.

One article in the final issue dealt with the impact of divorce on students. It named one student and quoted four others about their parents' behavior. A second article discussed teen pregnancy. It included the experiences of three unnamed students, but with enough details that students could identify them from the few pregnant teens at the school.

Before the paper was printed, the teacher who served as the newspaper's advisor asked the principal to approve the page proofs, a normal procedure. The principal pulled the two pages containing these articles. He found them to be inappropriate, highly personal, and too sensitive for the younger high school students. He was also concerned that, because it was the last issue of the school year, the people in the articles wouldn't have an opportunity to respond.

Cathy, Leslie, and Leanne, all seniors, disagreed with the principal's decision, claiming that it violated their First Amendment right to freedom of expression (see the **Bill of Rights** on pages 19–20). They wanted to change the school policy that gave the principal authority to censor the paper. With their parents' help, the girls went to court to challenge the extent of editorial control a school may have over the content of a school newspaper.

YOU BE THE JUDGE

- **Do you think the principal's decision violated the students' First Amendment rights? Why or why not?**

- **How much discretion should students have over the content of the school newspaper or yearbook? Should the faculty or administration have any say about what's published?**

- **Do you think the students should have asked for consent from the parents of the students who were covered in the articles? Why or why not?**

The Ruling:

Before deciding whether the students' rights were violated, the U.S. Supreme Court discussed the nature of a school newspaper. The Court decided it wasn't a public forum—available for anyone to voice their opinion. Rather, it was a supervised learning experience for students interested in journalism.

The Court stated that education is primarily the responsibility of parents, teachers, and school officials—not the courts. A school isn't required to tolerate student speech that's inconsistent with its basic educational mission. Therefore, schools are allowed to control the newspaper's content within reason and to restrict other forms of student expression, including theatrical productions.

Justice Byron R. White wrote the majority opinion in *Hazelwood,* which is summed up best in these words: "[E]ducators do not offend the First Amendment by exercising editorial control over the style and content of student speech in school-sponsored expressive activities so long as their actions are reasonably related to . . . [a] . . . valid educational purpose."

> "[T]he First Amendment rights of students in the public schools are not automatically coextensive with the rights of adults in other settings, and must be applied in light of the special circumstances of the school environment."—U.S. Supreme Court, *Hazelwood School District v. Kuhlmeier* (1988)

In a strong **dissent,** Justice William J. Brennan Jr. (with two other justices agreeing) argued that just as the public on the street corner must tolerate speech that tempts the listener to throw the speaker off the street, public educators must allow some student expression, even if it offends them or offers views or values that contradict those the school wishes to promote.

> "If all printers were determined not to print anything till they were sure it would offend nobody, there would be very little printed." —Benjamin Franklin (1730)

Leanne Tippett, now an environmental specialist with the State of Missouri, is married and has two young daughters. Looking back on the case eleven years later, she said: *"Tinker* gave schools the authority to stave off anarchy, but *Hazelwood* went too far in limiting student expression. Someday another challenge may result in a more favorable decision to students."

Leslie Smart, who has worked as a journalist and in television, is now a teacher in Missouri. Although the student journalists lost their case, Leslie believes it was a worthwhile fight. She commented in 1999, "Quiet, thoughtful, appropriate protest can be an effective way to get your voice heard."

The action taken by these students may not have changed censorship in schools, but it did open the subject for discussion. The Court's decision encourages schools to look closely at a student activity before imposing restrictions and to balance the school's goal of setting high standards for both student speech and the student's right to free expression.

Related Cases:

The word *censorship* raises many eyebrows. The debate over censoring information continues in regard to books, music, newspapers, and the Internet. Something that may not be restricted in one place may be in the school setting. Your school has the authority to reasonably limit or restrict the content of all forms of expression. This includes plays, the school yearbook, newspapers, and Web sites that may disrupt the school.

■ Can you be disciplined in school for something you did off campus?

Sixteen-year-old Brandon Beussink was a junior at Woodland High School, in Marble Hill, Missouri. He created his own home page on the World Wide Web, which criticized people in his school, including one of his teachers and the school principal. Although he created this Web page at home, school officials told him to remove it from the Web, which he did. A few students saw his site, but there was no evidence of any disruption at school. Yet, the school suspended Brandon for ten days. These missed school days were counted as absences, which brought Brandon over the limit for unexcused absences. As a result, he failed four classes that semester, which meant that he might not graduate with his class in 1999. (The incident had occurred in February 1998.)

Brandon filed a lawsuit, asking the court to restore his grades and to give him the chance to graduate with his class. He claimed that the school had violated his free speech and that he shouldn't be disciplined in school for comments he made off campus, even though they were in cyberspace.

The federal trial court agreed with Brandon and ordered the school to impose no further discipline against him. His ten-day suspension no longer could be counted as absences, which consequently reinstated Brandon's senior status. The court said that a function of free speech is to invite dispute—that free speech serves its highest purpose when it creates unrest or dissatisfaction with present conditions, or even stirs people to anger.

Beussink v. Woodland School District (1998)

▪ Can students restrict the type of advertisements that are accepted in student-run publications?

Natalie Berger and Dow-Chung Chi, high school seniors in Massachusetts, were co-editors of the Lexington High School yearbook. Ivan Chan, also a senior, was editor of the school newspaper, the *Musket*. Both publications were student-run and funded by sales and advertisements. They each had a policy of not running political or advocacy advertisements.

Douglas Yeo was a parent who lost a campaign against condom distribution at the school. He submitted ads to the school newspaper and yearbook advocating abstinence. Following their policy, Natalie, Dow-Chung, and Ivan decided not to accept the ads. They stuck to their position, even when the principal asked them to reconsider to avoid a lawsuit and media attention. After a number of meetings, the school left the decision to the students. The editorial judgment of the editors, acting independent of the school, was upheld by the Fifth Circuit Court of Appeals.

Yeo v. Town of Lexington (1997)

▪ Can material in an underground newspaper lead to school discipline?

Justin Boucher, a student at a high school in Greenfield, Wisconsin, wrote and distributed an underground newspaper called *The Last*. (He distributed the paper in school bathrooms, in school lockers, and in the cafeteria.) The June 1997 issue included an article titled "So You Want to Be a Hacker"—a how-to blueprint for invading the school's computer system. In the article, Justin not only encouraged doing this but also offered to "teach you more" after mastering the first lesson. Justin was suspended and later expelled for endangering school property. Based on the reasonable forecast rule, whereby substantial disruption of a school activity was possible, Justin's expulsion was upheld by the Seventh Circuit Court of Appeals. (For more on the reasonable forecast rule, see page 99.)

Boucher v. School Board of Greenfield (1998)

▪ Can you be suspended for passing out an underground newspaper at school?

Cory Bystrom and Adam Collins attended a high school in Fridley, Minnesota. They distributed an underground newspaper called the *Tour de Farce*. Under school policy, school officials had the right to review any publication before it was distributed on campus; if the officials found it vulgar, indecent, or obscene, they could prohibit its school distribution. Cory and Adam were suspended for violating this policy. The students and their parents sued the principal and the school district for violating their civil rights—exercise of free speech at school. The court ruled in favor of the school, having determined that the policy was reasonable.

Bystrom v. Fridley High School (1987)

Get on the Case:

▪ What is the purpose of a school newspaper? To incite and provoke, or to inform and entertain? Should there be any limits on student reporters and editors? Who decides where the line is drawn between acceptable and unacceptable journalism? What if your school or the school newspaper has its own Web site—should limits be set on its content? Should your school paper be sensitive to certain issues based on the age of the audience? Why or why not?

▪ What about a student's off-campus activities? Do you think the school ever has a right to restrict what a student does away from school? If so, under what circumstances?

▪ The *Hazelwood* decision has been criticized as giving too much authority to school officials and not adequately protecting a student's First Amendment rights. What do you think? Some states have passed laws further protecting high school journalists (including Arkansas, California, Colorado, Iowa, Massachusetts, and Nebraska). You might want to check into the laws of your state to see if any exist regarding your rights as a journalist. Call your local newspaper and ask to speak with the reporter who covers education issues (major metropolitan papers have education sections and reporters who should be aware of the laws). Or go to the library to learn more about laws in your area.

- Interview the editor or advisor of your school newspaper. Has this person ever experienced censorship first-hand? If your school doesn't have a student newspaper, talk to the journalism or writing teacher about this issue.

ISSUE:

Can you be forced to say prayers at school?

Case: *Lee v. Weisman* (1992)

In 1636, Providence, Rhode Island, was founded as a place where families could freely practice their religion. Three hundred and fifty years later, a young girl from Providence, Deborah Weisman, and her parents continued the fight for religious freedom. Although the Constitution's principle of separation of church and state remains valid, it's been blurred in the school setting by recent cases and decisions. This case, and the decisions that followed, have shed further light on the religious freedoms you have as a student.

The Facts:

It was June 1989, and fourteen-year-old Deborah Weisman was preparing to graduate from Nathan Bishop Middle School in Providence, Rhode Island. Her school district had a practice of inviting members of the clergy to the graduation ceremonies to offer a blessing and say a prayer. The district had written guidelines for composing a public nonsectarian prayer. A rabbi was invited to Deborah's graduation.

Four days before the event, Deborah and her father asked the school to cancel the rabbi's part of the ceremony. They argued that the public school, and therefore the state, was forcing students to participate in a religious exercise—a violation of the **Establishment Clause** of the First Amendment (see the **Bill of Rights** on pages 19–20). The school said it was too late to change the ceremony, and the event continued as planned. Deborah and her father then sued the school district to prevent future ceremonies from including prayers. She didn't want to face the same situation four years later at her high school graduation.

> "[T]he lessons of the First Amendment are as urgent in the modern world as in the eighteenth century when it was written."
> —*Lee v. Weisman,* 1992

YOU BE THE JUDGE

- **Do you think that including a blessing and a prayer in a graduation ceremony violates the separation of church and state included in the First Amendment? Why or why not?**

- **Do you think a school is promoting religion by including prayer in a ceremony? Why or why not?**

The Ruling:

The U.S. Supreme Court, in a five to four decision written by Justice Anthony M. Kennedy, found that prayer at a graduation ceremony was a state-approved religious exercise, in which the student was forced to participate. Although Deborah could have chosen not to attend the ceremony and still receive her diploma, the Court dismissed this option as unrealistic, saying: "Everyone knows that in our society and in our culture, high school graduation is one of life's most significant occasions."

In this case, the motives for prayer were good, but the danger of promoting religion outweighed its benefits. The Court said that religious beliefs and expression are too precious to be prohibited or ordered by the government—they are best left as private, individual matters.

The Court summed up its interpretation of the Establishment Clause by stating that the development and preservation of religious beliefs is an individual choice, with each person promised the freedom to pursue that choice. The Court also stated, in a few words, the philosophy behind many First Amendment decisions: "[S]peech is protected by ensuring its full expression."

The First Amendment begins with these words: "Congress shall make no law respecting an establishment of religion." This phrase is referred to as the Establishment Clause (this is where the concept of separation of church and state comes from). It means that the government may not promote or affiliate itself with any religious teaching or organization. Government may not advance or inhibit religion, or aid, foster, or promote one religion over another. Federal and state governments are to be neutral in all religious matters.

Religious freedom guaranteed by the First Amendment often collides with the concept of separation of church and state. On one side is the position that religious education and school prayer should exist in public school. Opponents argue that school prayer of any sort conflicts with the Establishment Clause.

Deborah graduated from Hope High School in Providence, where no graduation prayers were said. She went on to Rhode Island College and majored in communications and marketing; she's now in retail management. In recent comments about her case, she noted: "Although not always easy, stand up for what you believe in. . . . What seemed like a small complaint about a commonsense issue became a situation which has had a great effect on me. I have truly come to understand, from reactions we received, that hatred often comes from ignorance."

In a similar case, where a "moment-of-silence" at school was prohibited, Justice O'Connor made this comment in her **dissent:** "It is difficult to discern a serious threat to religious liberty from a room of silent, thoughtful schoolchildren."

Taking a stand on something you feel strongly about may be difficult. Deborah and her family did so, and after several years, they succeeded in changing public school graduation ceremonies. The process may not always be smooth or risk-free. But positive change, however attained, is worth the effort.

Related Cases:

Although our country was founded on the belief of separating church and government activities, the debate continues to this day. And, as you'll see from the following cases, courts don't always agree with each other. A case may be decided one way in one **jurisdiction,** with the opposite result in another.

▪ What if a prayer at a school function is voluntary and not required? Does it violate the separation of church and state in these instances?

In Houston, a student named Pamela Jones, her father, and two other students and their parents challenged Clear Lake High School's policy of allowing seniors to voluntarily write and present an invocation at their graduation ceremony. (It was strictly a choice of the senior class and, if voted in, had to be performed by a volunteer from the class.) Past functions included references to Christianity, including the words *Lord, Gospel,* and *Amen.* After considering the U.S. Supreme Court ruling in *Weisman,* the federal court upheld the Texas policy—finding no violation of the Establishment Clause. The difference between this case and *Weisman* is that this one concerned a *voluntary,* not mandatory, activity arranged by students themselves.

Jones v. Clear Creek School District (1992)

▪ What about prayers at school sporting events?

In June 2000, the U.S. Supreme Court ruled against voluntary, student-led, student-initiated prayer at school football games. The Sante Fe School District in Galveston County, Texas, allowed students to read a prayer over the public address system at home football games. Several students and their parents objected to the policy, and the Court agreed.

Santa Fe Independent School District v. Jane Doe (2000)

▪ Can religious groups meet on school grounds?

Senior Emily Hsu and several of her friends asked their high school in Roslyn, New York, for permission to form an after-school Christian Bible

Club and to meet on campus. The purpose of "Walking on Water" was to pray and study the Bible. The proposed rules of the club required all officers to be Christian. They were told that this provision was unacceptable, and therefore the club couldn't form on campus. Emily and her parents sued the school district, the school superintendent, and district board members, claiming **discrimination**—denial of access to school facilities for her club.

Emily won in court based on the federal 1984 Equal Access Act. This law "guarantees public school students the right to form extracurricular groups that engage in religious, philosophical, or political discourse."

Note: In a 1990 U.S. Supreme Court case *(Westside Community Schools v. Mergens)*, the Court determined that a Bible club at school doesn't violate the Establishment Clause if other noncurricular groups are allowed and no school officials participate in the club.

Hsu v. Roslyn Union Free School District (1996)

▪ Can you hand out religious material on school property?

Tracy Hemry and Kristi Jones attended Wasson High School in Colorado Springs, Colorado. They identified themselves as Christian students and believed that part of their religious duty was to distribute their church publication, *Issues and Answers,* to their fellow students. The principal allowed the girls to distribute the publication on the sidewalk in front of the school but not on campus. The girls and their parents sued the school board, school principal, and superintendent, claiming a violation of civil rights by restricting distribution on campus.

The Colorado federal court decided that the restrictions placed on the paper's distribution were appropriate, saying: "[T]he hallways of Wasson High School are not a public forum for indiscriminate use by the general public."

Hemry v. School Board of Colorado Springs (1991)

▪ What if you want to give your classmates an invitation to attend a church meeting? Is this okay?

Andrew Muller was in fourth grade at Jefferson Lighthouse Elementary School in Racine, Wisconsin. He asked his teacher if he could hand out a flyer inviting the public to a religious meeting at his family's church. The principal told Andrew that he couldn't hand out the invitation at school. The Seventh Circuit Court of Appeals agreed with the school's rules governing distribution of nonschool publications, saying: "School officials may impose reasonable restrictions on the speech of students, teachers, and other members of the school community."

Muller v. Jefferson Lighthouse School (1996)

■ Can public schools have religious holidays as vacation days?

Chicago public school teacher Andrea Metzel didn't think Good Friday should be a school holiday, and she sued the state superintendent of education. Illinois state law allowed twelve holidays each school year—nine for nonreligious celebrations, two that are religious in origin (Thanksgiving and Christmas) but secularized, and Good Friday—a purely religious holiday, celebrated by believing Christians.

On the other hand, the U.S. Supreme Court in January 2000 let stand a Maryland law that required public schools to close on Good Friday. The Court didn't comment on the case, leaving the issue unresolved among the states. The Court may take up the issue at another time, though, because a dozen states have similar laws. On the same subject, the Court (in March 2000) rejected a challenge to Indiana's designation of Good Friday as a state holiday.

The Seventh Circuit Court of Appeals ruled that the law violated the Establishment Clause and was therefore unconstitutional. It said schoolchildren may be excused on religious holidays, but mandatory school closure in favor of one belief or religion is prohibited.

Metzel v. Leininger (1995)

■ Is prayer at school acceptable if the majority of students are in favor of it?

At Wingfield High School in Mississippi, several students asked the principal, Dr. Bishop Knox, for permission to read a prayer each morning over the school's intercom. The school's student body voted 490 to 96 in favor of the prayers. After three days of allowing the prayer readings, Dr. Knox was suspended for the remainder of the school year by the school district's board of trustees. The court affirmed Dr. Knox's suspension due to his total disregard of the law—knowing that school prayer was unconstitutional.

Board of Trustees of Jackson School v. Knox (1997)

Get on the Case:

- Why do you think it's important, from the standpoint of the nation's courts, to keep religion out of public schools? Why was this dictate included in the First Amendment? Do you think the amendment should be reconsidered? Why or why not? What dangers might be posed by a repeal of this part of the amendment?

- Besides public schools, where else are religious events restricted? Why do you think this restriction is important for adults?

- Do you see any First Amendment violations in the situations in the list below? How would you decide these issues? Discuss your answers and reasons in support of each. See the court decisions at the end of this section.

1. Kentucky state law required that the Ten Commandments be posted in every public grade school classroom.

2. Attendance was required at a human sexuality class by all students in public school in New Jersey.

3. A Maryland school board required students to say the Lord's Prayer or read from the Bible each morning.

4. Alabama allowed a one-minute moment of silence for meditation in public schools.

5. In West Virginia, students were to salute the flag and say the pledge of allegiance each morning at school. Noncompliance meant expulsion.

How the courts ruled in each case:

1. The main purpose of posting the Ten Commandments on schoolroom walls was plainly religious and therefore prohibited. *Stone v. Graham,* 449 U.S. 39 (1980)

2. "[T]he 'free exercise clause' was adopted to protect the one individual who is sincere in a conscientious religious conviction." Sex education classes are to be optional, not mandatory. *Valent v. New Jersey Board of Education,* 274 A.2d 832 (1971)

3. The daily prayer wasn't allowed, as the state must remain neutral in matters of religion. *Murray v. Curlett,* 374 U.S. 203 (1963)

4. The moment-of-silence rule was struck down—because it had a religious purpose. *Wallace v. Jaffree,* 472 U.S. 38 (1985)

5. A compulsory salute of the flag violates the principles and spirit of the First Amendment. *West Virginia Board of Education v. Barnette,* 319 U.S. 624 (1943)

ISSUE:

Do school officials have the right to discipline you?

Case: *Ingraham v. Wright* (1977)

While you're at school, your teachers and the school's administrators are responsible for making sure that you learn a number of subjects. Because they also have this responsibility for the other students in your school, they may need to discipline you if you create classroom disruptions or break other school rules. Perhaps your school disciplines students by sending them to detention or by making them write an essay about their behavior. Or maybe you live in a state that allows **corporal punishment** in school. If so, you may have lots of questions about how this punishment is carried out and what your rights are under the law.

The Facts:

James Ingraham was fourteen years old and in the eighth grade at Drew Junior High School in Miami, Florida. In October 1970, James was in the school auditorium, onstage with other students. A teacher thought James was being disruptive and told him to leave the stage. Because James was slow in doing so, he was taken to the principal's office to get five swats with a paddle. (This form of discipline was allowed in the school district.) James claimed that he hadn't done anything wrong and refused to be paddled. Consequently, he was held down by two of the principal's assistants while the principal gave him twenty swats. The paddle was about two feet long, three to four inches wide, and a half-inch thick. James suffered some bruising and required medical attention, which kept him out of school for ten days.

He and his mother sued the principal, assistant principal, and school superintendent, claiming that the paddling violated James's Eighth Amendment's protection against cruel and unusual punishment (see the **Bill of Rights** on pages 19–20). They also claimed that James's **due process** rights were violated, because the school didn't hold a hearing or give James advance notice of the twenty swats he received.

YOU BE THE JUDGE

- **Do you think paddling in schools is cruel and unusual punishment? (Remember, the school policy allowed it.)**

- **What about James's due process rights? Do you think he should have been given a chance to tell his side of the story before he was punished?**

The Ruling:

The U.S. Supreme Court considered both of James's claims in deciding this case. At the time, a national debate raged in the schools on whether corporal punishment could be used, or whether it violated the Eighth Amendment. The Court began by looking at the history of the Eighth Amendment and determined that it didn't apply to discipline in public schools. In a five to four decision written by Justice Lewis F. Powell, the Court ruled that the Eighth Amendment was designed to protect convicted criminals only. The justices refused to extend its protection to situations outside criminal cases.

> The *Ingraham* court took a historical view of discipline at school: "The use of corporal punishment in this country as a means of disciplining school children dates back to the colonial period."

The Court, however, did state that teachers and principals must be cautious and use restraint when giving a physical punishment. The justices suggested using a test to determine if paddling is necessary, recommending that the school should consider (1) the seriousness of the offense, (2) the student's attitude and past behavior, (3) the nature and severity of the punishment, (4) the age and physical condition of the student, and (5) the availability of a less severe but equally effective means of discipline. The school district should also create a school-wide policy on discipline and make sure everyone in the school is aware of it.

The Court also rejected James's due process argument. It decided that because public schools are open to the community, students are sufficiently protected against abuse. Therefore, there's no need to hold a full hearing before disciplining a student.

On the other hand, the Court determined that due process should be followed before suspending or expelling a student. Corporal punishment is meant to quickly correct a student's behavior without interrupting his or her education. Suspension and expulsion have a greater impact on a student's education, requiring at least an informal "give-and-take between student and disciplinarian."

This case demonstrates that reasonable discipline at school doesn't violate the U.S. Constitution. The U.S. Supreme Court left this matter up to the states to address. State laws regarding discipline in school vary, so if you want to know more about your state's laws regarding this issue, check with your local police.

Related Cases:

When considering the issue of physical discipline at school, a balance must exist between the offense and the punishment. In states that permit physical discipline at school, the discipline may not be excessive and must be administered fairly. Other forms of punishment, such as expulsion or suspension, must also comply with a student's due process rights. This means giving students notice of the punishments and an opportunity to be heard.

▪ Can you be suspended or expelled without a hearing?

Nineteen-year-old Dwight Lopez was a student at Central High School in Columbus, Ohio. The school had experienced some tension regarding Black History Month, such as racially motivated demonstrations, disorderly conduct, and property damage. Dwight was in the lunchroom when a few black students entered and started overturning tables. Dwight and his friends got up and left, taking no part in the activity. Dwight was suspended—but no reasons were given, and no hearing was scheduled. There was some confusion about the length of his suspension, and he stayed out a week longer than he was supposed to. After a month, the school transferred him to another school in the district.

Dwight, along with eight other students who'd been suspended from various schools in the district, took his complaint (that he was suspended without any notice or hearing) to court and ultimately won. The U.S. Supreme Court, in a five to four decision written by Justice Byron R. White, held that Dwight's due process rights were violated. In cases of suspension or expulsion, due process requires that schools give students notice and an opportunity to tell their side of the story.

Goss v. Lopez (1975)

▪ Can teachers use physical discipline in some states or is this considered assault?

Anita Holbrook was a fourth-grade teacher in Kentucky. When one of her students failed to complete an in-class assignment, she gave her three swats with a paddle. The girl was slightly bruised but by the next morning, her buttocks "didn't sting bad or hurt." Ms. Holbrook was arrested and convicted of assault. She **appealed** and her conviction was eventually reversed by the Kentucky Court of Appeals. It held that she wasn't reckless in her actions and that the student didn't suffer serious

Some states ban corporal punishment at school, including California, Hawaii, Illinois, Maine, Maryland, Montana, Nebraska, Washington, and Wisconsin.

physical or mental harm. "A teacher is justified in the use of physical force within certain bounds," the court said.

Holbrook v. Commonwealth of Kentucky (1996)

▪ Can you be expelled for using a weapon in school?

D. B. was twelve years old when she got into a fight at school and stabbed another student. D. B. was expelled from all public schools in her county in Georgia. She and her parents asked the court to reverse this decision, arguing that it violated her right to a public education. The court ruled that the expulsion was valid due to the circumstances and zero tolerance for weapons at school. Although D. B. has a right to a free public education, she doesn't have an absolute right to attend a public school. She may be required to attend an alternative program or be homeschooled.

D. B. v. Clarke County Board of Education (1996)

▪ Are physical threats unacceptable or are they a form of free expression?

Fifteen-year-old Sarah Lovell spent hours one day attempting to change her class schedule at her school in California. When she thought she was finally done, the school counselor told her she may not get into certain classes because they were overloaded. Frustrated and irritated, Sarah put her head in her hands and said, "If you don't give me this schedule change, I'm going to shoot you."

The counselor reported the incident to the assistant principal, and Sarah was suspended for three days. She and her parents filed a lawsuit against the school district, the school principal, and the assistant principal, claiming a violation of free speech. The court held that threats of physical violence aren't protected by the First Amendment, saying: "[W]idespread violence in schools throughout the Nation significantly interferes with the quality of education." Sarah lost her case; her statements weren't protected by the First Amendment.

Lovell v. Poway Unified School District (1996)

▪ What if you're expelled after you finish your senior classes?

Can you still graduate? David P. Shuman, a senior at Cumberland Valley High School in Mechanicsburg, Pennsylvania, was caught selling LSD at school on May 16, 1985. The school scheduled a disciplinary hearing for June 30. In the meantime, David was allowed to finish his classes, take his final exams, and receive his grades. On June 30, the day of graduation, the school board voted to expel David. David asked the court to overturn this decision. The Pennsylvania Commonwealth

Court ruled that the expulsion was lawful, but because David had completed all the graduation requirements, he was entitled to receive his diploma.

Shuman v. Cumberland Valley School District (1988)

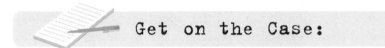

Get on the Case:

- Should teachers and the administration be granted immunity from lawsuits or prosecution for doing their jobs? Who determines when the line has been crossed and a student's rights have been violated?

- Is in-school suspension an effective disciplinary tool in your school? Is it taken seriously by teachers and students? If not, what would you suggest in those cases that don't merit suspension or expulsion?

- Interview a local attorney—either a prosecutor or a defense attorney—about the issue of discipline in school. What has this person's experience been with this issue? Does he or she think the laws need to be changed? Can this person offer any stories from personal experience? If you find it difficult to arrange such a meeting, ask a teacher to invite an attorney to visit your class and talk about the law and discipline.

- Assemble a panel of people who are knowledgeable about discipline in the school. You could invite your school principal, school board members, teachers, students, parents, and police officers. Work with your class to develop a specific list of questions to be addressed. Hold the panel discussion during class or in the evening, as an informational event.

ISSUE:

Can your parents discipline you however they see fit?

Case: *Joshua DeShaney v. Winnebago County Social Services* **(1989)**

If you act out at home or school, do your parents discipline you? That's what parents often do to help their children learn the difference between right and wrong, and between what's acceptable and unacceptable. The law respects parents' right to discipline their children; however, there *are* limits. Courts, by looking at what's reasonable under all the circumstances, decide whether parents have crossed the line. Although this case is about a young child, the ruling applies to all **minors,** including teens.

The Facts:

Four-year-old Joshua DeShaney lived with his father and his father's girl-friend. Over a two-year period, nurses, police officers, and the department of social services made and received numerous reports about Joshua being physically abused at home. At one point, Joshua was removed from his father's home but was returned three days later. (His father agreed to see a counselor and enroll Joshua in preschool, but he didn't follow through.) Then, in March 1984, Joshua was hospitalized with severe brain damage. He was in a coma, and bruises covered his body. Although he survived, he's permanently paralyzed and mentally disabled now.

Joshua's mother, Melody DeShaney, sued the Winnebago County Department of Social Services in Wisconsin for returning Joshua to his father. She argued that the department had a duty to protect her son from his father and should now be held responsible for the abuse.

YOU BE THE JUDGE

- **Do you think the county should be held responsible for what happened to Joshua? Why or why not?**

- **Is the government responsible for protecting children from their parents?**

The Ruling:

In a six to three decision written by Justice William H. Rehnquist, the Court held that the government doesn't have a "constitutional" duty to protect children from their parents. Therefore, the department wasn't at fault and couldn't be held responsible. Joshua's father caused the boy's injuries, and he was prosecuted and sent to prison as a result.

The U.S. Constitution doesn't require states to protect the life, liberty, and property of its citizens from acts by private individuals. The government is prohibited from doing certain things without affording you **due process,** but the government isn't required to guarantee you protection from others.

Although the government isn't *required* to protect children, all states assume this responsibility under **child protection laws.** Social services departments exist to provide services for families, and the departments have a duty and a responsibility to protect children when they're in their care—but not while the children are in a *parent's* care. However, even when children are removed from a parent's home, the government has only a limited liability if something goes wrong.

The U.S. Supreme Court has consistently respected parents' rights to discipline their children. Recognizing that each state's civil and criminal laws must be followed (there are no federal laws regarding parental discipline—it's a matter left to the states to legislate), the Court has deferred to state and local **jurisdictions** to do just that—enforce their laws regarding the protection of children. Unfortunately, these protections aren't always enough to prevent harm to children by their parents.

Related Cases:

Excessive discipline in the home may amount to child abuse, which is illegal in all states. But determining what's excessive and what's acceptable isn't always easy. Because individual parents hold a wide range of beliefs on how to best raise their children, children are disciplined in many different ways. And some parents might never even consider using some forms of discipline that are legal, such as spanking.

▪ What if your parents spank you so hard that you're bruised afterward?

Is this against the law? R. A. lived with her father and stepmother in Iowa. When she was nine years old, her father spanked her with a leather belt, which left bruises on her buttocks and thighs. The bruises were still visible three days later when she reported the abuse to her family therapist. Her father was convicted of **child endangerment** and sentenced to 180 days in jail. The Iowa Supreme Court stated that a parent's right to discipline his or her child "clearly has its limits." When they're exceeded, the parent may be criminally liable. However, the court noted: "American courts are not in full agreement on how to define the limits of the parental right to discipline a disobedient child."

State v. Arnold (1996)

▪ Can your parents discipline you using a paddle or switch?

Eight-year-old Amanda lived with her mother and visited her father, a noncustodial parent (meaning he didn't have custody). One weekend, her father told her to wash her hair, bathe, and get ready for some photographs. Because Amanda wasn't ready when her father arrived, he spanked her three times with a wooden spoon over her denim jeans. Red marks were visible for several days.

Amanda's father was charged with child abuse, but the Iowa Supreme Court ruled in his favor. The court decided that parents "have a right to inflict reasonable **corporal punishment** in rearing their children." It also said that "welts, bruises, or similar markings are not physical injuries *per se.*"

Hildreth v. Iowa D. H. S. (1996)

> In most states, child abuse, endangerment, and assault are considered a **felony** with jail or prison time possible.

▪ Is physical punishment always considered child abuse?

Brandon, ten, and Andrew, nine, were regularly disciplined by their parents with wooden or plastic spoons and a belt. The boys often had slight bruises, but no serious physical injuries. In a case filed by the North Dakota Department of Human Services in Fargo, the parents explained that their religious beliefs, based on the Bible, allowed corporal punishment to train their children to do what's right. Although the North Dakota Supreme Court determined that there wasn't enough evidence to support child abuse charges in this case, it remarked: "[T]he regular use of corporal punishment is a practice to be avoided."

Raboin v. North Dakota D. H. S. (1996)

> "Parental autonomy is not . . . absolute. The state is the guardian of society's basic values. . . . the state has a right, indeed, a duty, to protect children. State officials may interfere in family matters to safeguard the child's health, educational development, and emotional well-being."
> *In re Phillip B.* (1979)

Get on the Case:

- What forms of discipline do your parents use? Do you think these rules or punishments are effective? Why or why not? What would you suggest as alternatives?

- With your mom or dad, develop a fair discipline plan for your home. List the rules of your household and the consequences for breaking them. Post the rules where everyone in the family can see them.

- How do you balance a parent's right to raise a family with a child's right to protection from abuse? Do you think that parents have too little or too much freedom concerning discipline? Teachers, medical professionals, social workers, and other people who are responsible for children have a legal responsibility to report suspected abuse or neglect. What do you think about these laws? Should they be extended or limited in any way? Why or why not?

Can you be hospitalized for mental health treatment against your will?

Case: *Parham v. J. R.* (1979)

Do parents know best when it comes to raising their kids? Are their decisions always right? Regardless of mistakes parents may make in child-rearing, the law gives them a certain amount of authority over their kids. But along with this authority comes a high level of responsibility concerning your health and well-being. This case explores the rights children have to challenge their parents' decisions and get their opinions heard.

The Facts:

When J. L. was six years old, he was expelled from school for two months. He received outpatient therapy and was eventually diagnosed as having a "hyperkinetic reaction to childhood." His mother and step-father then asked a mental health hospital to admit him indefinitely. The physician who interviewed J. L. and his parents before he was admitted to the hospital said J. L. was uncontrollable and aggressive. J. L. was admitted to the hospital and after several unsuccessful attempts to return him home (his parents said they couldn't control him), his parents signed papers surrendering custody of the boy to the county. J. L. remained in the hospital for several more years, even though the hospital recommended at one point that he be moved to a special foster home. A lack of funds prevented the move. When he was twelve, J. L. and another boy, J. R., took legal action to change their situation.

At only three months old, J. R. had been placed into foster care because of his parents' neglect. He spent the next seven years in seven different foster homes. In 1970, he was diagnosed as borderline retarded, mentally ill, unsocialized, and aggressive, and he was placed in a mental health hospital. Three years later, the hospital recommended that J. R. be moved to a foster home or an adoptive home because "he will only regress if he does not get a suitable home placement, and as soon as possible." Two years later, J. R. was thirteen and still under hospitalization.

J. L. and J. R., along with their attorneys, filed a lawsuit representing approximately 140 children and teenagers in mental health institutions in the state of Georgia. They sued James Parham, the director of the state's mental health programs, and the medical director of the hospital where the boys were confined. The basis of their suit was that the procedures in Georgia allowing a parent or guardian to hospitalize a **minor** without his or her consent violated the minor's **due process** rights.

YOU BE THE JUDGE

- **Should parents have the right to commit their child to a mental health hospital against his or her wishes? Why or why not?**

- **Who should have the final say on whether a child remains hospitalized—a parent or the hospital? Why?**

- **How does a child's due process right fit into this decision? Should the child have the right to express his or her opinion? If so, how much weight should this opinion have in the decision to place the minor in a psychiatric hospital?**

The Ruling:

In making its decision, the U.S. Supreme Court first looked at Georgia's state law on committing children to psychiatric hospitals and whether the procedures protected children from unnecessary hospitalization. The law allowed parents to apply for hospitalization, which was reviewed by the hospital superintendent. This person could admit any child for "observation and diagnosis"—usually for a few days. If, during this stay, an evaluation showed that the child had a mental illness and was in need of treatment, the child would be hospitalized until a doctor determined that the child was no longer a threat to self or others.

The Court then studied the admission procedures at each of Georgia's mental health hospitals, as well as the child's right to not be hospitalized and to receive treatment in a less restrictive setting. Although the Court recognized that parents are responsible for raising their own family, it found that they alone don't have the authority to institutionalize their child. Before hospitalization, an independent

States have different laws about the length of hospitalization. Some set a maximum length of stay depending on the final diagnosis. For example, if the person is a danger to himself or herself, the stay is three months; if the person is a danger to others, the stay is six months, with regular reviews scheduled.

medical evaluation must show the need for inpatient treatment. In a six to three decision written by Justice Warren E. Burger, the Court concluded that without the opinion of a neutral person, minors may be unnecessarily hospitalized.

In a **concurring opinion,** Justice Potter Stewart pointed out that not only does commitment to a mental institution result in loss of liberty, but the person is also affected by the stigma attached to treatment in a mental hospital. Consequently, hospitalization must be accomplished through procedures that comply with due process. An independent evaluation, with regular reviews of the patient's condition and the patient's right to be heard at an impartial hearing must be in place.

When a child in psychiatric care turns eighteen, he or she may remain hospitalized but must proceed through the adult commitment process—the patient isn't automatically discharged due to age. An adult can be hospitalized against his or her wishes through the **civil commitment laws,** which vary by state.

In upholding Georgia's process for voluntary commitment of children by the parent, the Court declared that an independent process that includes a thorough psychiatric investigation, followed by periodic reviews of the child's condition, would protect children who shouldn't be admitted. The boys lost the case.

On the balance between parent and child in the decision-making process, the Court wrote: "Simply because the decision of a parent is not agreeable to a child or because it involves risks does not automatically transfer the power to make that decision from the parents to some agency or officer of the state. . . . Most children, even in adolescence, simply are not able to make sound judgments concerning many decisions, including their need for medical care or treatment."

If you, a family member, or a friend is hospitalized for mental health care, you may have questions about the rights of patients. For example: What happens to your privacy or your ability to communicate with the outside world? Do you retain any rights while in treatment, or is it like being in jail?

The laws in each state differ slightly regarding your specific rights while in treatment. In general, patients have privacy rights and the use of personal possessions and storage space. You may be allowed to wear your own clothes and will have the opportunity to make telephone calls (to a limited number of approved people), write letters, and have personal visits during certain hours. Depending on the circumstances, these rights may be suspended or restricted to protect your safety or the welfare of others. You may also have the right to refuse certain types of treatment, such as shock therapy, psychotherapy, or extreme behavior modification programs. There are also laws that protect you from unreasonable restraints (mechanical, isolation, medication). A violation of your rights may result in civil or criminal penalties. A local lawyer or librarian can point you to the law in your **jurisdiction.** If you're going into treatment, ask the doctor or hospital staff for a written copy of your rights as a patient.

Teenagers and children no longer have to worry about being locked up in a mental hospital and forgotten. States now have procedures and policies for admission, interviews, evaluation, and periodic reviews for continued care. Patients' rights apply to minors, as well as their parents. Outpatient counseling is another alternative available to teens. Your parents may arrange for counseling, and as long as you're a minor under your parents' authority, you have to go. In some states, you may find your own counselor and attend without your parents' knowledge or consent. These laws are usually limited to drug counseling and health care regarding sexually transmitted diseases and contraceptives.

Related Cases:

Because one person isn't solely responsible for committing someone into a mental health facility, it's highly unlikely that a child would be wrongly hospitalized. Although parents have a certain degree of authority to make mental health decisions for their children, a nonrelated, neutral decision-maker who has evaluated the minor determines whether confinement for mental health treatment is necessary. After treatment, and at a point at which the person is no longer a danger to self or others, he or she may receive a less restrictive placement (like a foster home).

■ Are your parents violating your civil rights if they force you into a psychiatric hospital, or do they have a duty to make sure you receive such care?

At her mother's request, seventeen-year-old R. J. D. voluntarily entered a hospital in Birmingham, Alabama, for drug screening and counseling. After four days, she was released. Her mother then placed R. J. D., against her will, in the secure ward of a psychiatric hospital. Two weeks later, her father smuggled her out. (Her parents were divorced.) She and her father sued the hospital and the admitting psychiatrist, claiming false imprisonment and violation of R. J. D.'s civil rights. The Alabama Supreme Court held that a parent may seek medical care for a child against the child's will. The court also noted that parents have a legal responsibility to care for their child; failing to do so may result in civil and criminal penalties. R. J. D.'s claims were dismissed.

R. J. D. v. Vaughan Clinic (1990)

■ What if you need psychiatric hospitalization but the state hospital is full? Does this violate your rights to receive treatment?

D. W. was a seventeen-year-old boy in Alabama, who had a history of mental illness. He was diagnosed as schizophrenic and was potentially dangerous to himself and others. Because of this, an Alabama juvenile court ordered D. W. into the state psychiatric hospital until his condition improved. However, the hospital was full, so the court allowed D. W. to stay at home with his mother, while he was on a waiting list. D. W. continued to display dangerous behavior, including threatening the lives of his mother, grandfather, brother, and five-year-old sister. D. W.'s mother arranged for private hospitalization until the state hospital could take him the next month.

D. W. and his mother claimed a violation of D. W.'s civil rights to care and treatment, because children over twelve were put on waiting lists, unlike younger children or adults. The court didn't agree with D. W. He wasn't denied mental health services; he only had to wait until a bed was available at the hospital. The court said the right to treatment begins when hospitalized, not while waiting for an opening. In the meantime, treatment on an outpatient basis was available. In D. W.'s case, private hospitalization with the help of Medicaid (government assistance) was also available.

D. W. v. Rogers (1997)

Individual states have different laws about rights to mental health treatment and care. For example, some states give minors the right to seek treatment without their parents' consent or the right to refuse treatment. In Wisconsin, minors who are fourteen and older may receive treatment if their parents refuse to arrange for mental health services. In Iowa, if the parent seeks help for the child and the child refuses, the matter goes to juvenile court for a decision.

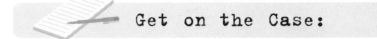

Get on the Case:

■ Have your parents ever forced you into doing something that you didn't want to do? How did that make you feel? Did you understand their reasons? If so, did that help you accept their demand? If some time has passed since this incident, do you feel differently now than you did at first?

■ Do you think minors should have a voice in all decisions concerning their health? Why or why not? What if a child has a life-threatening disease, such as AIDS or cancer? What roles should the child and his or her parents have in deciding on medical care? Does it matter how old the minor is? Why or why not? What if an alternative therapy is being considered? Who should have the final say in which treatment to use?

ISSUE:

Can your grandparents visit you against your parents' wishes?

Case: *Parkerson v. Brooks* (1995)

Times change, and with change comes new laws. Grandparents' visitation rights wasn't as big of an issue ten years ago, but it is today. Because of the nation's high divorce rate and the larger number of blended families in the country, courts are facing many more custody and visitation questions.

Balancing the rights of family members and other loved ones with the best interests of the children involved isn't always easy or clear-cut. The right solution in one case may not make sense in another, as you'll see in the cases that follow.

The Facts:

Under Georgia's grandparent visitation law, Mrs. Parkerson asked the court for an order allowing her to visit her four-year-old granddaughter (her daughter's child). The child's parents, Stacy and William Brooks, wanted the court to deny the visitation request. The Brooks had decided that it wasn't in their daughter's best interests to see her grandmother and that the law invaded their right, as parents, to raise their child without government interference.

YOU BE THE JUDGE

- **Do you think the Georgia law was unconstitutional? Do grandparents have a right to see their grandchildren even if the parents object?**

- **Should parents have the final say regarding who their children see and don't see? Or, put another way, should grandparents or other relatives be able to force contact with family members?**

- **Do you think the government has a right to interfere with the way parents raise their children?**

The Ruling:

The Georgia Supreme Court determined that the law was unconstitutional, because it violated parents' right to raise their children without state interference under the Fourteenth Amendment (see page 151). An **appeal** by Mrs. Parkerson to the U.S. Supreme Court was unsuccessful. The Court declined to review the Georgia court's decision. This left the Georgia Supreme Court decision in effect.

In deciding whether Mrs. Parkerson could obtain court-ordered visitation with her granddaughter against the wishes of the girl's parents, the Georgia Supreme Court reviewed the history of parent and child relationships under the law. The court studied cases dating back to 1923 and found a common thread—state interference with parents' rights to custody and control of their children is permissible only when the health or welfare of a child is threatened. Otherwise, the law protects the authority of the immediate family.

As a result, the court found that parents in Georgia, as well as parents throughout the United States, have a fundamental right to raise their children as they see fit, without excessive government intrusion. The court was also worried that forcing children to spend time with someone against their parents' wishes would negatively affect the children.

Quoting from an earlier Georgia case, the *Parkerson* court also stated: "[T]he law's concept of the family rests on a presumption that parents possess what a child lacks in maturity, experience, and capacity for judgment required for making life's difficult decisions."

So, although the court understood that grandparents can enhance a child's life, it stood by tradition in its decision, saying: "Having found wisdom, learned patience, and journeyed in faith, many grandparents have much to give their grandchildren in the way of a vision of the world, as models of action, and may, as well, provide children with a very profound sense of connection with others. However, as important as grandparents can be in the lives of their grandchildren, the relationship between parent and child is paramount."

When contacted in 1999, Stacy Brooks noted that cases such as theirs can be hard on families: "When an agreement cannot be reached regarding visitation of grandparents, and the judicial system becomes involved, everyone needs to first weigh the financial cost, and emotional toll of a courtroom battle on an already strained relationship."

The issue of visitation, as you'll see in the related cases, has been expanded beyond just your parents. Whether you have a say in who you visit depends on your state's law. Every state has a grandparent visitation law, with different rules and requirements. Your chance to go to court and talk with the judge is better as you get older. Once you reach your teens, the court will want to know your wishes on such matters. The judge may speak with your lawyer, if you have one, or talk to you directly. If you get to appear in court, take advantage of this opportunity to tell the judge how you feel and why.

Related Cases:

During the past twenty years, courts have split over the issue of grand-parent visitation. Some have ruled on the side of parents' rights, while others have held that grandparent visits may occur—even over parents' objections. As you'll see in the following cases, visitation rights are also being sought by siblings, stepparents, aunts and uncles, and people who aren't related to the child in question.

In 2000, the U.S. Supreme Court considered the constitutionality of Washington state's grandparent visitation law. The Court's decision upheld the fundamental right of parents to make decisions concerning the care, custody, and control of their children. The Washington case involved the children of Brad Troxel, a man who committed suicide in 1993. Brad wasn't married, but he left behind two young daughters, Natalie and Isabelle. Brad's parents, Gary and Jenifer Troxel, obtained a court order under the Washington grandparent law, granting them one weekend each month with the girls. Their mother, Tommie Granville, later married and her husband, Kelly Wynn, adopted the girls in 1996. Tommie opposed the court-ordered visitation, arguing that it violated her authority over the girls' lives. The Supreme Court of the state of Washington agreed and ruled that the law was an unconstitutional invasion of parents' rights. The U.S. Supreme Court agreed.
Troxel v. Granville (2000)

■ Can you sue for rights to visit your underage siblings?

When Pennsylvania resident C. R.'s parents divorced in 1981, she continued to live with her mother, Mary Jane. After remarrying, Mary Jane had two more daughters, Heather and Alison. Due to alleged sexual contact with her stepfather, sixteen-year-old C. R. moved to her father's home. Mary Jane refused to allow C. R. to see her half-sisters at all.

C. R. and her father sued for visitation rights but were unsuccessful. The Pennsylvania Supreme Court stated that because the law didn't provide for sibling visitation, the court had no right to overrule Mary Jane's decision to prevent C. R. from contacting Heather and Alison.

Ken R. on Behalf of C. R. v. Arthur and Mary Jane Z. (1996)

On the other hand, a South Dakota court wrote that "it is universally recognized that in the absence of compelling reasons to the contrary, the best interests of siblings require that they be raised together whenever possible." The court also said that this also applies to half-siblings. Although this statement was issued in a custody case, the principles apply to visitation issues as well. "Family unity between siblings often promotes their best interests," the court said.
Crouse v. Crouse (1996)

■ Do people who are gay or lesbian have any legal rights to their partners' children?

In 1999, the U.S. Supreme Court was presented a case involving visitation between a birth mother, L. M. M., and her former same-sex partner, E. N. O, a couple in Massachusetts. The women had been together for thirteen years and had agreed to jointly raise a child. Through artificial insemination, L. M. M. became pregnant and gave birth to Baby O. M. in February 1995. In 1998, the couple's relationship began to deteriorate, and they separated that spring. L. M. M. would no longer allow E. N. O. to see the child, who was now three years old. E. N. O. went to court, seeking enforcement of their agreement to jointly raise O. M. Based on their three-year history as a family, and the psychological best interests of O. M., the Supreme Court of Massachusetts gave E. N. O. visitation with O. M. The court noted that the only family O. M. had ever known had broken up and that the child was entitled to be protected from further trauma of the separation of his parents. The U.S. Supreme Court didn't accept the case for review, meaning the decision of the Massachusetts court stands.

E. N. O. v. L. M. M. (1999)

■ What about relatives who help raise a child? Do they have any visitation rights?

Michelle Guchereau asked her sister and brother-in-law, Cindy and Richard LaHaye, to care for her one-year-old daughter, Josie, while she served a jail sentence. This involved Michelle giving the couple temporary legal custody of Josie. Cindy and Richard, who lived in Louisiana, ended up keeping Josie for fourteen months.

When Michelle was released from jail, she moved to Chicago and sought sole custody of Josie. Based on Josie's best interests, the Louisiana court granted Michelle's request, but against her wishes granted liberal visitation to Josie's aunt and uncle—up to six days on each alternating holiday (Christmas, New Year's, Easter, and Thanksgiving), three weeks each summer, and weekly telephone access with the child.

In the Interest of Baron (1996)

■ Can grandparents be denied visitation with their grandchildren if the courts don't approve of their behavior?

Missouri resident Leah Mack had three children, Christina (age five), Arthur (age one), and William (one month). Leah's mother, Bernice E.

Young, had a court order to visit the children on alternating weekends, on holidays, and during two one-week periods each summer. Due to increasing problems between the grandmother and Leah's husband, Leah asked the Missouri court to reduce the visitation order. Among other things, the grandmother brought her mother to the visits, and this woman spoke negatively about the children's father. According to the visitation order, the grandmother was prohibited from smoking around the children, which she did anyway. Christina returned from visits smelling of tobacco smoke; she pretended to smoke with a stick or pencil; and on one occasion, she reported that she'd been burned with a cigarette. The grandmother also took Christina to a halfway house to visit a relative, against Leah's wishes. All in all, the court determined that the grandmother's conduct harmed the parents' authority and that restrictions were appropriate. Visits with Christina were limited to once a month for six hours; visits with the boys were restricted to once a month for one and a half hours at their parents' home.

D. F. S. v. Ellis (1994)

■ Do death-row inmates have a right to see their children?

W. G. T., a prisoner on Florida's death row, wanted to see his son, who lived with his aunt and uncle. The court held that supervised visits were possible but only if the boy's therapist approved. W. G. T. was entitled, however, to photographs and regular reports about his son's health, education, and overall well-being.

W. G. T. v. B. C. (1996)

■ What if a parent uses illegal drugs? Does this affect his or her visitation rights?

During a paternity trial in Washington, Michael Waters argued that the court's restrictions placed on his visits with his son, Alex, were unreasonable. Michael admitted to using alcohol and cocaine in the past. The Washington court also found that he had committed acts of domestic violence and that his daily use of marijuana could negatively affect Alex's general welfare. The court withheld visitation until Michael provided thirty days of drug-free urine samples. The court didn't accept his argument that his religion encouraged his daily drug use.

State v. Waters (1998)

Get on the Case:

- What other circumstances might lead to visitation disputes? How do you think the court would rule on such cases, based on what you've read here?

- Are your parents divorced? If so, are you satisfied with your visitation arrangements? What type of challenges are involved? Are there any changes you'd like to make?

ISSUE:

Do you have any rights if you break the law?

Case: *In re Gault* (1967)

Even if you break the law, you still have rights. The court system has been carefully set up to protect those accused of a crime and to be sure that people in power—such as police officers, lawyers, and judges—don't abuse their authority. The court system recognizes the importance of treating people humanely and with a certain level of respect while they're involved with the courts. This means being fair, allowing people to tell their story, and helping them make their way through a system they may not understand.

The Facts:

On June 8, 1964, fifteen-year-old Arizona resident Gerald Gault made an indecent telephone call to his neighbor, Mrs. Cook. She reported the call to the police, who traced it to Gerald's house. Gerald, who was already on **probation** for theft, was picked up by the police and arrested. Gerald's parents weren't told of their son's arrest or of any charges filed against him. Two **delinquency** hearings were held during the week, which Gerald attended without the assistance of an attorney. He didn't have an opportunity to question Mrs. Cook because she failed to attend the hearings. Gerald and his parents weren't given a copy of the charge against him (obscene phone calls) or told what may happen to him. On June 15, the judge determined, based on the testimony of Gerald's probation officer, that Gerald was a delinquent and ordered that he attend the state reform school (today called the Department of Juvenile Corrections) until he turned twenty-one. This was for an offense that, if committed by an adult, carried a two-month sentence.

Gerald and his parents **appealed,** claiming that the laws and procedures for **minors** who got into trouble were inadequate. Gerald wasn't provided **due process**—specifically, he wasn't able to confront his accuser in court; he wasn't given any legal assistance; and his parents weren't notified of the charges.

YOU BE THE JUDGE

- **Do you think Gerald's case was handled fairly? Should the courts and police have made sure that Gerald's parents knew about his arrest and the case against him? Why or why not?**

- **Was the sentence that Gerald received reasonable, especially considering the sentence an adult would have received for the same crime? Why or why not?**

- **Should Gerald have been given the chance to confront Mrs. Cook about her version of the incident?**

The Ruling:

In deciding Gerald's case, the U.S. Supreme Court reviewed the sixty-year history of juvenile law in the United States. In a seven to two decision written by Justice Abe Fortas, the Court concluded that juvenile court procedures must be fair and follow due process guidelines. In other words, Gerald and his parents shouldn't have been kept in the dark about the charge against Gerald, and Gerald should have been given an opportunity to tell his side of the story in court, with the help of a lawyer. The Court noted that the possibility of losing one's freedom is as significant (if not more so) to a minor as to an adult. The Court looked at each step in Gerald's original case and made three separate rulings:

1. **Notice of charges**—Defendants must be told of the charges far enough in advance to allow them a reasonable amount of time to prepare for the court proceeding. This means that the court should have ensured that Gerald's parents knew about the case.

2. **Right to counsel**—Minors who are suspected of breaking a law should receive an attorney's help in court.

3. **Confrontation, self-incrimination, cross-examination**—The right to face your accusers and question them **(cross-examination)**, as well as your right to remain silent, is guaranteed by the Fifth Amendment (see the **Bill of Rights** on pages 19–20). The Court couldn't find a reason why juveniles shouldn't have these rights. Gerald should have been afforded all of these rights before being sent to the state school for boys.

In the first *Gault* decision by the Arizona Supreme Court (before the case went up to the U.S. Supreme Court), Justice Charles C. Bernstein commented on the purpose of juvenile courts: "Juvenile courts do not exist to punish children for their transgressions against society. The juvenile court stands in the position of a protecting parent rather than a prosecutor. It is an effort to substitute protection and guidance for punishment. . . . The aim of the court is to provide individualized justice for children . . . [and] authoritative treatment for those who are no longer responding to the normal restraints the child should receive at the hands of his parents. The delinquent is the child of, rather than the enemy of society, and their interests coincide."

Finding that due process had not been followed in Gerald's case, the U.S. Supreme Court reversed the Arizona Supreme Court decision and sent the case back with an order to follow due process. Gerald spent five months at the reform school and was released.

The U.S. Supreme Court's position regarding the rights of juveniles was clear from several comments by Justice Fortas. He wrote: "Neither the Fourteenth Amendment nor the Bill of Rights is for adults alone." The Fourteenth Amendment to the U.S. Constitution uses several phrases that apply to every U.S. citizen, regardless of age: due process and **equal protection.** Again, due process, in its simplest form, means fairness. Gerald wasn't treated fairly—his opportunity to defend himself or even know what he was charged with was limited. Equal protection is the principle that everyone in the same group or classification should be treated the same. A person can't be singled out of a group and treated differently.

Gerald Gault was a Job Corps student in California when the decision in his case was announced. He later became a computer technician, joined the army, and served in Korea. He's married and has two sons. When interviewed twenty-five years later, he commented: "I had no rights, but now my children and the children of the community have rights—the right to an attorney and to be able to question their accuser. It was well worth the fight."

In the 1800s, children were tried, convicted, and sentenced as if they were adults. Children who were abandoned or neglected were institutionalized. The concepts of rehabilitation, treatment, and best interests brought about the first juvenile court in Chicago, Illinois, in 1899. At this time, the emphasis shifted

> Fourteenth Amendment, Section 1.: All persons born or naturalized in the United States, and subject to the **jurisdiction** thereof, are citizens of the United States and of the State wherein they reside. No State shall make or enforce any law which shall abridge the privileges or immunities of citizens of the United States; nor shall any State deprive any person of life, liberty, or property, without due process of law; nor deny to any person within its jurisdiction the equal protection of the laws.

to providing services for children and teens rather than simply locking them up. Sixty-eight years later, the U.S. Supreme Court in *Gault* fully recognized minors as people with specific rights when charged with a crime. Juveniles in the justice system were now afforded the same rights as adults. Recently, there's been a slight shift back toward punishment and community protection. Juvenile drug use and violence has resulted in legislation that's changing the focus of juvenile law. Yet, the *Gault* decision still applies to all minors facing criminal charges.

Related Cases:

The test used most often by the courts in determining whether a person's statements are admissible evidence (can be used at trial) is "totality of circumstances." In other words, all factors surrounding the statement or confession are considered. These include age, maturity, ability to communicate, criminal history, mental and physical state, and environment at the time of questioning. The following cases offer examples of admissible and inadmissible statements.

▪ If you confess to a crime but your parents aren't with you, can the confession be used against you in court?

Ten-year-old B. M. B. was convicted of raping his four-year-old neighbor, J. in Sedgwick County in Kansas. During the investigation, B. M. B. was taken from school to the police station and questioned. His mother wasn't present for the interview, which lasted thirty-one minutes. The Supreme Court of Kansas ruled that B. M. B.'s statements weren't admissible as evidence against him, due to his age, the absence of a parent during questioning, and the inappropriate interview techniques used by the officer.

In the Matter of B. M. B. (1998)

▪ Does your age and background affect whether your confession is admitted as evidence?

In December 1994, seventeen-year-old Calvin Jones and Darrell Johnson robbed a convenience store in Minnesota, shot the clerk, and escaped with $600 and four packs of cigarettes. Later, when they were caught, Calvin was read the **Miranda rights,** but he agreed to speak with the police. Calvin told several stories of what happened before finally confessing to shooting the clerk, who later died. After an hour of questioning, Calvin asked to speak with his mother.

The Minnesota Supreme Court ruled that Calvin's confession was admissible under the totality-of-circumstances test. The court took into consideration everything it knew about Calvin—his past, his education, and his contact with law enforcement, before determining his ability to understand his Miranda rights. Calvin had finished the eleventh grade, had ten **felonies** on his record, and was read his rights before being questioned. Calvin was convicted of first-degree murder.

State v. Calvin Jones (1997)

▪ After you're taken into custody, can police question you without reading you your rights?

In Colorado in January 1995, D. F. L., a minor in Colorado, was at a friend's apartment with three men when the police arrived. They had a **warrant** to search the apartment and the people found there. D. F. L. was searched, placed in handcuffs, and taken into custody. When asked by the police, D. F. L. stated that a brown purse found in the apartment was hers. It was searched, and a dried mushroom was found inside a cigarette pack. D. F. L. said she was holding it for a friend. Although the police hadn't read her the Miranda rights, she was charged with possession of a controlled substance.

The Colorado Supreme Court threw out D. F. L.'s statement admitting ownership of the purse. She should have been advised of her rights first and told she could have a parent present before being questioned. The case was sent back to the trial court.

In the Interest of D. F. L (1997)

▪ If you report a crime, can police question you without reading you your rights and without your parents present?

T. C. was eleven years old when he was charged with robbery and first-degree murder of Luis Gutierrez in Denver, Colorado. He and his best friend's older brother, Leroy, were at a park early one evening where they saw Luis, an elderly man who was apparently drunk. Leroy pushed Luis to the ground, and both he and T. C. kicked him in the head. They stole Luis's soda can and a dime, and Leroy stabbed the man three times in the chest, killing him. T. C. was afraid of getting into trouble and reported the stabbing to the police. He was in custody at the police station where he was questioned without a parent present and without having been read his rights. An appeals court ruled that the resulting statements couldn't be used against him in court. The case was sent back to trial court to evaluate the evidence without the excluded statements.

People v. T. C. (1995)

▪ What if you confess, but the police didn't follow the rules?

Fifteen-year-old Jacqueline Montanez was arrested in Illinois on May 13, 1992, for the murders of Hector Reyes and Jimmy Cruz, committed the day before. The victims had been shot in the head. Jacqueline was taken to the police station at 9:00 P.M. and read her Miranda rights. Police called her mother at 10:00 P.M. and told her that Jacqueline was involved in a murder and was in protective custody. She asked to see her daughter and was told that they'd let her know when she could. At 2:00 A.M., her mother went to the station and waited until 8:00 A.M. to see her daughter. In the meantime, police had questioned Jacqueline throughout the night without the presence of an attorney, and at 6:15 A.M. she signed a written confession. A jury in Chicago, Illinois, found Jacqueline guilty, and she was sentenced to life in prison.

The Illinois Court of Appeals found that the police had violated Jacqueline's rights in their attempt to obtain a confession. She should have been allowed to have her mother with her during questioning and should have been given the opportunity to ask for the assistance of a lawyer. Her conviction was reversed, and a new trial was ordered without her confession as admissible evidence.

People v. Montanez (1995)

■ Can the police do whatever they want to get you to confess?

In an Illinois case, ten-year-old V. L. T. was found guilty of involuntary manslaughter in the death of a twenty-two-month-old child she was baby-sitting. She was sentenced to five years of probation. V. L. T. was taken into custody around 10:00 P.M. while in her pajamas. She had little food, drink, or sleep. She asked for her grandmother, who got to see her around 3:00 A.M., after V. L. T. had given a written confession. The Illinois Court of Appeals ruled that her confession was involuntary, considering all of the circumstances (she was deprived of sleep, proper clothing, and contact with her grandmother, even though she asked to see her). The confession therefore couldn't be used as evidence.

In re V. L. T. (1997)

Get on the Case:

■ Where do parents fit in when a teenager becomes involved with the court? Do parents need to be involved with their child's probation officer and help in rehabilitation, or should the parents leave this matter entirely to the court system?

- Why should a child's parent be with him or her during police questioning? Do you think the presence of a parent might affect the questions asked? The way they're asked? Or perhaps the answer the child gives?

- Role-play an interview between police officers and suspects at the police station. (Some of the role-players can be the police, while others act as suspects, parents, or attorneys.) If possible, interview an actual police officer or legal expert to learn more about how such questioning is conducted.

ISSUE:

Does the whole world have to know about a mistake you made as a teenager?

Case: *Josh Davis v. Alaska* (1974)

Let's face it, everybody makes mistakes. That's how we learn. Yet some errors in judgment carry greater consequences than others—just ask anyone who's ever seen the inside of a police station. If you get in trouble with the law before you're eighteen, your case is usually handled by a juvenile court and kept confidential. However, this doesn't necessarily mean that your record will be sealed forever or destroyed when you turn eighteen.

The Facts:

Sixteen-year-old Richard Green's mother asked him to run an errand. On his way to the store, he saw two men standing by a blue car, along a little-used side road. Richard asked them if they needed any help; when they said no, he continued on to the store. On his way back, he saw them again. This time, one of the men was standing near the trunk of the car, holding a crowbar.

Later that day, Richard and his stepfather discovered a safe on the road where the blue car had been parked. They called the police and were both interviewed. Richard explained what he saw and later identified the two men in police photos. It turns out that someone had broken into a local bar and stolen a 200-pound safe containing more than $1,000 in cash and checks. When Richard and his stepfather found the safe, its bottom had been pried open and it was empty. Police eventually found the blue car at Josh Davis's home. Paint chips and insulation from the safe were found in the trunk.

Richard's testimony and identification of Josh Davis was important to the state's case. However, Richard was a **minor** on **probation** for an unrelated burglary. Josh's lawyer wanted to question Richard about his criminal background in court and argue that Richard quickly and falsely identified Josh, so the police wouldn't consider him a suspect. He knew that his probation would probably be revoked if he was thought to be involved with the crime.

The Alaska trial court didn't allow Josh or his attorney to bring up Richard's history or the fact that he was on probation at the time of the burglary. Josh was found guilty. He **appealed,** asking the U.S. Supreme Court to set aside the conviction since his right to **confrontation** was limited.

> If a person breaks the terms of his or her probation, the court may impose more serious consequences, such as time in **detention** or stricter probation conditions.

YOU BE THE JUDGE

- **Do you think Richard's right to privacy (of his juvenile record) outweighed Josh's right to cross-examine him in court? Why or why not?**

- **Why did the Alaska court refuse to allow Richard's history to be presented at the trial?**

The Ruling:

Although this case is named after Josh Davis, he wasn't the person the U.S. Supreme Court was concerned with. Josh was tried and convicted of burglary and theft. During the trial, Josh's lawyer wanted to tell the jury about Richard Green's criminal record and probation, so they'd have a reason to question his credibility as a witness—a reason to suspect that he was lying.

The U.S. Supreme Court discussed the purpose of confrontation at trial, looking at the Sixth Amendment which gives criminal defendants a right to confront witnesses in court (see the **Bill or Rights** on pages 19–20).

The goal of cross-examination is to challenge the accuracy of a witness's memory and to reveal any bias or prejudice that he or she has toward the defendant or ulterior motives for a given testimony. Because Richard's testimony was critical to the case against Josh, the Court ruled that Josh's lawyers should have been allowed to ask Richard questions that might show a bias. The jury should have been given the opportunity to judge Richard's trustworthiness after knowing all the facts, not just some of them. In a seven to two decision written by Justice Warren E. Burger, the U.S. Supreme Court ruled that limiting the examination of Richard was an error. The case was sent back for a new trial.

The U.S. Supreme Court did make a point of saying that the right to confrontation isn't unlimited. They held that there's a duty to protect the juvenile from questions designed merely to harass, annoy, or humiliate.

Josh Davis was later convicted of possession and sale of heroin, and sentenced to twenty years in prison.

Related Cases:

There's some truth to the expression that the past may come back to haunt you; the mistakes you make while growing up may ripple through your adult life. Ten percent of America's teenagers are involved with the justice system. Most will become law-abiding, responsible adults. Even so, some will carry with them the scars of their earlier years— the effects of having a juvenile record.

■ Does your school need to know about your past trouble with the law?

N. P., a Louisiana resident, had been in gifted classes since the first grade. When he was fourteen, the school bus driver caught him with a gun. N. P.'s friend had stolen the gun from N. P.'s older brother, who was a security guard. His friend gave the gun to N. P. and asked him to return it to his brother. N. P. was expelled from school and charged with carrying the gun. He was placed on probation for two years. One of his probation terms required that he tell the principal of his new school about his probation and provide the name and phone number of his probation officer. N. P. objected on grounds of confidentiality.

Because this probation requirement was intended to ensure N. P.'s continued progress in school, the juvenile court didn't consider the disclosure to the principal to be a violation of confidentiality. The court said it served a legitimate purpose and wasn't intended to harass or jeopardize N. P.'s future.

State in the Interest of N. P. (1989)

■ Can your juvenile record affect later adult sentences?

As an adult, Steven LaMunyon was convicted of marijuana possession with intent to sell and sentenced to three to ten years in prison. When determining Steven's sentence, the Kansas court considered his juvenile offenses—two thefts, a burglary, and property damage—which increased his adult sentence. Steven argued that it was unconstitutional to punish him as an adult for crimes he committed and had been punished for as a juvenile. The Kansas Supreme Court disagreed and upheld the sentence, stating that Steven was considered a repeat offender and his sentence was based on his criminal history, not on the specific offenses he committed as a minor.

State v. LaMunyon (1996)

■ Can DNA blood tests required for an offense as a minor be held on file after you're eighteen?

In 1996, two juveniles in Arizona were charged with and plead guilty to child molestation. At sentencing, each boy was put on probation and placed at a residential treatment center. They were also ordered to submit to DNA blood testing, the results of which would be filed with a local law enforcement agency. Both teens and their lawyers challenged this part of their sentence. They claimed an invasion of privacy and sought protection from use of the test results after they turned eighteen. The Arizona Court of Appeals ruled against them on both counts. It stated that the primary purpose of DNA testing is to guard the public safety and that this outweighs the minor inconvenience in obtaining the blood sample. Furthermore, it said that ordering DNA testing isn't a form of punishment, and the records of such may be kept beyond a minor's eighteenth birthday. (Similar rulings have been made in the case of mandatory HIV and AIDS testing, following sex offense convictions.)

Appeal in Maricopa County Juvenile No. JV-512600 (1997)

■ Can a juvenile's name and case be used in the news?

J. E. W. was sixteen when he was arrested for murder and theft in Arizona. The prosecutor wanted to try him as an adult, and a hearing to decide this issue was scheduled. The news media asked for and received the court's permission to attend the hearing. J. E .W. appealed, asking that the hearing be closed to the media and general public. J. E. W. lost his appeal. The Arizona Supreme Court determined that the public has an interest in knowing how a juvenile court works and that they operate fairly and effectively. Closed or private hearings create suspicion about the court's operation.

Wideman v. Garbarino (1989)

■ Does the news media always have the right to cover juvenile hearings?

Three teenagers and an adult were charged in 1994 with civil rights violations and alleged hate crimes. They were suspected members of the New Dawn Hammerskins, a white supremacist group in Massachusetts. A local newspaper asked the court for permission to cover the hearings. The court denied the request, ruling that it wasn't possible to protect the juvenile offenders from public exposure and the stigma of a criminal record if the media was allowed to attend. The federal court of appeals was concerned about how releasing the case details would affect the juveniles.

United States v. Three Juveniles (1995)

Get on the Case:

■ What do you think of the decisions in these cases about juvenile records? Should the mistakes of your teen years be buried in the "graveyard of the forgotten past," as one court put it? Or should you have to live forever with the consequences of breaking the law? Should the type of crime committed play a role in this decision? Why do you think a juvenile's criminal record is treated differently than an adult's record?

■ What about using a person's juvenile record to increase the sentence of an adult? Is this fair? Why should a shoplifting conviction at age fourteen affect a sentence at age twenty? On the other hand, if your only offense was the shoplifting when you were fourteen, shouldn't your record be cleared now that you're twenty, responsible, and independent?

■ In most states, juveniles and adults who are found guilty of a sex offense are subject to a number of health and safety requirements. They may be ordered to register with law enforcement as a sex offender. At the victim's request, they may also be ordered to submit to an HIV test or provide a DNA sample for law enforcement information purposes. What do you think of the long-term effect of sex-offender registration and DNA testing? Should there be a limit on how long an offender is subject to these state laws? Or does the overall best interests and protection of the community justify permanent application? Talk this over with your friends and teachers. You could also ask your community relations department of your local police station to talk to your class about such laws in your community.

ISSUE:

Can you request a jury of your peers?

Case: *McKeiver v. Pennsylvania* (1971)

A jury is a group of six to twelve people who have been brought together to decide a particular case. The jury listens to the evidence and arguments of the two sides, considers the law that applies to the case (which the judge tells the jury about), and reaches a verdict. Jurors are usually comprised of ordinary people, but they have an awesome responsibility.

The Facts:

Three teenagers were in Fairmont Park in Philadelphia, Pennsylvania, when they were approached by a group of twenty to thirty boys. One of the boys, who was on a bike (sixteen-year-old Joseph McKeiver), demanded money from the teens. When one of the victims refused, Joseph punched him. The victim then gave Joseph a quarter, and he rode off. The victim later identified Joseph as the thief in this incident.

Joseph, who had never been arrested before, was charged with robbery, larceny (theft), and possession of stolen property. He pleaded not guilty, and the case was set for trial in the juvenile court. Joseph requested a jury trial, which the court denied. His case was tried by a juvenile court judge who found him guilty and placed him on **probation**. Joseph **appealed** this decision, arguing that his Sixth Amendment rights (see the **Bill of Rights** on pages 19–20) were violated because he was denied a trial by jury.

YOU BE THE JUDGE

- **Do you think Joseph had a right to a jury trial? Why or why not?**

- **Do juvenile courts have to follow the same rules as courts for adults?**

"Teen court" or "peer court" is a high school program where students become the judge, prosecutor, defense attorney, and jury. A teenager who's a first-time offender may appear before the teen court. This program is usually limited to nonviolent, **misdemeanor,** or low **felony crimes.** The offender must admit responsibility for the offense, and the teen jury decides the consequences. If the consequence is completed successfully and on time, no formal charges are filed in juvenile court. Consequences may include writing a paper on a particular subject, completing community service work, paying **restitution,** or writing a letter of apology to the victim. The offender may also be required to serve once or twice on a teen court jury. Participants in teen court are trained by local attorneys, **probation officers,** and judges.

The Ruling:

Before addressing the main issue in this case, the U.S. Supreme Court reviewed earlier Supreme Court decisions about juvenile rights: the use of a juvenile's confession as evidence, **waiving** a **minor** into adult court, and the level of proof required to convict a minor. The Court concluded that minors aren't guaranteed all of the rights that adults receive in the adult criminal process, including the right to a jury.

Over the years, courts and legal scholars have expressed different views on the use of juries in juvenile court. In previous cases, some of the justices thought jury trials were a fundamental right of the criminal justice system in the English-speaking world. Justification for juvenile court juries was also argued in cases where the minor was charged with a crime that, if the person were an adult, would be triable by jury.

Depending on the type of case, a defendant may prefer a jury over a trial before a judge alone. The theory is that it may be easier to convince a few jurors of your position than a single trial judge. The decision to ask for a jury, or not, should be made after consulting with a lawyer.

The Court in *McKeiver* needed to strike a balance between the different responsibilities of the juvenile courts. On the one hand, juvenile courts need to make minors realize that they're in a serious situation. A jury could help provide a dose of reality to minors. On the other hand, juvenile courts need to be informal, as the philosophy of juvenile justice is treatment and rehabilitation, not punishment. The Court determined that of all the **due process** rights that could be applied in juvenile court, the right to a jury was the one that would most likely disrupt the unique nature of the juvenile process. In fact, the Court said: "[T]he addition of the trial by jury might well destroy the traditional character of juvenile proceedings."

However, Joseph's attorney argued that juvenile proceedings are very similar to criminal trials held in adult court and, therefore, minors should have the same rights that adults have. The Court stuck to its position that juvenile proceedings aren't criminal prosecutions and that juvenile due process requires fundamental fairness. It wrote: "[O]ne cannot say that in our legal system the jury is a necessary component of accurate fact-finding." A trial before a judge alone is sufficient.

Several justices **dissented** in this decision (the vote was four to three), voting to grant juveniles the right to a jury. Equating the court experience of adults with juveniles, Justice William O. Douglas wrote: "The experience of a trial with or without a jury is meant to be impressive and meaningful. The fact that a juvenile realizes that his case will be decided by twelve objective citizens would allow the court to retain its meaningfulness without causing any more trauma than a trial before a judge. . . . Who can say that a boy who is arrested and handcuffed, placed in a lineup, transported in vehicles designed to convey dangerous criminals, placed in the same kind of cell as an adult, deprived of his freedom by lodging him in an institution where he is subject to be transferred to the state's prison and in the 'hole' has not undergone a traumatic experience?"

Although the U.S. Supreme Court didn't give minors an automatic right to a jury trial, it didn't go so far as to prohibit states from allowing juries in juvenile court. It stated: "If, in its wisdom, any State feels the jury trial is desirable in all cases, or in certain kinds, there appears to be no impediment to its installing a system embracing that feature. That, however, is the State's privilege and not its obligation."

If you're called to jury duty someday, you'll hear several terms, including *voir dire, challenge,* and *sequester.*

In order to select an impartial (unbiased) panel to hear and decide the case, the lawyers and judge involved will ask you questions about yourself. This is *voir dire,* which is a French term meaning "to speak the truth." *Voir dire* takes place during the jury selection process—at the beginning of the case. You'll be asked to state your name, age, occupation, family status, whether you've been on a jury before, and whether you know anyone involved with the case. More specific questions relating to the case will then be asked. The purpose of *voir dire* is to determine whether you have any bias or prejudice that may affect your decision-making ability.

After *voir dire,* the lawyers are given a chance to strike or challenge a set number of jurors. For example, if a group of twenty people went through *voir dire,* and a jury of twelve is needed for the case, each lawyer will be allowed to strike four people from the group. This would leave a panel of twelve to be sworn in to hear the case. Reasons for striking a panel member aren't required to be given.

In certain cases, jurors are kept together night and day during the trial—known as sequestering the jury. The court bailiff is responsible for your living arrangements—where you eat, sleep, and relax when you're not in court. Once the case is over and you've reached a verdict, the judge thanks you for your service and sends you home. Sequestering a jury is rare; it's only done in high-profile cases that have extensive media coverage. The costs and the level of inconvenience often dictate whether a jury will be sequestered.

Related Cases:

People who are tried before a jury learn to appreciate the role of a jury. But there are other ways of experiencing the jury system. Juries are used in both criminal and civil cases. You may be called as a victim or a witness to testify before a jury. Your chances are even better of being summoned to jury duty. It's both a duty and an honor to participate in government by sitting on a jury. The cases presented here discuss the function of a jury and your right to one in particular situations.

■ If a state allows minors to have jury trials, do the jurors also need to be under eighteen?

In a Minnesota case, sixteen-year-old J. K. B. was charged with terrorist threats, assault, unlawful possession of a handgun, and possession of stolen property. His case was moved to adult court, and he was given the option of having a jury trial.

Although J. K. B. and his lawyer agreed that juveniles don't have a constitutional right to a jury trial, they claimed that since Minnesota extended this right to minors when they were tried in adult court, the jury must be made up of the defendant's peers—meaning other sixteen- and seventeen-year-olds. The Minnesota Court of Appeals didn't accept J. K. B.'s argument, saying: "A juror must have the maturity and understanding to do what may often be an unpleasant task." J. K. B. was found guilty by the jury (made up of legal adults) on all counts.

Welfare of J. K. B. (1996)

■ Are juvenile proceedings and criminal prosecutions the same thing?

In an Oregon case, thirteen-year-old Brad Reynolds was charged with sexual abuse and giving obscene materials to a minor. He asked the court for a jury trial, which was denied. Brad was found guilty and sentenced to two years of probation. He and his lawyer appealed, claiming that the trial phase of the juvenile proceeding was, in fact, a criminal proceeding, entitling Brad to a jury.

The Oregon Supreme Court reviewed the history of juries in Oregon, noting the differences in how **juvenile delinquents** were treated in the 1800s versus the 1900s. More than one hundred years ago, children were treated the same as adults and could therefore have a jury trial. Since then, the philosophy of juvenile court has changed from punishment to rehabilitation. Juvenile justice often focuses on reforming and protecting.

The court also discussed the ideas behind juvenile hearings as opposed to adult criminal proceedings, saying: "The message of the juvenile code is clear . . . rehabilitation of children in trouble is a family affair." This isn't the case in adult criminal court, where punishment and deterrence are the goals. Consequently, the court determined that a juvenile trial isn't a criminal prosecution. The ruling of the lower court was upheld.

State v. Reynolds (1993)

■ Does the possible sentence for breaking a particular law determine whether an adult has the right to a jury trial?

In a California case, Jerry Nachtigal, a legal adult, was charged with driving under the influence of alcohol in a national park. Jerry asked for a jury trial and was refused. He appealed, claiming that this decision violated his Sixth Amendment rights (see the Bill of Rights on pages 19–20). The U.S. Supreme Court disagreed. In 1993, the Court decided that the right to a jury trial doesn't always exist but depends on the seriousness of the offense. If the crime is serious enough that the law demands a maximum sentence of longer than six months, then you may request a jury trial or you may decide to waive this right. If the possible sentence is for less than six months or is considered a **petty offense,** your request will be denied. Because the maximum penalty for Jerry's crime was six months in jail, he was denied a jury trial. (He was fined $750 and placed on one year of probation.)

This ruling applies only to legal adults—people who are eighteen or older, unless you live in a state that allows jury trials for minors. States that currently provide for juries in juvenile proceedings include Alaska, Colorado, Kansas, Massachusetts, Michigan, Montana, New Mexico, Oklahoma, Texas, West Virginia, Wisconsin, and Wyoming.

U.S. v. Nachtigal (1993)

Get on the Case:

- Do you think teens who are sixteen and seventeen years old should be allowed to serve on juries? In your opinion, do teenagers have the experience and wisdom to sit in judgment on another person—teen or adult? Or should teens be limited to participating in teen court? Is age eighteen much different than seventeen or sixteen? Or should the age be raised to twenty or twenty-one?

- Are you ready to serve on a jury? Why or why not? How do you think your life experiences would help you in deciding the fate of someone else? If you're eighteen, maybe you've already been summoned for jury duty. If so, what did you think of the experience? Did you find it difficult to decide the case or vote because someone close to your age was on trial?

- Play the role of a journalist and write an article about a teen or peer court. Interview local participants, including the jurors, the teens on trial, and the judges. If you can't find a peer or teen court in your area, visit a neighboring city. You may need special permission to attend the court session.

ISSUE:

Can a teenager be sentenced to death?

Case: *Thompson v. Oklahoma* (1988)

Murder is a **capital crime.** This means it's a crime that may be punishable by death. Whether you personally believe in the death penalty, it's a reality in thirty-eight states in our country. When **minors** commit horrific crimes and are transferred to adult court, they may face the death penalty, depending on which state they live in. The question is, at what age is a person fully accountable for a capital crime and therefore old enough to be sentenced to death?

The Facts:

In January 1983, fifteen-year-old William Wayne Thompson; his older brother, Anthony Mann; and two friends, Bobby Joe Glass and Richard Jones, brutally murdered Charles Keene in Grady County, Oklahoma. Charles was married to William's sister and had been physically abusing her. Before the murder, William told his girlfriend, Donetta, that they were going to kill Charles. He and the others abducted Charles from his home, beat him, broke his leg, shot him, and stabbed him in the neck and chest. His body was then chained to a concrete block and thrown into the Washita River, where it remained for four weeks.

Afterward, William told Donetta that he had shot Charles in the head and cut his throat. Mr. and Mrs. Brown, who lived near the river, heard one of the attackers say during the murder: "This is for the way you treated our sister." The Browns couldn't identify any of the men, because the incident occurred late at night.

All four were tried and convicted of first-degree murder. Each received the death penalty. Because William was a minor (the others were legal adults), his attorney **petitioned** the U.S. Supreme Court to determine whether the death penalty violated the Eighth Amendment as cruel and unusual punishment (see the **Bill of Rights** on pages 19–20). The attorney argued that William was too young to fully appreciate the consequences of his acts and shouldn't be punished as if he were an adult. A psychologist, Dr. Helen Kline, testified that William would probably commit additional criminal acts of violence and that he was a threat to society.

YOU BE THE JUDGE

- Do you think a fifteen-year-old should be sentenced to death? Does age matter in such a crime?

- Did the death penalty violate William's Eighth Amendment rights, even if it was acceptable for the other participants in this crime?

- Do you think fifteen-year-olds are prepared to accept responsibility for their behavior, even a prison sentence or the death penalty?

The Ruling:

The ultimate question before the Court was whether age alone was enough to spare someone from the death penalty. The Court analyzed the issue by looking at the nation's attitude about crime and punishment, particularly the use of the death penalty. In order to determine if **capital punishment** was "cruel and unusual" under the Eighth Amendment, the Court first reviewed current state laws to see how society viewed punishment. (Because laws are passed by state representatives, they're assumed to represent the beliefs of people who live in that state.) Then it looked at capital cases around the country and what sentences were ordered by the courts and juries.

In a decision written by Justice John Paul Stevens, the Court found that historically the law recognized that children and adults have different rights and duties. For example, minors are usually restricted from entering into contracts by themselves, voting, getting married, being a juror, and buying alcohol or cigarettes. Most states treat people under sixteen as minors. All of the states (eighteen at the time) that set a minimum age in their death penalty laws recommended age sixteen as the limit. In a five to three decision, the Court found a national agreement against sentencing juveniles under sixteen to death.

> The death penalty is legal in thirty-eight states, but only nineteen of these states allow the sentence for juveniles who are sixteen and seventeen years old: Alabama, Arizona, Arkansas, Delaware, Florida, Idaho, Louisiana, Mississippi, Missouri, Montana, Oklahoma, Pennsylvania, South Carolina, South Dakota, Utah, Vermont, Virginia, Washington, and Wyoming.

The Court accepted the argument that the average fifteen-year-old isn't "prepared to assume the full responsibilities of an adult." The Court considered adult versus juvenile behavior and said that less experience, education, and intelligence makes teenagers less able to evaluate the consequences of their conduct. Teenagers are much more likely than adults to be motivated by emotion or peer pressure. Therefore, the Court reasoned, juveniles aren't trusted with the privileges and responsibilities of an adult, and their crimes aren't as morally unacceptable as those of adults. The Court said: "Crimes committed by youths may be just as harmful to victims as those committed by older persons, but they deserve less punishment because adolescents may have less capacity to control their conduct and to think in long-range terms than adults."

Following the Court's decision, William's sentence was reduced to life imprisonment.

Related Cases:

Courts are constantly being pressed to decide what types of punishment are fair, reasonable, and acceptable in the eyes of society. The justices who consider these cases can't rely solely on their personal values; they must also carefully review the Constitution and the beliefs of the citizens of this country in reaching a conclusion. And at no time will their decisions satisfy everyone.

■ What about sixteen- or seventeen-year-olds? Can they be sentenced to death?

A year after the *Thompson* decision, the Court faced two unrelated cases questioning whether minors older than fifteen could be sentenced to death. Kevin Stanford (seventeen) and Heath Wilkins (sixteen) had both been convicted of murder and sentenced to death. The U.S. Supreme Court considered the cases together and issued one opinion, in Kevin's case, that applied to both young men.

In January 1981, Kevin shot and killed twenty-year-old Baerbel Poore in Kentucky. She was Kevin's neighbor and was working at a gas station when Kevin and a friend robbed the store and sexually assaulted her. Kevin shot Baerbel in the face and in the back of the head. He was convicted and received a sentence of death for the murder, plus forty-five years imprisonment on related charges (sexual assault, robbery, and receiving stolen property).

In a close decision (five to four), the Court upheld the death penalty, stating that it was unable to find societal agreement, in either the past or the present times, forbidding the death penalty for sixteen- or seventeen-year-olds who commit murder.

Stanford v. Kentucky (1989)

■ Should people who are severely mentally challenged receive a lesser sentence?

In 1979, twenty-two-year-old Johnny Paul Penry raped, beat, and stabbed Pamela Carpenter in her home in Texas. Johnny was already on **probation** for rape. He had the mental age of a six-year-old and had been physically abused as a child. Despite this, he was found guilty of Pamela's murder and sentenced to death.

The U.S. Supreme Court, in a five to four decision written by Justice Sandra Day O'Connor, didn't rule out capital punishment for people who are diagnosed as mentally retarded. It stated, though, that mental disabilities are a factor that may well lessen a person's responsibility for a capital crime. In 2001, the Supreme Court agreed to reconsider the issue, and it heard arguments in Penry's case.

Penry v. Lynaugh (1989)

▪ What about sentencing a minor to life in prison without the possibility of parole? Is this cruel and unusual punishment?

Sixteen-year-old Stephen Launsburry and a friend wanted to leave town and flagged down a car driven by a pregnant woman. While attempting to steal the woman's car, Stephen shot and killed her. He was sentenced to life without the possibility of parole. The Michigan Court of Appeals upheld the sentence, stating it "does not constitute cruel and unusual punishment."

People v. Launsburry (1996)

▪ What if the juvenile is only thirteen? Is life without the possibility of parole acceptable then?

For a year, thirteen-year-old Khamsone Naovarath had been molested by his thirty-eight-year-old neighbor, David Foote, who was confined to a wheelchair. On January 1, 1987, Khamsone forced his way into David's house and brutally tortured him, until finally stabbing him several times and strangling him with an electrical cord. Khamsone confessed to the murder, saying he didn't know why he did it.

He was sentenced to life in prison without the possibility of parole. On **appeal,** the Nevada Supreme Court reduced the sentence to life with a possibility of parole. It said: "[A] flicker of light should be kept alive in the hope that he may some time in the future be rehabilitated and become an acceptable member of society."

Naovarath v. State (1989)

▪ What if parole isn't possible for at least thirty years? Is this cruel and unusual, no matter what the crime?

In November 1994, fifteen-year-old Eric Mitchell robbed a convenience store in Minnesota with seventeen-year-old Harley Hildenbrand, who acted as a lookout. Eric went into the store and confronted the nineteen-year-old clerk, Mickey Wilfert. Although the security cameras showed no resistance by Mickey, Eric shot him in the face. Eric was tried as an adult, and a jury convicted him of intentional first-degree murder.

He was sentenced to the mandatory adult sentence—life imprisonment with no possibility of parole for a minimum of thirty years. He and his lawyer appealed, arguing that his sentence was cruel and unusual punishment based on his age. The Minnesota Supreme Court upheld the sentence, finding no violation of Eric's rights or that the sentence was cruel and unusual. It said: "Mitchell committed one of the most heinous crimes, murder in the first degree. . . . [W]e cannot say that his punishment was out of proportion to his crime."

State v. Eric Mitchell (1998)

■ Do the circumstances of a case affect whether a sentence is appropriate?

In August 1993, Jason Pilcher and Brandy Wiley (both fifteen) ran away together. They stole a car and a loaded .38 revolver. Jason was driving when he lost control of the car and crashed into a ditch. They walked to a nearby house and asked to use the phone. Phyllis Albritton's eleven-year-old son, Justin, brought them a cordless phone. His thirteen-year-old sister, Amanda, brought them each a glass of water. Without provocation, Jason pulled the gun out and killed Mrs. Albritton. He chased Justin to his room and killed him. Amanda ran out the back door and was shot at, but not hit. Jason was convicted in Louisiana of two counts of murder. He received two life sentences, to be served one after the other. He appealed and the court ruled that the sentences, without the opportunity of parole, probation, or suspension, were not excessive or illegal under the circumstances of this case.

State v. Pilcher (1995)

Get on the Case:

- Do you think a fourteen- or fifteen-year-old should be locked up for the rest of his or her life for committing a murder or sexual assault? Should the circumstances of the incident be considered and the jury or court given the ability to decide the length of sentence? How much consideration should be given to the victim and the victim's family?

- Do you think the death sentence is cruel and unusual punishment for anyone—adults and minors alike? Or do you agree that it's an appropriate sentence for some crimes? What about the different forms of execution—lethal injection, electrocution, gas chamber, hanging, or firing squad? Some controversy exists about whether one form is more humane than another, and some forms are rarely used anymore. What do you think? Are some forms of execution more acceptable than others? Why or why not?

- With your classmates or family, hold a mock debate on the death penalty as it pertains to minors. Assign or choose sides of the issue, and then research the arguments and start the debate.

Glossary

Accomplice. A person who voluntarily helps someone commit, or attempt to commit, a crime.

Age of majority. In most states, eighteen is recognized as the age of adulthood, entitling you to make your own decisions and manage your personal affairs.

Appeal. A right that is sometimes available to the losing party of a case, depending on the type of case. It allows you to ask a higher court (called an *appellate court*) to review a decision made by a lower court. The appellate court decides the case by reviewing a transcript of what took place in the lower court. The court doesn't consider new evidence; there are no witnesses called to testify; and there is no jury. The attorneys involved make their arguments to the court in writing (called **briefs**), and they may be allowed to present oral arguments, if the court thinks it would be useful in deciding the issues. The appellate court has the power to reverse the decision of the lower court and send the case back for a new trial, affirm the trial court's decision, or modify the decision.

Bill of Rights. The first ten amendments to the United States Constitution.

Brief. A concise written statement about a case, with arguments about issues raised by the lawyers. Briefs are read by the appellate court and help in making decisions about these issues.

Capacity to sue. The ability of a person to come into court under his or her own name. This right is usually limited to adults and **emancipated minors.**

Capital crime. Crime that may be punishable by death.

Capital punishment. The death penalty.

Censorship. The act of limiting access to material found objectionable; for example, books, movies, and music with explicit sexual content, violence, or profanity. Schools also have the right to limit what is contained in a student publication or play.

Child endangerment. This term is defined by each state. Sometimes it's considered the same thing as child abuse, and usually involves the intentional harm of a child. The Iowa definition of endangerment, for example, is the intentional use of physical force that results in physical injury.

Child protection laws. Laws in every state that provide for the protection of minors from abuse and neglect.

Civil commitment laws. The right to hospitalize people who are a danger to themselves or others against their will—without being charged with a crime.

Civil detention. Detaining someone to protect him or her from possibly harming himself or herself, or others.

Concurring opinion. A separate opinion written by a justice of an appellate court that agrees with the majority decision.

Confrontation. Questioning a witness in court. Every person charged with a crime has the right to **cross-examine** people who are accusing or testifying against him or her in court.

Contempt of court. Anything that interferes with the work of the court, including failing to follow a judge's order. The penalty may be a fine or jail time.

Corporal punishment. Physical discipline such as swats, paddling, and spanking.

Criminal detention. Detaining a minor who has been charged with a crime in a juvenile facility. State laws dictate the type and length of confinement.

Cross-examination. Questioning a witness in court. Every person charged with a crime has the right to face people who are accusing or testifying against him or her in court.

Delinquent. A minor who violates a criminal law. If found guilty, he or she is called a **juvenile delinquent.**

Detention. Temporary confinement of a minor in a locked facility. Although it isn't considered jail, the juvenile can't leave. This may be a consequence of an action committed by the minor or for the safety of the minor or the community between hearings. A person with a mental illness may also be held (detained) for certain periods of time if authorities believe the person is a danger to self or others.

Discrimination. The act of treating an individual or a group differently than others because of race, gender, religion, nationality, or disability. Not all discrimination is illegal. Teenagers have age restrictions regarding employment, curfew, alcohol, and driving, all of which is legal.

Dissenting opinion. An opinion written by a justice of an appellate court that explains why the justice disagrees with the majority decision. Other justices may also join the dissenting opinion.

Due process. Also called *due process of law,* this is your right to enforce and protect your basic rights to life, liberty, and property. It means that you have the right to be notified of any action against you and the right to be heard and confront the opposing side. Essentially, it's the right to fair treatment.

Emancipation. The process of becoming legally free from your parents or guardian. This may be the result of a court order, an act on your part (marriage, enlistment in the armed services), or other circumstances your state's law allows. If you're emancipated, your parents lose their authority over you and are no longer responsible for you.

Equal protection. The principle that everyone in the same group or classification should be treated the same. A person can't be singled out of a group and treated differently.

Establishment Clause. A part of the First Amendment. It means that the government may not promote or affiliate itself with any religious teaching or organization. Government may not advance or inhibit religion, or aid, foster, or promote one religion over another. Federal and state governments are to be neutral in all religious matters.

Felony. A classification of the criminal laws that carries the strictest penalties, usually a minimum of one year in jail. A felony is more serious than a **misdemeanor** or **petty offense.**

Guardian. An individual with the legal power and duty to take care of another person, including his or her property and financial affairs. The court may appoint a guardian for a minor if necessary, and sometimes the minor may select a guardian or object to the one being considered. A guardian may also be selected by your parents and named in their will.

Guardian ad litem. Latin for "guardian at law," this is a person that the court appoints to represent a minor in a specific case. Once the case is over, the guardian is dismissed. This person's job is to present to the court what he or she thinks is in the minor's best interest, and that may not be what the minor is asking for. A lawyer, on the other hand, is responsible for presenting his or her client's position in a case. That is why a minor may have both a lawyer and a guardian ad litem.

Judicial bypass procedure. A procedure used when a minor seeks an abortion and doesn't want to tell her parents, for whatever reason. In this situation, the minor may show the court that she is mature enough and well enough informed to make a decision, in consultation with her doctor, and independent of her parents' wishes. If not mature enough, she may show that the abortion is in her best interests.

Jurisdiction. The legal right of a judge and a court to exercise its authority—the power to hear and determine a case. Specific rules exist regarding jurisdiction. Without it, a court is powerless to act. Under some circumstances, a juvenile court may **waive** its jurisdiction over you and ask an adult court to consider your case.

Juvenile delinquent. A minor who has broken the law and has either admitted the offense or been found guilty by a court.

Minor. Someone who's not yet legally an adult.

Miranda rights. These are the rights that suspects are read when in police custody. You have the right to remain silent; a right to a lawyer before you talk to the police; if you can't afford to hire a lawyer yourself, one will be appointed to you; and the right to have your parents with you during questioning. If, after you've been told of these rights, you choose to talk to the police, whatever you say may be used against you later on.

Misdemeanor. A criminal offense less serious than a felony, with a jail sentence of one year or less.

Negligence. Doing something that a reasonable and careful person wouldn't do, or failing to do something that a reasonable and careful person would do under similar circumstances. As a result of the person's act or omission, an injury occurs.

Petition. Asking the court, in writing, to take a specific action regarding a person or company.

Petty offense. A crime with a maximum penalty of (usually) a few months in jail or a fine. No prison time is given, and the fines are often set by law up to several hundred dollars.

Probation. A program in which you're supervised by the court or probation department for a period of time. Special terms of probation may include time in detention, community service hours, counseling, a fine, or **restitution.**

Probation officer. An officer of the court assigned to a minor or an adult placed on probation. This person arranges for appropriate services to assist with rehabilitation, provides supervision and guidance, and reports results to the court.

Restitution. The act of restoring a victim to the position the victim was in before suffering property damages or loss or personal injury. A minor placed on probation may be required to pay the victim back for any loss that the minor caused.

Search and seizure. The ability of a person in a position of authority (police or schoolteacher) to search you or your property (room, car, locker) and take anything unlawful or not legally in your possession.

Sexual harassment. Any unwelcome sexual advances, request for sexual favors, or other verbal or physical contact of a sexual nature—to be unlawful, it must be so offensive and severe that the conduct affects or disrupts the victim's education or ability to do his or her job.

Social file. A file separate from the court's legal file. It contains a person's social history, previous evaluations, and probation officer's reports.

Statutory rape. Unlawful sexual relations with a person under the age of consent, which may be sixteen, seventeen, or eighteen, depending on your state. It's a crime even if the underage person consents.

Subpoena. A formal written document that commands an individual to appear in court to testify as a witness. Failure to appear will result in a penalty.

Transfer. In juvenile law, this is the process by which a minor is charged with a crime and tried in adult court rather than juvenile court. Due to the seriousness of the charge and the juvenile's history, he or she may be treated as an adult, making the juvenile eligible for adult consequences including life imprisonment or the death penalty.

Waive. To voluntarily give up or transfer a right. For example, a person can waive their right to a trial by jury; juvenile courts can waive their jurisdiction of a trial to an adult court.

Warrant. A written order from a court directing law enforcement to either arrest an individual or search a specific place for evidence of a crime.

Zone and expectation of privacy. The area that a reasonable person would expect to be protected from the intrusion of others—an area outside of public view or where one has taken precautions to preserve his or her privacy.

Bibliography

Rachel Kingsley v. Gregory Kingsley (1993)

A Kind and Just Parent: The Children of Juvenile Court by William Ayers (Boston, MA: Beacon Press, 1997).

No Matter How Loud I Shout: A Year in the Life of Juvenile Court by Edward Humes (New York: Simon & Schuster, 1996).

Taming the Lawyers: What to Expect in a Lawsuit and How to Make Sure Your Attorney Gets Results by Kenneth Menendez (Morton, PA: Silver Lake Publishing, 1996).

Meyer v. Nebraska (1923)

Abandoned in the Wasteland: Children, Television and the First Amendment by Newton N. Minow, Craig L. Lamay (New York: Hill and Wang, 1995).

"Holding Parents Criminally Responsible for the Delinquent Acts of Their Children: Reasoned Response or 'Knee-Jerk Reaction'?" by Christine T. Greenwood, 23 *Journal of Contemporary Law* 401 (1997).

"Killer Party: Proposing Civil Liability for Social Hosts Who Serve Alcohol to Minors" by Matthew C. Houchens, 30 *John Marshall Law Review* 245 (1996).

Gebser v. Lago Vista Independent School District (1998)

"A Rose By Any Other Name . . . The Gender Basis of Same-Sex Sexual Harassment" by Robert Brookins, *Drake Law Review,* Vol. 46., No. 3, page 441 (1998).

Sexual Harassment and Teens: A Program for Positive Change by Susan Strauss with Pamela Espeland (Minneapolis: Free Spirit Publishing, 1992).

Sexual Harassment: High School Girls Speak Out by June Larkin (Toronto: Second Story Press, 1994).

Sexual Harassment on Campus: A Guide for Administrators, Faculty, and Students by Bernice R. Sandler, Robert J. Shoop, and Carolyn S. Bratt (Needham Heights, MA: Allyn & Bacon, 1996).

Sexual Harassment: What Teens Should Know (Issues in Focus) by Carol Rust Nash (Springfield, NJ: Enslow Publishers Inc., 1996).

Beth Ann Faragher v. City of Boca Raton (1998)

You Want Me to Do What? When, Where and How to Draw the Line at Work by Nan DeMars (New York: Fireside, 1998).

Sexual Harassment: A Practical Guide to the Law, Your Rights, and Your Options for Taking Action by Tracy O'Shea and Jane Lalonde (New York: St. Martin's Griffin, 1998).

Everything You Need to Know About Sexual Harassment (Need to Know Library) by Elizabeth Bouchard (New York: Rosen Publishing Company, 1997).

Rights and Respect: What You Need to Know About Gender Bias and Sexual Harassment by Kathyln Gay (Brookfield, CT: Millbrook Press, 1995).

Sexual Harassment and Teens: A Program for Positive Change by Susan Strauss with Pamela Espeland (Minneapolis: Free Spirit Publishing, 1992).

Vernonia School District v. Jimmy Acton (1995)

Addiction: The High That Brings You Down by Miriam Smith McLaughlin (Springfield, NJ: Enslow Publishers Inc., 1997).

"The Constitution Expelled: What Remains of Students' Fourth Amendment Rights?" by Darrell Jackson, *Arizona State University Law Journal* (1996).

Drugs and Sports by Rodney G. Peck (New York: Rosen Publishing Group, 1998).

"Examining Random Suspicionless Drug Testing of Public School Athletes" by Nancy D. Wagman, *Villanova Sports and Entertainment Law Journal* (1996).

"High School Students Lose Their Rights When They Don Their Uniforms" by Jonathan M. Ettman, 13 *New York Law School Journal of Human Rights* 625 (1997).

New Jersey v. T. L. O. (1985)

"The Constitution Expelled: What Remains of Students' Fourth Amendment Rights?" by Darrell Jackson, 28 *Arizona State Law Journal* 673 (1996).

"Minors and the Fourth Amendment: How Juvenile Status Should Invoke Different Standards for Searches and Seizures on the Streets" by Lourdes M. Rosado, 71 *New York Law Review* 762 (1996).

New Jersey v. T.L.O., Drug Searches in Schools by Deborah A. Persico (Springfield, NJ: Enslow Publishers Inc., 1998).

The Right to Privacy by Ellen Alderman and Caroline Kennedy (New York: Knopf Publishers, 1995).

"Strip Searches of Students: What Johnny Really Learned at School and How Local School Boards Can Help Solve the Problem" by Scott A. Gartner, 70 *Southern California Law Review* 921 (March 1997).

Tariq A-R Y v. Maryland (1998)

"And a Small Child Shall Lead Them: The Validity of Children's Consent to Warrantless Searches of the Family Home" by Matt McCaughey, 34 *University of Louisville Journal of Family Law* 747 (Summer 1995–1996).

Mind Your Own Business: The Battle for Personal Privacy by Gini Graham (Insight Books, 1995).

"Minors and the Fourth Amendment: How Juvenile Status Should Invoke Different Standards for Searches and Seizures on the Streets" by Lourdes M. Rosado, 71 *New York University Law Review* 762 (1996).

The Right to Privacy by Ellen Alderman and Caroline Kennedy (New York: Knopf Publishers, 1995).

"Who's Been Searching in My Room? Parental Waiver of Children's Fourth Amendment Rights" 17 *University of California Davis Law Review* 359 (1983).

Kent v. United States (1966)

"Dennis the Menace or Billy the Kid: An Analysis of the Role of Transfer to Criminal Court in Juvenile Justice" by Eric K. Klein, 35 *American Criminal Law Review* 371 (Winter 1998).

"49 Black Faces, Brown Faces . . . Why Are We Different Than White Faces? An Analytical Comparison of the Rate of Certification of Minority & Non-Minority Juvenile Offenders" by Keisha L. David, 2 *Scholar: St. Mary's Law Review on Minority Issues* 49 (2000).

"The Rush to Waive Children to Adult Court" by Robert E. Shepherd Jr., 10 Sum. *Criminal Justice* 38 (1995).

Bellotti v. Baird (1979)

The Abortion Battle: Looking at Both Sides by Felicia Lowenstein (Springfield, NJ: Enslow Publishers Inc., 1996).

Dear Diary, I'm Pregnant: Teenagers Talk About Their Pregnancy by Annrenée Englander (Toronto: Annick Press, 1997).

Griswold v. Connecticut: Contraception and the Right of Privacy by Susan C. Wawrose (Danbury, CT: Franklin Watts, 1996).

"Sex Education and Condom Distribution: John, Susan, Parents, and Schools" by Jeffrey F. Caruso, *Notre Dame Journal of Law, Ethics and Public Policy,* Vol. 10, No. 2 (1996).

"Sex, Sectarians and Secularists: Condoms and the Interests of Children" by Yvonne A. Tamayo, 29 *Indiana Law Review* 593 (1996).

Sex Smart: 501 Reasons to Hold Off on Sex by Susan Browning Pogany (Minneapolis: Fairview Press, 1998).

Planned Parenthood Locator Service
1-800-230-7526
www.plannedparenthood.org
Planned Parenthood believes in the fundamental right of each individual, throughout the world, to manage his or her fertility, regardless of the individual's income, marital status, race, ethnicity, sexual orientation, age, national origin, or residence. Contact them to find a clinic in your area.

Tinker v. Des Moines Independent School District (1969)

The Struggle for Student Rights: Tinker v. Des Moines and the 1960's by John W. Johnson (Lawrence, KS: University Press of Kansas, 1997).

"Student Activism Forces Schools to Revisit Free Speech Policies" by Mark Walsh, *Education Week* (2-16-91).

Tinker v. Des Moines: Student Protest by Leah Farish (Springfield, NJ: Enslow Publishers Inc., 1997).

Olff v. East Side Union High School District (1972)

Ferrell v. Dallas Ind. School District—Hairstyles in Schools by Karen L. Trespacz (Springfield, NJ: Enslow Publishers Inc., 1998).

"No Shoes, No Shirt, No Education: Dress Codes and Freedom of Expression Behind the Postmodern Schoolhouse Gates" by Alison G. Myhra, *Seton Hall Constitutional Law Journal* 337 (Spring 1999).

"Public School Dress Codes: The Constitutional Debate" by Amy Mitchell Wilson, 1998 *BYU Education and Law Journal* 147 (Spring 1998), pages 147–172.

"Undressing the First Amendment in Public Schools: Do Uniform Dress Codes Violate a Students' First Amendment Rights?" by Alison M. Barbarosh, 28 *Loyola University (Los Angeles) Law Review* 1415 (1995).

Education Week
www.edweek.org
Education Week is for people interested in education reform, schools, and the policies that guide them.

Hazelwood School District v. Kuhlmeier (1988)

Hazelwood v. Kuhlmeier—Censorship in School Newspapers by Sarah Betsy Fuller (Springfield, NJ: Enslow Publishers Inc., 1998).

"Kids Surfing the Net at School: What are the Legal Issues?" by Sally Rutherford, 24 *Rutgers Computer & Technology Law Journal* 417 (1998).

"Viewpoint Discrimination" by Marjorie Heins, 24 *Hastings Constitutional Law Quarterly* 99 (1996).

Student Press Law Center
(703) 807-1904
www.splc.org
Since 1974, the Student Press Law Center has been the nation's only legal assistance agency devoted exclusively to educating high school and college journalists about the rights and responsibilities embodied in the First Amendment and supporting the student news media in their struggle to cover important issues free from censorship.

Youth Guide to the First Amendment, Freedom Forum
www.freedomforum.org
The Freedom Forum is a nonpartisan, international foundation dedicated to free press, free speech, and free spirit for all people. The foundation pursues its priorities through conferences, educational activities, publishing, broadcasting, online services, fellowships, partnerships, training, research, and other programs.

Lee v. Weisman (1992)

Church and State: Government and Religion in the United States by Kathlyn Gay (Brookfield, CT: Millbrook Press, 1992).

The First Amendment: Freedom of Speech, Religion, and the Press by Leah Farish (Springfield, NJ: Enslow Publishers Inc., 1998).

Religious Liberty in the Supreme Court: The Cases That Define the Debate over Church and State by Terry Eastland (Washington, DC: Ethics & Public Policy Center, 1993).

Religious Schools v. Children's Rights by James G. Dwyer (Ithaca, NY: Cornell University Press, 1998).

School Prayer: A History of the Debate by Tricia Andryszewski (Springfield, NJ: Enslow Publishers Inc., 1997).

Ingraham v. Wright (1977)

"Corporal Punishment in Public Schools: A Violation of Substantive Due Process?" by Cynthia Denenholz Sweeney, 33 *Hastings Law Journal* 1245 (1982).

"Corporal Punishment in Public Schools: The Legal and Political Battle Continues" by John Dayton, 89 *Education Law Reporter* 729 (1994).

Joshua DeShaney v. Winnebago County Social Services (1989)

"Parricide: States are Beginning to Recognize that Abused Children Who Kill Their Parents Should Be Afforded the Right to Assert a Claim of Self-Defense" by Merrilee R. Goodwin, 25 *Southwestern University Law Review* 429 (1996).

"Spanking and Other Corporal Punishment of Children by Parents: Overvaluing Pain, Undervaluing Children" by David Orentlicher, 35 *Houston Law Review* 147 (1998).

"Spare the Rod, Embrace Our Humanity: Toward a New Legal Regime Prohibiting Corporal Punishment of Children" by Susan H. Bitensky, 31 *University of Michigan Journal of Law Reform* 289 (1998).

"When is Parental Discipline Child Abuse? The Vagueness of Child Abuse Laws" by Scott A. Davidson, 34 *Journal of Family Law* 403 (1996).

Parham v. J. R. (1979)

Fighting Invisible Tigers: A Stress Management Guide for Teens by Earl Hipp (Minneapolis: Free Spirit Publishing, 1995).

Talk With Teens About Self and Stress: 50 Guided Discussions for School and Counseling Groups by Jean Sunde Peterson and Pamela Espeland (Minneapolis: Free Spirit Publishing, 1993).

When Nothing Matters Anymore: A Survival Guide for Depressed Teens by Bev Cobain (Minneapolis: Free Spirit Publishing, 1998).

Parkerson v. Brooks (1995)

"The Best Interests of All Children: An Examination of Grandparent Visitation Rights Regarding Children Born Out of Wedlock" by Nicole Miller, 42 *New York Law Review* 179 (Summer 1997).

"Breaking Up a Family or Putting it Back Together Again" by Carolyn Wilkes Kaas, 37 *William and Mary Law Review* 1045 (1996).

My Parents are Getting Divorced: A Handbook for Kids (Chicago, IL: American Bar Association Family Advocate, 1996). Call 1-800-285-2221 to order a copy of this guide.

"A Quest for Sibling Visitation: Daniel Weber's Story" by Christine D. Markel, 18 *Whittier Law Review* 863 (1997).

"Sibling Rights to Visitation: A Relationship Too Valuable to Be Denied" by Joel V. Williams, 27 *University of Toledo Law Review* 259 (Fall 1995).

Teens with Single Parents: Why Me? by Margaret A. Schultz (Springfield, NJ: Enslow Publishers Inc., 1997).

In re Gault (1967)

"Good Kids, Bad Kids: A Revelation About the Due Process Rights of Children" by Cecilia M. Espenoza, 23 *Hastings Constitutional Law Quarterly* 407 (Winter 1996).

In re Gault (1967): Juvenile Justice by Susan Dudley Gold (New York: Twenty-First Century Books, 1995).

"Miranda in a Juvenile Setting: A Child's Right to Silence" by Larry E. Holtz, 78 *Journal of Criminal Law & Criminology* 534 (1987).

No Matter How Loud I Shout: A Year in the Life of Juvenile Court by Edward Humes (New York: Simon & Schuster, 1996).

Josh Davis v. Alaska (1974)

"Disclosing the Identities of Juvenile Felons: Introducing Accountability to Juvenile Justice" by Arthur R. Blum, 27 *Loyola University Chicago Law Journal* 349 (Winter 1996).

"A Mere Youthful Indiscretion? Reexamining the Policy of Expunging Juvenile Delinquency Records" by T. Markus Funk, 29 *University of Michigan Journal of Law* Ref. 885 (1996)

"Privacy v. Public Access to Juvenile Court Proceedings: Do Closed Hearings Protect the Child or the System?" by Jan L. Trasen, 15 *Boston College Third World Law Journal* 359 (1995).

McKeiver v. Pennsylvania (1971)

The Jury: Disorder in the Court by Stephen J. Adler (New York: Main Street Books, 1995).

Jury Trials in the Classroom by Betty M. See and Diane Elizabeth See (Englewood, CO: Teacher Ideas Press, 1998).

Last Chance for Justice: The Juror's Lonely Quest by Laurence H. Geller and Peter Hemenway (Dallas, TX: NCDS Press, 1997).

"The Right to a Public Jury Trial: A Need for Today's Juvenile Court" by Joseph B. Sanborn, 76 *Judicature* 230 (1993).

Thompson v. Oklahoma (1988)

"The Constitutionality of Executing Juvenile Offenders: *Thompson v. Oklahoma*" by Steven H. Gerstein, 24 *Criminal Law Bulletin* 91 (1988).

Dead Man Walking (1995) This movie takes a powerful, but balanced, look at capital punishment, starring Susan Sarandon and Sean Penn.

"The Decency of Capital Punishment for Minors: Contemporary Standards and the Dignity of Juveniles" by Lawrence A. Vanore, 61 *Indiana Law Journal* 757 (1986).

"The Dignity of the Condemned" by Richard J. Bonnie, 74 *Virginia Law Review* 1363 (1988).

"The Efficacy of Harsh Punishment for Teenage Violence" by Victor L. Streib, 31 *Valparaiso University Law Review* 427 (1997).

Slow Coming Dark: Interviews of Death Row by Douglas Magee (Cleveland, OH: Pilgrim Press, 1980).

"Too Young to Die—Juveniles and the Death Penalty—A Better Alternative to Killing Our Children: Youth Empowerment" by Sherri Jackson, 22 *New England Journal of Criminal & Civil Confinement* (1996).

"When Will It Stop? The Use of the Death Penalty for Non-Homicide Crimes" by Jeffrey C. Matura, 24 *Journal of Legislation* 249 (1998).

Young Blood: Juvenile Justice and the Death Penalty by Shirley Dicks (Amherst, NY: Prometheus Books, 1995).

Index

About the Author

Photo by Sharon Dennis, Phoenix, Arizona

Thomas A. Jacobs attended Loyola University at Los Angeles and Arizona State University College of Law. He served as an Arizona Assistant Attorney General from 1972 to 1985 handling civil, criminal, and child welfare matters. In 1985, he was appointed to the Maricopa County Superior Court, Juvenile Division, where he presides over delinquency, dependency, severance, and adoption cases. He has published several books and articles on extradition, habeas corpus, children's rights, and other juvenile law topics. A regular speaker and instructor at community functions and educational programs, he also serves as an adjunct professor at the Arizona State University School of Social Work.

Other Great Books from Free Spirit

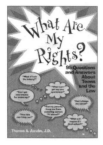

What Are My Rights?

95 Questions and Answers About Teens and the Law
by Thomas A. Jacobs, J.D.

Teens need to know about the laws that affect them to make informed decisions about what they should and shouldn't do. This fascinating book helps teens understand the law, recognize their responsibilities, and appreciate their rights. For ages 12 & up.
$14.95; 208 pp.; softcover; 6" x 9"

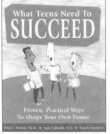

What Teens Need to Succeed

Proven, Practical Ways to Shape Your Own Future
by Peter L. Benson, Ph.D., Judy Galbraith, M.A., and Pamela Espeland

Based on a national survey, this book describes 40 developmental "assets" all teens need to succeed in life, then gives hundreds of suggestions teens can use to build assets at home, at school, in the community, in the congregation, with friends, and with youth organizations. For ages 11 & up.
$14.95; 368 pp.; softcover; illus.; 7¼" x 9¼"

When Nothing Matters Anymore

A Survival Guide for Depressed Teens
by Bev Cobain, R.N.,C.

Written for teens with depression—and those who feel despondent, dejected, or alone—this powerful book offers help, hope, and potentially life-saving facts and advice. Includes true stories from teens who have dealt with depression, survival tips, resources, and more. For ages 13 & up.
$13.95; 176 pp.; softcover; illus.; 6" x 9"

To place an order or to request a free catalog of
Self–Help for Kids® and Self–Help for Teens® materials,
please write, call, email, or visit our Web site:

Free Spirit Publishing Inc.

217 Fifth Avenue North • Suite 200 • Minneapolis, MN 55401-1299
toll-free 800.735.7323 • local 612.338.2068
help4kids@freespirit.com

teaching systems (1965). The adaptive teaching procedure which these men propose requires the student to reveal, by making some sort of error, the kind of instruction he should receive next. This requirement, they suggest, need not conjure up an image of an aversive and threatening situation in which the student is forced to reveal his ignorance. If adaptive control is competently designed, a student's weaknesses are revealed by his selection of response alternatives. Where no adaptive procedures are available for dealing with error, the minimization of error is forced upon a teaching procedure.

Error minimization advocates might suggest that the adaptive system could do better by preventing errors from occurring in the first place. Lewis and Pask react to this by pointing out that the presence of error is tacitly acknowledged by the error minimizers when they cue or prompt in the course of a program to adjust a program to the population of students being taught. These nonadaptive programs remove error factors without allowing them to be manifested in the form of overt mistakes. This necessarily involves working in the dark; and hence programs which forestall error often make provisions for far more error possibilities than any one student is likely to have, and, hence consist of less-than-challenging tasks.

Adaptive teaching systems, in contast to error minimization, take seriously the view that students profit from their mistakes. In addition, an instructional sequence should require that students discover things for themselves, and in the course of self-discovery the student will undoubtedly make mistakes. Thus, there is a basic incompatibility between this self-discovery process and error minimization.

At this point, I am sure of one thing: I have not resolved any issues. But I do hope that I have laid out for inspection what seem to me to be relevant variables and nuances that are involved in learning by discovery. On the basis of my review of the kind of learning situations that have been included under this label, I have pointed out that the hallmarks in this kind of learning involve two identifying characteristics: induction and errorful learning. And I have attempted to look further into these two aspects to provide some specific variables for their operational handling.

Task Properties

So far I have discussed the characteristics of learning by discovery in general. This really does not get us very far in efforts at instructional design because the characteristics of a teaching sequence interact with the properties of the terminal tasks that are being taught. Therefore, induction and errorful learning take on differential usefulness depending upon whether we are teaching response precision, simple associations, concepts, rules and principles, or higher-order strategies.

Consider first the establishment of response precision. An evident characteristic of the educational process that leads to subject-matter mastery is the increasing precision of the student's response. The student's initial performance is variable, crude, and rarely meets the criteria of subject-matter competence. An effective instructional procedure tolerates this initial state and gradually takes him toward mastery. In order to accomplish this, the teaching process involves the progressive establishment of narrower limits for correct performance. Increasing competence in performing such new skills as learning to write or learning precise timing in music is accomplished by gradually contracting performance tolerances. This can be done progressively so that each successive range of successful performance includes a major portion of the range of variations already in the student's repertoire. Over the sequence of instruction, the range of observed performance will align itself with a particular range of acceptable performance defined as subject-matter competence. I would suggest that this can be done and should be done with a minimum amount of errors, since a sudden or inappropriate constriction of performance criteria can lead to extinction and loss of motivation. The use of errors and induction for this kind of learning seems not especially appropriate.

Consider next the learning of associations: The process involved is attaching the increasingly precise responses being learned to particular subject-matter stimulus situations so that subject-matter mastery is attained because the precise responses are under the command of detailed subject-matter discriminative stimuli. In learning translation in a second language, for example, the precise expression of a word meaning already in the learner's repertoire is transferred to new subject-matter stimuli. The transfer of stimulus control is a major process in teaching students to make precise subject-matter discriminations and teaching them to use previously learned skills in response to new stimuli. This process, like the establishment of response precision, does not seem to require induction and errorful learning. Through the use of mediators, associations can be taught so that errors are minimized. As Gilbert (1958) has pointed out, in learning the correspondence between the number one and the color brown, and zero and black, in teaching the resistor color code, it is possible to teach such associations on almost one trial by the use of mediating stimuli. The student learns by means of statements such as 'one brown penny' and 'zero black nothingness.' The procedure of stimulus fading, used widely in operant conditioning and in programmed instruction, can also be used to transfer existing associations to new ones with little error.

With respect to the learning of concepts, I have already indicated that induction may be a useful procedure. Whether or not errorful learning is useful may be debated in light of the work of Terrace in discrimination learning. The question here centers around whether, in the discrimination-training aspects of concept formation, errorful learning has useful consequences.

In the learning of rules, principles, and higher-order strategies, I can be less than definitive although the use of induction and error seem indicated. At this point it is a matter of some systematization and experimental analysis along the lines of variables I have been discussing.

In summary, learning by discovery, when analyzed, appears to involve not only the properties of induction and errorful learning, but also interactive effects with task properties.

TEACHING FOR DISCOVERY

I turn now, briefly, to teaching for discovery, or learning to discover. This is much easier to talk about. Since we know so little about it, one can say anything and enjoy his own speculations without the constraints of knowledge. Again the problem is analysis of the behavior involved because it is unlikely that we can teach discovery behavior adequately until the component behavior repertoires have been analyzed. Once we specify or at least postulate relevant situational and behavioral variables, discovery behavior should be more amenable to instructional manipulation. Right off, it seems likely that discovery behavior is specific to the subject matter domain in which discovery takes place. Discovery requires different concepts and logical combinations when one is working in microbiology or botany, or breaking hieroglyphic codes. Presumably, there is some communality of behavioral repertoires, but there will be much significant specific variance.

Mechner in a recent chapter on "Science Education and Behavioral Technology" (1965) lists subdivisions of scientific method and research skills which seem to be manageable pieces of discovery in science. He lists such things as deductive reasoning skills, inferential reasoning skills, skill in generating hypotheses, skill in selecting "fruitful" hypotheses, skill in testing hypotheses and deciding which experiments to perform, skill in formulating problems that can be solved by the scientific method, and generalized traits such as patience, perseverance, and curiosity. Skill in generating hypotheses is described as a type of scanning, like free association, except that it involves statements about the world. Each statement is checked against experience until it is refuted. If it is not refuted it becomes a scientific contribution. Mechner writes:

> The terminal behavior test for this skill would require the student to generate and test, at a certain minimal rate, hypotheses about a universe with which he has had some previous experience. The behavioral technologist, in developing the terminal behavior specifications, would have to (a) make the behavior overt rather than covert, (b) circumscribe the universe for the hypotheses, and (c) circumscribe the range of data against which the successive hypotheses are tested by the student. Here, the use of a computer suggests itself. It should be possible to develop a program for the computer that would make the computer behave like a small, artificial, circumscribed universe. This universe would be described by a set of specific input-output relationships, some of them determined and others probabilistic. The student of "creativity" [discovery] would start out by learning his "subject matter," i.e., how this computer behaves under various specific conditions. At the end of this subject-matter training, there would still be a great deal about the computer-universe that would be unknown to him. Here he must begin to generate hypotheses and test them. A program could be designed to develop this skill. The program would teach the student in the standard step-by-step fashion how to generate hypotheses on the basis of some available data and then to test the hypotheses in brute force manner against other available data until the hypothesis is refuted or until the data are exhausted. At the end of the program, the student would be generating and testing hypotheses at the desired rate.

Another way of looking at discovery behavior is suggested by the work on computer simulation of information processing. The work pioneered by Simon and Newell (1964) identifies elementary information processes which combine into compound processes. The processes identified might be considered as heuristics which are teachable behaviors which can be combined by the learner to produce discovery behavior. For example, a paper by Simon and Simon (1962) identifies certain heuristics for discovering and verifying mating combinations in chess. The discovery heuristic involves a tree of move possibilities which explores branches that turn out to be false leads. This exploration tree consists of move possibilities in which the attacker has to discover a branching sequence of moves, one subtree of which leads to a checkmate. The authors write that, "The exploration tree is precisely analogous to the paths tried out by a subject in a maze-running experiment, except that it includes branches for defender's choices as well as branches for the attacker's trees" (p. 427). A heuristic program simple enough to be simulated by hand is able to discover mating combinations in about 52 of the 136 chess positions. Slight modification of the program adds 10 more mating combinations that would be discovered. Simon and Simon conclude:

> The conclusion we reach from our investigations is that the discovery of 'deep' mating combinations by expert chess players requires neither prodigious memory, ultra-rapid processing capacities, nor flashes of insight. Combinations as difficult as any that have been recorded in chess history will be discovered by the selective heuristics we have outlined. . . . The evidence strongly suggests that expert chess players discover combinations because their programs incorporate powerful selective heuristics and not because they think faster or memorize better than other people (1962, p. 429).

A third line of endeavor which is of interest for consideration as an influential variable in teaching for discovery has to do with the study of curiosity and exploration. An increasing amount of research has been directed to the study of this area in the past decade (Fowler, 1965). Research, much of it with infra-human organisms, has indicated that the strength of exploratory behavior is positively related, within limits, to the degree of change in the stimulus situation provided by novel, unfamiliar, complex, surprising, or incongruous situations introduced into the environment. Too great or too abrupt a change, however, is disrupting and may preclude exploration. In complex situations, an individual encounters change by way of his interaction with or manipulation of the elements involved. Such interaction provides the stimulus change which can elicit curiosity and exploratory behavior. Investigations have also demonstrated that behaviors are learned that lead to a change in the stimulus display. Thus, in addition to stimulus change eliciting exploratory behavior, experiments show that organisms will respond in order to secure novel, unfamiliar stimuli. In general, these findings demonstrate that stimulus change or sensory variation may be employed to selectively reinforce behaviors which result in change, and that this variation in the situation will serve concomitantly to elicit exploratory behavior. When stimulus change is used as a reinforcing stimulus, it seems reasonable to hypothesize that learning variables which influence acquisition and extinction will influence the acquisition and extinction of exploratory and curiosity behavior as they do other learned behavior. This suggests that a student's curiosity and explorations which enhance discovery may be elicited and maintained in an instructional environment which provides for appropriate variation in the stimulus characteristics of the subject materials confronting him.

In summary, interesting leads for studying 'learning to discover' come from operant analysis, cognitive simulation and studies of exploratory drive. Finally, the excursion that this paper has taken into the intricacies of 'discovery learning' brings to mind the admonition of Edward L. Thorndike who wrote the following: ". . . if we avoid thought by loose and empty terms, or if we stay lost in wonder at the extraordinary versatility and inventiveness of the higher forms of learning, we shall never understand man's progress or control his education."

Chapter III

The Meaning of Discovery In Learning

QUITE APPROPRIATELY, THE FIRST DISCUSSION BEGAN WITH A QUESTION on the nature of discovery as a method of teaching.

A participant raised the issue of whether what we call discovery teaching must always be inductive, and nondiscovery teaching, deductive. He referred to experiences of his own where the rule-example method had, in fact, elicited discovery experiences, as he suddenly discovered what the teacher had been talking about during an earlier rule-example sequence. Hence, teaching by discovery may not be synonymous with inductive teaching, but rather the discovery process can result from either inductive or deductive teaching.

Another discussant demurred. He felt that such a definition of learning by discovery fell into the box of looking at discovery as an intervening process in the learner. Instead, he maintained that in the literature we traditionally view discovery only as manipulative, that is, something teachers do. When people advocate discovery, they are advocating the withholding of answers from pupils. The teacher knows how an answer is obtained, but the students do not. Hence, the major question in the issue of learning by discovery is the extent to which you get better pedagogy by not telling the student what the teacher already knows.

This discussion brought out a theme which was to appear and reappear throughout all of the discussions of the conference. In attempting to clarify the meaning of learning by discovery for teaching, is it more valuable to focus upon what the teacher must do (the independent variable), is it more important to find out what it is the learner does when he learns by discovery, or is it best to look primarily at the end product in the form of what the learner has finally learned to do (the dependent variable)? The danger to avoid is that of assuming a necessary isomorphism between the independent and intervening variables. Just because the teaching is inductive, it does not follow that the learner is discovering. Conversely, simply because the teacher is instructing didactically, discovery experiences on the part of the learner are not precluded.

If we are to consider the possibility that discovery refers to an intervening process in the learner, what form shall our descriptions of this process take? For one participant, discovery was essentially a mediational process in the learner, and he asserted that the terms which are generally utilized to describe or distinguish among mediational processes are equally useful in discussing processes of discovery.

A slightly different attack was suggested by another participant. He maintained that in these processes a student confronted with a set of concrete experiences is led to scan through a range of stored models of different kinds and try to fit these models to the data or problem at hand. What is discovered is not something outside the learner, but an appropriate internal structure for handling the situation or problems. He must translate these experiences into his own language frames rather than learn a formal list which is already in his own language. What we need to investigate is the linkage between the complex language forms we are aware of and the kinds of experiences we control for the pupil while he is learning.

A great advantage of learning this linguistically is that the relationship is now in a form that has enormous substitution possibilities. Hence, the crux of the discovery process is recognition and understanding of the relationships among concrete experiences and the operation of putting these experiences into the compact form of language.

It was suggested that the idea of language alone was too restricting. The key point in discovery learning is that of stimulus change. The child learns concepts and abstractions by being asked to pick out the invariants. This requires not only providing for stimulus change so that the child may pick out these invariants, but more important, arranging for the child to seek to change the stimuli himself in order to discover these invariants. This ability is more than simply learning a heuristic. Heuristics can be subject-matter specific; one used for code-breaking is not likely to be the same as one used for chess-playing. One participant pointed out that learning by pure induction rarely exists. What the learner does is to scan through a range of stored models of different kinds and to try and fit these models to the data or problems at hand. The role of language represents a major means by which one codes stored models and retrieves them. Linguistic cues help tell the learner which model to bring out with respect to the kinds of data being dealt with.

A discussant now suggested that within any of these definitions of discovery, a particular way of looking at the nature of what is taught is implied. To be amenable to learning by discovery, what is taught can never be meaningless, senseless, or arbitrary. Instead, it must be somehow rational and structured. You cannot discover the irrational except by accident. You must take as your subject matter for research or pedagogy things that are amenable to rationality, such that something in your head can in fact match something 'out there.' When this happens, the resulting match is essentially a reinforcement of an important educative response. The problem for the child is to find an order out there that fits the order he has figured out in his head. This approach was dubbed the 'cultivation of rationality.'

It was suggested that, no matter what kinds of discovery you are concerned with, you must never lose sight of the importance of the antecedent explorations of the field. In Piaget's terms, we have been talking about the jump from the level of concrete perceptual experiences to abstract formulations and verbally stated conceptualizations. This is not a large single jump· it is rather a process. The finding of a language code of appropriate linguistic structure is mediated by a process one might call abstraction. This is nonverbal, or even preverbal in many ways and, most important, is a function of the richness of the antecedent crisscrossing of an exploratory field by the individual in order that patterns may begin to emerge. It is wrong for us, as it was for Poincaré, to speak of the triumphant moment of discovery without emphasizing the antecedent richness of preparation from which, and only from which, this pattern of discovery can emerge. Poincaré was not adept at introspection and so he thought that his ideas just popped into his mind, but he worked for a long time with the discoveries before the harvest was possible. The importance of language is that it is the universal vehicle of patterns. Therefore, the problem is one of finding an appropriate linguistic pattern which fits our experiences and is adequate to provide the appropriate exploration of the field.

The discussion now turned to consideration of discovery as a terminal behavior. In this sense the construct can take on two very different forms, analogous to Piaget's distinction of assimilation and accommodation. First, we have discovery within an accepted framework, and then, we have discovery which is in fact the reconstruction of an accepted framework and the development of a new one. Psychological research has traditionally looked only at the first kind, which is probably trivial, because we can understand these phenomena within frameworks we have already overlearned. The development of the revolutionary insight, which is really a totally different way of looking at things, is a much more difficult psychological phenomenon. Here, the notion that we have a process of finding structures in our own coded language system to fit what is out there does not seem to be the case, because it is very often precisely the problem of giving new meaning to our old words or even making new words, that makes this the second kind of discovery. We do not know how to set up instructional conditions which will elicit these revolutionary discoveries, but it is quite certain that the little 'coding' types of experiments that characterize the psychological literature of learning by discovery, e.g., seeing that something is spelled backwords, have absolutely nothing to do with the second kind of discovery.

This distinction between a minor discovery and a major one was sharpened even further by the suggestion that different terms should be used to describe these two phenomena. Minor, or assimilation type, discovery might be simply called *discovery*. On the other hand, major discovery should probably be called by some other name, *conceptual invention*. These two phenomena are quite different and should be treated as such.

PART TWO

THE RESEARCH

Chapter IV

The Learning By Discovery Hypothesis

M. C. WITTROCK

Introduction

MANY STRONG CLAIMS FOR LEARNING BY DISCOVERY ARE MADE IN EDU-cational psychology. But almost none of these claims has been empirically substantiated or even clearly tested in an experiment. In this chapter we will state the learning by discovery hypothesis; briefly look at the many interests in the hypothesis; analyze it into the independent, intervening, and dependent variables it denotes; review the literature related to each of these variables; and make suggestions for future empirical research. The independent–intervening–dependent variable approach has proven useful with other problems in psychology and education. Perhaps it can help us to comprehend some of the complexities and to avoid some of the tautologies in the research on learning by discovery. The value of this chapter rests on this assumption.

Statement of the Hypothesis

To call learning by discovery an hypothesis will come as a surprise to some readers who accept it as a postulate supported by data, intuition, and common sense. However, one of its leading proponents also considers it an hypothesis. In a well known article Bruner (1961) discusses four benefits said to accrue from discovery learning: greater intellectual potency, intrinsic motivation, memory processing, and the learning of the heuristics of discovery. Concluding the section on intellectual potency, he presents the learning by discovery hypothesis:

> It is, if you will, a necessary condition for learning the variety of techniques of problem solving, of transforming information for better use, indeed for learning how to go about the very task of

33

learning. Practice in discovering for oneself teaches one to acquire information in a way that makes that information more readily viable in problem solving. So goes the hypothesis. It is still in need of testing. But it is an hypothesis of such important human implications that we cannot afford not to test it—and testing will have to be in the schools (p. 26).

In the above quote, Bruner makes several important points. He states that learning by discovery is an hypothesis, and that the solving of problems is an appropriate dependent variable to index its results. Practice at problem solving is an independent variable. As we shall see at the end of this chapter, he makes another point—the hypothesis is still in need of testing.

The Dilemma

In another article, he is apparently less convinced that learning by discovery is an unproven hypothesis. After commenting on the passivity of knowledge-getting in the classroom (peaches are grown in Georgia; New York is our largest port, etc.) which lacks thinking as a reward for learning, Bruner writes:

One experiment which I can report provides encouragement. It was devised and carried out by the research group with which I am associated at Harvard in collaboration with teachers in the fifth grade of a good public school. It is on the unpromising topic of the geography of the North Central States and is currently in progress so that I cannot give all of the results. We hit upon the happy idea of presenting this chunk of geography not as a set of knowns, but as a set of unknowns. One class was presented blank maps, containing only tracings of the rivers and lakes of the area as well as the natural resources. They were asked as a first exercise to indicate where the principal cities would be located, where the railroads, and where the main highways. Books and maps were not permitted and "looking up the facts" was cast in a sinful light. Upon completing this exercise, a class discussion was begun in which the children attempted to justify why the major city would be here, a large city there, a railroad on this line, etc.

The discussion was a hot one. After an hour, and much pleading, permission was given to consult the rolled up wall map. I will never forget one young student, as he pointed his finger at the foot of Lake Michigan, shouting, "Yipee, *Chicago* is at the end of the pointing-down lake." And another replying, "Well, OK: but Chicago's no good for the rivers and it should be here where there is a big city (St. Louis)." These children were thinking, and learning was an instrument for checking and improving the process. To at least a half dozen children in the class it is not a matter of indifference that no big city is to be found at the junction of Lake Huron, Lake Michigan, and Lake Ontario. They were slightly shaken up transportation theorists when the facts were in.

The children in another class taught conventionally, got their facts all right, sitting down, benchbound. And that was that. We will see in six months which group remembers more. But whichever does, one thing I will predict. One group learned geography as a set of rational acts of induction—that cities spring up where there is water, where there are natural resources, where there are things to be processed and shipped. The other group learned passively that there were arbitrary cities at arbitrary places by arbitrary bodies of water and arbitrary sources of supply. One learned geography as a form of activity. The other stored some names and positions as a passive form of registration (Bruner, 1959, pp. 187–188).

In this second quote from Bruner, some of the complexities of the learning by discovery hypothesis become apparent when one applies the independent-dependent variable framework suggested above. It is important that children be taught to discover on their own, to be able to solve problems, to transfer to related situations (including further study in the same discipline), to be motivated to continue to learn, and to increase in independence. However, the quote from Bruner includes not only ends but means. A particular way of learning is hypothesized to produce these important ends.

After observing the children's overt behavior, Bruner concludes that the children presented with the blank maps were thinking. No doubt they were. But it would be better to have empirical data to index their thought. It seems that regardless of which group performs better six months after learning, the group that received the blank maps received the better treatment. Herein lies the crux of the dilemma among educational psychologists about discovery learning. When learning and discovery are measured by one event, discovery cannot be given as a cause for learning. It does no good to say tautologically that those who discover learn. For example, the desired result is an event named *learning by discovery*. The treatment designed to produce the result is also an event named *learning by discovery*. A tautological conclusion easily follows. The discovery learners learned by discovery, therefore their treatment was the better one, regardless of the data.

The treatment and its results must be kept separate from each other. The treatment is an independent variable. It may or may not produce transfer, savings, retention, or ability to discover as well as, or better than, some other treatment.

To evaluate discovery learning, we should obtain empirical data on its consequences. These data will have common sense and intuition to complement or refute them. Many people feel that, surely, practice at discovering is the best treatment to teach children to discover information by themselves. In any event, it may be difficult to convince many that one can learn to discover best by some route other than simply practicing the terminal behavior.

The Dialectic

Any individual whose intuitions favor discovery learning, both for its results and its treatments, will find himself with many colleagues. According to many of its proponents, learning by discovery produces knowledge which transfers to new situations. Through practice at problem solving it develops problem solving ability. It is intrinsically motivating and is its own reward. By being taught to solve problems, to behave in a scientific and inductive fashion, and to go beyond the data, a student is helped to become a mature person. It is a useful conceptualization for the teaching of many subjects in schools. Left to his own resources, the student's individual history will determine the proper sequence of learning activities. It is an important end in its own right. It deserves attention, and students should have some practice at discovering answers for themselves. One must learn to produce rather than to reproduce answers and knowledge. So goes the argument for learning by discovery.

According to some people less enthusiastic about it, only those students who have already learned how to discover may learn by discovery. It assumes that every individual can best be taught by one method, learning by discovery, when individual differences may require several different approaches.

The hypothesis confuses means with ends. To produce the ability to discover (an end) may involve more than simple practice at discovering (a means). Discovery is time consuming. The essence of a culture is that everyone need not discover for himself everything anew but that he can profit from the experiences of others as summarized in language. Even the motivation produced by discovery may be an attempt to escape, and later to avoid, the subject matter because the problems may threaten rather than challenge the student's intellect and self-concept. As an end, the ability to solve problems is important, but it is not the only important end. One must learn to acquire and comprehend much of his culture as well as to discover new knowledge and to solve problems.

So goes the opposition to learning by discovery, and so goes the dialectic. We shall analyze the fundamentals of this dialectic and discuss the research on these components after a discussion of the widespread interest in learning by discovery. With the variety of subject matter and students encountered in schools, it is surely futile to expect one method of learning to be consistently superior or inferior to other plausible procedures. The dialectic should be replaced by better issues, ones that will allow alternatives to the all-or-none positions common in the literature.

THE INTEREST IN LEARNING BY DISCOVERY

Current Interest

Among writers on human learning and education, there are definite ideas about the sequence and arrangement of stimuli which should be presented to students to produce transfer, savings, ability to discover, intrinsic motivation, and self-confidence. To present some of the excitement and some of the flavor which accompanies the learning by discovery hypothesis, several quotes are presented below. They help to convey accurately some of the enthusiasm and reasons for teaching and learning by discovery.

Suchman (1961) states many of the advantages claimed for teaching and for learning by discovery. About a program to improve inquiry skills, he writes:

> The need for improvement is great. Current educational practice tends to make children less autonomous and less empirical in their search for understanding as they move up the elementary grades. The schools must have a new pedagogy with a new set of goals which subordinate retention to thinking.
>
> It is clear that such a program should offer large amounts of practice in exploring, manipulating and searching. The children should be given a maximum of opportunity to experience autonomous discovery. New goals must be set for the children. Instead of devoting their efforts to storing information and recalling it on demand, they would be developing the cognitive functions needed to seek out and organize information in a way that would be the most productive of new concepts. Both the teacher and the pupil would have to be cast in new roles. The pupil must become more active and aggressive in his learning role. Direction of the concept formation process should be his own, and he should come to re-

gard his environment (including the teacher) as a potential source of information which can be obtained through his own acts of inquiry. The teacher must abandon his traditionally directive mode and structure an environment that is responsive to the child's quest for information. The teacher must see to it that the child's efforts at inquiry are rewarded by success, that the child is able to obtain the information he needs, and that he does discover new concepts on his own. The teacher can help the child by posing problems that are reasonably structured and will lead to exciting new discoveries. The teacher can also coach him in the techniques of data collection and organization that will lend power and control to his searching. The educator should be concerned above all with the child's process of thinking, trusting that the growth of knowledge will follow in the wake of inquiry.

For the past four years, we have been attempting to design and test just such a program to be employed in the elementary school. The following section describes our method, which we call *Inquiry Training* (p. 151).

Interest in the hypothesis is not limited to individual researchers. As early as 1952, the University of Illinois began to prepare materials and teachers to improve the teaching of secondary school mathematics. Max Beberman (1964, pp. 9–34) describes some of the careful organization of materials and some of the objectives of the program. He gives (pp. 11, 23) two operationally defined desiderata for the understanding of mathematics: (1) precision of textbook language and teacher language and (2) student discovery of generalizations. Cause and effect may be somewhat confounded here. These desiderata of the dependent variables of meaning and understanding are also the independent variables—the treatments—which are supposed to produce the understanding of mathematics. For example, by practicing discovery, mathematics is supposed to be made meaningful. How do we know this? Because discovery has been practiced.

But more important than the desiderata is the set of materials developed by the University of Illinois Committee on School Mathematics (UICSM). The Department of Mathematics, the College of Education, and the University High School cooperated in preparing, trying out, and testing the materials. The terminal behavior of students who complete the program seems to indicate that some important improvements in the teaching of mathematics in the secondary school have been introduced.

The UICSM is only one of the groups working on the improvement of the teaching of mathematics. A national effort, rather than a state or local one, is presented by the School Mathematics Study Group

(SMSG), which is financed by the National Science Foundation, and was begun in 1958. A brief history of SMSG is presented by William Wooten (1964, pp. 35–53). The sample textbooks and other materials prepared by this group are characterized by a careful sequencing and structuring of basic mathematical concepts (e.g., numeration, number systems, and intuitive plane geometry in grade 7) and also by involvement of the student in discovery of mathematical concepts. These materials have been enthusiastically received by many teachers, administrators, parents, and students.

The preference among scholars for teaching by discovery is not limited to mathematics. The Chemical Education Material Study (CHEM) by 1963 produced a new course in chemistry (Campbell, 1964, pp. 82–93). With movies, text, and laboratory manual, a series of laboratory experiments was prepared. Through laboratory experiments the student discovered (p. 87) the basic ideas of the course, including such fundamentals as kinetic theory and atomic structure. The discovery precedes the discussion of these concepts in the text. The third major part of the text includes applications of the concepts.

The many dimensions of change these new projects and their courses produce in students are difficult to evaluate. Although these projects are quite new, apparently for many students they present advances in teaching.

However, it is equally clear that the courses themselves involve many complicated dimensions in addition to those of careful sequencing and student discovery. The success of these programs does not, in any serious sense, support or refute the contention that learning by discovery is important for learning the subject matter, for learning a way of solving problems, or, for that matter, important for any other educational objective.

So far as these curricular demonstrations are concerned, learning by discovery is still an hypothesis—an untested one at that. In the sense that learning by discovery involves student selection of the sequence of materials, it is not involved in these projects. They have sequences very carefully designed by scholars and schoolmen. In the sense that learning by discovery implies inductive encounters with problems and raw data and student derivation of concepts or principles, discovery is definitely involved.

One could name other recent curriculum projects, e.g., the American Institute of Biological Sciences (AIBS) project in the teaching of biology. Most of these projects are also sympathetic to a learning by discovery procedure.

Earlier Interest

The current interests described above are rooted in movements in philosophy, education, and psychology. Only a few of the directly relevant leaders of these movements will be mentioned here: J. J. Rousseau, Maria Montessori, and John Dewey. J. J. Rousseau in his book *Emile* insisted that the proper role of the environment is to avoid interference with the internal processes of spontaneous maturation. Teacher direction, goals, and standards were to be replaced by a permissiveness which would allow the innately good child to realize himself best.

Maria Montessori (1912, 1917) pioneered a movement in education. She emphasized the freedom of the child and his choosing for himself the problems or subject matter he would study (1917). The teacher is to give little deliberate verbal direction to the child. She is not often to reinforce the child with words, smiles, or other verbal or social reinforcers.

For example, children are taught discrimination of form and sound by manipulating apparatus. The apparatus is designed to provide feedback to a child without the necessity of intervention of a teacher. In discussing how a child's senses are trained by having him insert objects into a form board, Montessori writes:

> Here instead it is the work of the child, the auto-correction, the auto-education which acts, for the *teacher must not interfere in the slightest* way. No teacher can furnish the child with the agility which he acquires through gymnastic exercises: it is necessary that the *pupil perfect himself* through his own efforts. It is very much the same with the *education of the senses*.
>
> It might be said that the same thing is true of every form of education. A man is not what he is because of the teachers he has had, but because of what he has done (1912, p. 172).

And in another volume, after giving examples of futile attempts of people to control the development of children's legs, noses, ears, heads, and the development of their character and intelligence, she writes:

> It is Nature, "creation," which regulates all these things. If we are convinced of this, we must admit as a principle the necessity of "not introducing obstacles to natural development"; and instead of having to deal with many separate problems—such as, what are the best aids to the development of character, intelligence and feeling?—one single problem will present itself as the basis of all education: How are we to give the child freedom? (1917, p. 5).

Later, she presents an episode important to her in the search for the discovery of a treatment required by the soul of the child which would be analogous to what hygiene prescribes for the body.

I think, therefore, that it is essential to record the fundamental fact which led me to define my method.

I was making my first essays in applying the principles and part of the material I had used for many years previously in the education of deficient children, to the normal children of the San Lorenzo quarter in Rome, when I happened to notice a little girl of about three years old deeply absorbed in a set of solid insets, removing the wooden cylinders from their respective holes and replacing them. The expression on the child's face was one of such concentrated attention that it seemed to me an extraordinary manifestation; up to this time none of the children had ever shown such fixity of interest in an object; and my belief in the characteristic instability of attention in young children, who flit incessantly from one thing to another, made me peculiarly alive to the phenomenon.

I watched the child intently without disturbing her at first, and began to count how many times she repeated the exercise; then, seeing that she was continuing for a long time, I picked up the little arm-chair in which she was seated, and placed chair and child upon the table; the little creature hastily caught up her case of insets, laid it across the arms of her chair, and gathering the cylinders into her lap, set to work again. Then I called upon all the children to sing; they sang, but the little girl continued undisturbed, repeating her exercise even after the short song had come to an end. I counted forty-four repetitions; when at last she ceased, it was quite independently of any surrounding stimuli which might have distracted her, and she looked round with a satisfied air, almost as if awaking from a refreshing nap.

I think my never-to-be-forgotten impression was that experienced by one who has made a discovery (1917, pp. 67–68).

With her willingness to observe children's behavior and to induce classroom innovations from these naturalistic observations, she has produced innovations in educational practice and thought. Unfortunately, she was less interested in the difficult problems of measuring the results of these innovations.

In a quite different way, John Dewey's (1910) preferences for problem solving, laboratory work, and a scientific method produced a decided effect upon education in our own century. He suggested concrete experience, active responses, problem solving projects, and do-it-yourself learning. Although he emphasized social interaction and problem solving as ways to learn, he also recognized three levels of the curriculum. In the third level, subject matter was organized according to the structure of the discipline and not necessarily in terms of the student's own needs or problems. The progressive education movement often seemed to depart from Dewey on this point.

From the above quotes and discussion, it is clear that learning by discovery is used to describe both an end and a means. By discovery a student is supposed to learn regularities and concepts within a discipline. But, more importantly, he is supposed to learn how to solve problems, to go beyond the data, and to behave as a junior scientist. He is supposed to become motivated and enthusiastic about the discipline. He is to know personal satisfaction because he has selected his own sequence of problems and, through active responses of his own, has succeeded at these problems. Attractive as these propositions appear on the surface, they are complicated and do not always survive careful examination.

Issues and Problems

The literature is fraught with conceptual issues, methodological problems, and semantic inconsistencies in the uses of the word discovery. Some of the problems and different uses of the term should be made explicit before the literature is reviewed.

Conceptual Issues

1. **Discovery as a way to learn subject matter versus as an end in its own right.** Not only is discovery thought to be a way to learn the structure of a subject, but it is a way to teach problem solving. Therefore, regardless of the subject matter a child learns, it is thought to be important for him to discover. These two ends should be kept separate from each other. They can be operationally defined and measured as dependent variables.

2. **What is to be discovered?** Is it a rule, generalization, or a more specific bit of information? Although it is difficult to define the difference between verbal statements of generalizations and more specific information, an attempt should be made to do so. Discovery may differ in its usefulness as a way to learn these ends.

3. **Induction vs. deduction.** Discovery learning is commonly equated with inductive learning where the subject proceeds from the specific to the general. It is just as plausible to assume that the learner begins with a higher order generalization, from which he derives more

specific conclusions and thus discovers answers and even generalizations. That is, there are probably several different processes involved in discovery. Induction has no exclusive identity with discovery learning. Discovery should be viewed as a set of very complex processes.

4. **The depreciation of verbal learning.** Much of the research on discovery learning is highly critical of a teacher's use of words. The argument centers on the necessity for a student to derive his own verbalizations rather than receiving them from teachers.

5. **Control of rate and sequence of stimuli.** For some unknown reasons, the effects of allowing a student to control his own rate and sequence of stimuli are relatively unstudied in the literature. Usually learning by discovery refers to a predetermined sequence beginning with problems and examples rather than with rules or generalizations.

6. **Variety of dependent variables.** From study to study one finds a wide variety of dependent variables: transfer, savings, retention, and especially ability to solve problems. Ability to verbalize rules and conclusions is sometimes an index of discovery. Another important dependent variable is affectivity. If the student discovers, he is supposed to display positive emotions, increased interest in subject matter and in solving problems. Such variety can be healthy, provided the results are carefully related to the particular dependent variables sampled in the study. Obviously, quite different findings cannot be contrasted with one another unless they pertain to the same types of dependent variables.

Methodological Problems

1. **Lack of replicability of the treatments.** In many of the empirical studies, the treatments are not operationally defined. They are complex and lengthy sequences of stimuli which often differ from other treatments in any number of ways. There often are no principles described which could be used by another researcher to generate the same types of treatments to replicate the study. The independent variable is not isolated or carefully varied.

2. **Failure to use random assignment.** Many of the studies called experiments are not experiments. Intact groups are frequently used. Little attempt is made to hold constant the effects of confounding variables.

3. **Inadequate statistical analysis.** Sometimes the statistical analysis of the data is omitted entirely or is given cursory treatment. In few studies is there a complete report of the data and its analysis.

4. **Extrapolation of results**. Although different subject matter and types of students are rarely studied in one report, the results are frequently extrapolated to a wide range of populations unsampled in the research. Discovery may be effective only when the students have already learned the necessary prerequisites and few competing responses. In an arbitrary situation, discovery learning may be highly ineffective and very discouraging.

Semantic Inconsistencies

1. **Labeling treatments in terms of responses they are said to produce.** *Rote* and *Discovery* are two most popular labels. These labels scarcely describe stimuli, but they do indicate responses and mediating processes. The words rote and discovery make it difficult to believe that the rank order of treatment means could be any other than discovery higher and rote lower. Less biased and emotionally loaded names are needed to describe the treatments. In addition, the rote treatment group of one study is sometimes indistinguishable from a discovery treatment of another study. One important function of experimental research on discovery is to determine if the stimuli produce the responses called discovery, not to assume that the issue is closed before the study begins.

2. **Lack of operational definitions and objective indices for the term discovery.** When a variety of specific problems, rather than rules or generalizations, are verbalized by a teacher or researcher, the situation is often labeled a discovery treatment. When concepts are verbalized by the teacher, the situation is usually not named discovery. Sometimes the verbalization of very general or vague cues, rather than specific ones, is also labeled a discovery procedure. Apparently, discovery applies so long as a specific rule or generalization is not mentioned by a teacher. It is usually confined to hierarchically arranged subject matter in which the learner has considerable background. With instructions he has a fairly high probability of deriving by himself correct answers and generalizations. If discovery were accurately indexed in terms of student behavior or knowledge, it would be easier to determine those situations which would preclude his producing that behavior without direction from a teacher.

Discovery is often used to denote a hypothetical, intervening cognitive event. One of the few researchers to try to index it objectively was Hendrix (1947). She used facial and other emotional processes rather than descriptions of teacher behavior or of student answers on a transfer test. If it is useful as an intervening event, we should try to find indices separate from measures of transfer or of treatments.

THE EMPIRICAL RESEARCH

The problems and issues discussed above will become more apparent in this section. In another chapter of this volume, Cronbach discusses some of the methodological mistakes common in the literature. Design and analysis problems will not be considered in detail here. The reader is urged to remember the conceptual and semantic problems described above, especially the comon practice of labeling different treatments with the same name.

Only a representative sample of the studies on learning by discovery can be presented. Any representative sample will include many studies which can scarcely be called research. Many researchers apparently were not aware of the complexity of the problems under study. Their procedures seem grossly inadequate to tease out the cause and effect relationships often boldly reported.

To provide some semblance of organization to the studies below, the independent–intervening–dependent variable framework is used. The studies do not always fall neatly into one of the three major categories, but more is gained than is lost by imposing some structure upon the diversity of studies. Research related to learning by discovery is described at the end of each of the major sections to indicate some of the ways to improve the quality of future research.

The reader is forewarned that the current state of research on discovery is very disappointing and precludes any important conclusions about teaching or learning. The reader is not expected to accept this comment on faith. Many studies are summarized in detail below, to allow one to become familiar with the problems and issues mentioned in the above section.

The literature on learning by discovery does not lend itself to terse summaries. The studies are seldom closely interrelated to one another. The procedures are sometimes naive and crude and evidence only the researcher's preference for a type of treatment. Only by summarizing a few studies in detail can one appreciate the several meanings of the learning by discovery hypothesis, the severe shortcomings of the research, the futility of an attempt to gloss over the particulars of a study, and the meaninglessness of generalizations based on these studies. For other attempts at summarizing these studies, see Ausubel (1963), Kersh and Wittrock (1962), and Wittrock (1963c). What follows below is a review of research only incidentally. Primarily, it is a description and analysis of the fundamental issues and complexities involved in the empirical work on learning by discovery.

The Intervening Variables

The Rote—Meaningful Dilemma. One segment of research began with an interest in deriving and comparing predictions from connectionism and field theory. The recent research on learning by discovery largely grew from this theoretical controversy.

Thorndike's extensive research upon the law of effect, including the relative effects of reward and punishment, stimulated much research upon discovery. A quote from Thorndike often appears in studies on discovery:

> . . . the attainment of active rather than passive learning at the cost of practice in error may often be a bad bargain. . . . The almost universal tolerance of imperfect learning in the early treatment of a topic, leaving it to be improved by the gradual elimination of errors in later treatments, is probably unsound, and certainly risky (1935, p. 147).

These sentences, and others of his, have been interpreted as an attempt to explain complex human learning in terms of simple learning and to de-emphasize the arrangement of stimuli, the meaningfulness of material, and the importance of discovery learning (e.g., Swenson, 1949). In two treatment groups, Swenson operationalized the distinction between meaning-discovery theory and connectionism. She added a third treatment to approximate her conception of the then current practice of the teaching of arithmetic. The subject matter was one hundred addition combinations (e.g., $3 + 4$ and $7 + 3$).

She assigned to the three treatment groups 332 children from 14 different second grade classes. The first group was a Generalization group. The combinations presented to these children were ordered according to an unspecified generalization. By grouping these number combinations, the teachers led the pupils to formulate their own generalizations. The second group, the Drill group, was presented the number combinations in different orders. The children were discouraged from producing answers in any but an automatized procedure. If a pupil hesitated or gave a wrong answer, he was instantly corrected. The third group, the Drill-Plus group, was supposed to approximate common practice in elementary schools. Each number combination was presented by pictures of concrete objects, and each new addition combination was followed by allowing the children to count and manipulate concrete objects. After the counting and manipulating of concrete objects, drill was used. The Drill-Plus method also presented the addition facts in groups organized by the size of the sum. Again, pupils were discouraged from making generalizations of number relations.

For all three groups, instruction lasted for a total of 20 weeks, and was divided into three major sections. An original set of facts (O) an interpolated set of facts (I), and a final set of facts (F) were taught. The 14 second grade classes were assigned by stratified random procedures to the three treatment groups. A test over the 100 addition facts was given on five different occasions: before the original learning (Test I), after the O instruction (Test II), after the interpolated learning (Test III), after two-and-a-half weeks of vacation (Test IV), and after the final instruction (Test V). After the fifth test of learning, three transfer tests were given. One was on 100 untaught subtraction facts. The second was on a test of 100 addition problems in which one of the two numbers to be added was a two-digit number. The third transfer test presented a variety of addition possibilities with one-digit, two-digit, and three-digit numbers.

She reports no means, standard deviations, standard errors, or analysis of variance tables, but states that she tested for homogeneity of variance, and used analyses of variance and covariance. Her analysis of results is complicated and it includes an analysis of gain scores from one of the five tests to the one which immediately followed it. The failure to report numbers and the use of the gain scores make it most difficult to summarize the results. On the learning of the original (O) facts, the Generalization group gained more than either of the other two groups. The Drill group was significantly superior to the Drill-Plus group. On the learning of the interpolated (I) facts, the three groups were not significantly different in gain scores. Neither were there any significant differences in gain scores on the learning of the final (F) facts, although the Generalization group performed better than either of the other two groups at the beginning of the F learning, and also at the end of the F learning.

On the learning of the three sets of facts, the gain scores were significantly different only in the case of the learning of the O facts, where the rank order was Generalization, Drill, and Drill-Plus. Each group was significantly better than the group which immediately followed it. There was no significant gain or loss in retention across the three methods for any of the retention periods.

After adjusting for Mental Age (MA), the transfer within the 100 addition facts favored the Generalization group on most of the tests. Occasionally the Drill-Plus group transferred more than the Drill group. When adjusted for MA and initial learning of addition facts, transfer to subtraction facts ranked, from highest to lowest, Generalization, Drill, Drill-Plus. All differences were statistically significant. On transfer to the upper decade facts, both the Drill and Generalization groups were statistically significantly better than the Drill-Plus group, while neither of the two former groups were statistically significantly different from each other.

Anderson (1949) also tried to compare connectionism and drill with generalization theory and active discovery by the pupils. Against relatively discrete elements and drill, he compared a highly organized system of principles. Practice came after, rather than before, the principles and their rationalization. Connectionism was depicted as a sterile system designed to avoid the practice of errors. He alternately described the two theories as Drill theory and Meaning theory (p. 41).

He also used arithmetic, elementary school children, and two treatments. In the Drill group there were 208 fourth grade students. The experiment lasted for approximately six months. Unlike the Swenson study, in which the teachers were assigned at random to the treatments, he assigned teachers on the basis of interviews and a measure of attitudes. There was no day by day control over the procedure for the teachers of the treatments (p. 44), nor were the teachers held responsible for definite objectives, content, or amount of time spent on instruction and drill.

The teachers of the Drill classes averaged about 11 minutes a day on instruction and 24 minutes a day on drill, while the teachers of the Meaning classes spent about 27 minutes a day on instruction and 18 minutes on drill. Anderson did not specify precisely how the treatments differed from each other. The intent was to implement connectionism in the Drill treatment (discrete elements, responses given to the learner, and repetition or drill on the discrete elements) and field theory in the Meaning treatment (organized patterns, responses not given to the learner, and practice at applying generalizations).

The dependent variables were tests of computational skills, problem solving, understanding of social concepts in arithmetic and vocabulary, and of mathematical thinking. The tests of computational skills included tests of addition, subtraction, multiplication, division, fundamental operations, and an interpolated test of subtraction. The significant differences which did occur indicated that the Drill method was superior for pupils who scored low on the Minneapolis School Ability test but high on the arithmetic pretest. The Meaning method tended to be superior for pupils who were high on the ability test but who were low on the arithmetic pretest. Anderson interprets this to mean that practice is probably most helpful to those who are low on the ability measure but are quite high on the achievement measure.

There were no significant differences among the two groups when social concepts and vocabulary tests were the dependent variables. On the tests of mathematical thinking, the difference between the high groups favored the Meaning group and was significant at the .01 level. The difference between the low groups favored the Drill method and was significant at the .01 level. On a test of long division over the learning exercise, the Drill method was better for both the high groups and the low groups.

In Anderson's study there was little control over the independent variables. It is impossible to draw any conclusions from his data. See Thiele (1938) and Forgus and Schwartz (1957) for further research.

Unverbalized Awareness. Interest in theory about discovery as an intervening variable also appears in Gertrude Hendrix's writings. Her work is interesting for its theoretical approach, not for its serious methodological shortcomings. Her theory departs from the connectionism–field theory dilemma. In several papers (1947, 1950, 1961), she argues that a period of unverbalized awareness is important for obtaining transfer. Here we have transfer as an operational definition of the effect of discovery. She indexed discovery, as described below, by facial and emotional responses. However, she is still using, as the treatment variables, covert responses rather than the stimuli which may or may not produce these covert responses.

In the earliest of the three papers (1947) she presents, in very brief form, her first three attempts at experimentation with discovery learning. With 40 college and high-school subjects, she compared three treatments. In Method I, the generalization was stated first by the teacher, then it was illustrated and applied to new problems. The generalization was, "The sum of the first n odd numbers is n-square."

In Method II, labeled the Unverbalized Awareness Method, a series of problems was presented. First the learners were asked to find the sum of the first two odd numbers, then the sum of the first three, the first four, etc. As soon as the subject noticed (discovered?) the relationship between the totals and the number of odd numbers he was asked to leave the room. The index of his discovering the relationship was, ". . . he started, or gasped a little, or smiled, or grew tense—that is he showed in some way that something had happened to him. Furthermore, he began to give the succeeding answers rapidly. . . ." (1947,

49

p. 199). In group III, labeled the Conscious Generalization Procedure, the method was the same as for Group II, except that when the indices of discovery occurred, the subjects were asked to state the rule they had discovered. The teacher then shaped the student's verbalization of the rule until it was accurate. Two weeks later, each group was given a transfer test whose items could be quickly solved by the generalization. The results were expressed as a ratio between the number of correct answers obtained by the short cut and the total number of correct answers. The groups ranked, from high to low, II, III, and I. A t-test showed that groups II and I differed at the .12 level, and that groups II and III differed at the .34 level. In other words, no difference was statistically significant at the conventional .05 level. Hendrix, and others subsequently, have cited her study as if the statistical results were significant. However, the n was small, 40 in all three studies combined.

Aside from the serious methodological problems, her results neither support nor refute the discovery hypothesis nor her hypothesis about unverbalized awareness. Hendrix's hypothesis deserves further study, if the treatments can be designed to differ from each other on a single dimension.

Motivation. Kersh (1958, 1962) presents two studies in which he was primarily interested in discovery as an intervening process. Kersh's work indicates a new interest and refinement in conceptualization about the intervening process. He argued that meaning may not be the intervening variable most useful in discovery learning. Instead, motivation may be the construct most useful in explaining the results. In particular, competence motivation may be a useful way to describe the intervening events produced by the discovery treatments.

In his first study (1958), 60 college volunteers were divided at random into six groups. Each subject was taught two rules of addition, the Odd Numbers Rule and the Constant Difference Rule. All the groups were given general instructions which specified the two types, and told that the first type of problem was called the Odd Numbers Problem while the second type of problem was called the Constant Difference Problem. They were then given a sample of the respective types of problems and were told some of the characteristics of the number series which occurred in the problems. Then the three groups, each with two different forms for the presentation of the problems, were given their first problem. The No Help groups were told to try to discover the rule. The two Direct Reference groups were told to discover the rule and were given some hints about the rule. For the two Rule Given groups, the problems and rule were given by the experimenter

(E). Each group then continued to work on six problems. Some of the individuals in the No Help groups were unable to discover the intended rules within the time period of 90 minutes. Immediately after the learning period, the first test was given. A retest was given to all subjects four to six weeks after the first test. On the retest, two problems were presented. The first problem asked each subject to sum the first 35 odd numbers. The second question asked them the sum of all the first 35 numbers. However, the dependent variables which interested Kersh were the answers to the following questions:

> Did you add the first 35 (odd) numbers to get your answer? (Yes or no) If your answer is no, explain how you obtained your answer.
> Did you try to recall the rule you learned (or attempted to learn) under our direction several weeks ago? (Yes or no)
> Were you successful in recalling the rule? (Yes or no)
> Describe how you recalled or attempted to recall the rule (1958, p. 287).

His primary interest was the method used in solving the problems, not whether the correct answer was produced. On the test of transfer to new examples of the rules he found that the No Help group produced ($p <$ .05) a greater incidence of "acceptable methods" than did either the Direct Reference group or the Rule Given group. On a dependent variable which asked the subject (S) to explain the rule, he found that only a small percentage of any group could explain either of the two rules. Initial learning was best for the directed groups. He concludes that motivation and consequent practice, greatest for the discovery group, produced the best performance on the acceptable test given approximately one month after learning.

One clear result of the study is that none of the treatments was very effective at producing transfer to new problems several weeks after learning. The second result is that the self-report data on motivation and practice are difficult to interpret and may not be very reliable. The third result is that a motivational explanation for the performance of the discovery groups is an interesting hypothesis.

Considerable guidance was given to all groups before they were allowed to begin to work on problems. They were all told the names of the types of rules and were given some experience with examples of the rules. It may be that Kersh had introduced into this study the effects of retroactive inhibition.

In his second study (1962) Kersh definitely was studying the effects of retroactive inhibition. He used the same two rules and taught them to 90 high school subjects by a program booklet procedure. After the rules were taught and practiced by each group, one-third of the subjects was given indivdual guidance in discovering an explanation for the rule. This was the Guided Discovery group. The second 30 students were given an explanation of the rules in a programmed booklet. This group was called the Directed Learning group. The last group, the Rote Learning group, was given no further instruction. The tests of retention and transfer, given three days, two weeks, and six weeks later, favored the Rote Learning and Guided Discovery groups. From the questionnaire, it appeared that the Guided Discovery group practiced rules after learning and before testing more than did the subjects in the other groups.

In both studies, he argues that some kind of directed discovery of explanations or relationships motivates the students to continue after the learning exercise is completed. As in the first study, Kersh again used as the primary dependent variable the method used by the students to arrive at answers to transfer items. This is not the same index of transfer often used in other studies on learning by discovery. In his second study, the label of rote learning was used to describe a control condition in which no instruction was given. In earlier studies, rote learning was made synonomous with drill and repetition.

Kersh's work is of interest because it represents recent experimental attempts to index the intervening events. His attention to motivation is described after White's (1959) concepts of competence and effectance. As is characteristic of the research on discovery primarily concerned with intervening processes, one finds less attention given to the independent and dependent variables. One result is that rote and discovery occur as the treatments. Another is that dependent variables, scarcely employed otherwise, become the primary variables of interest because they are likely to index the intervening events. Kersh makes one acutely aware of the problems of measurement of intervening events such as motivation.

Verbal Mediators. Gagné and Brown (1961) taught 33 males, in grades nine and ten, a program on some principles of a number series. All three experimental groups received an introductory program followed by one of three programs. The first treatment was labeled Rule and Example. The second treatment was labeled Discovery, and the third, Guided Discovery.

The Rule and Example program began with the correct formula, which S was asked to copy on his answer sheet; and was followed by several examples for S to work. The Discovery program began by asking S for a rule for the number series. The following frames contained hints to direct S to work at deriving the rule. The questions became more and more explicit; however, they never stated the rules for him. The Guided Discovery program also began with a question, but the question was more specific than the one asked in the Discovery program. The first question was followed by a second to introduce numbers and to make the steps in deriving the rule more apparent than they were in the Discovery treatment. Further items gave examples of the relationships within the number series.

On the second day, each S repeated the first day's program. In this respect, even the Discovery group was given considerable direction. They had seen the items and had been asked to produce the rule the day before. Gagné and Brown state:

> The procedure employed with the three learning programs insured that, although the Ss responded to different sets of learning materials, they all achieved successful answers to questions about the same four number series (p. 316).

The dependent variables were the time to solve the problems, the number of hints required to solve the problems, and the weighted time score combining these. In each case, S had to derive the formula for the sum of n terms in a number series. This type of dependent variable differs from those often used in studies in learning by discovery, where the subject is required to use a previously learned rule to work specific problems. Transfer of a more remote nature—transfer to new rules—is involved in the Gagné and Brown study.

Their results showed the best performance for the Guided Discovery group, the worst for the Rule and Example group, and intermediate performance for the Discovery treatment. All measures were significant by analysis of variance at less than the .01 level. Their results support a Guided Discovery procedure for the teaching of the derivation of new but related rules. However, one must remember that all the groups were given a second day's rehearsal over the material carefully directed the first day.

This study is one of the most carefully controlled ones on the intervening processes in learning by discovery. They described the intervening variable in terms of the subject's history. The concepts newly learned in an experiment were the mediators affecting problem solving and transfer. From this line of argument they state that, provided the concepts are learned, it should not matter how the concepts were learned. The result should be the same. It is not *how* you learn but *what* you learn that is important, according to the argument (p. 320).

Their discussion of the importance of what is learned rather than how it is learned scarcely seems appropriate for this study. This is especially the case since they were careful to mention, as stated above, that all groups learned to approximately the same criterion, and therefore must have differed only in terms of how it was learned. After an analysis of the Gagné and Brown tasks and programs, Della-Piana and Eldredge (1964), question the interpretation that the differences in their study were due to what was practiced rather than how it was practiced.

A study by Bruner (1961) represents an interesting, but not a rigorous, approach to the study of discovery as an intervening event. He used the concept of mediation to predict the results of learning a list of paired-associates. Generic mediation (a superordinate term or idea is the mediator), thematic mediation (a theme or story is the embedding material), and part-whole mediation (e.g., a sentence containing the word 'trees' mediates between chairs and forest) were three types of mediators he intuited and used to measure children's preferences for mediators.

He taught the 30 paired-associates to three groups of twelve year old children. The first group was told to remember the words. In the second group, each child was asked to select some word or mediator which could help to make the association meaningful to him. The third group was supplied with the words selected by the second group and was directed to use these words as their mediators. Since the second group learned in one trial the greatest percentage of the paired-associates (95 per cent), Bruner concluded that discovery was a method superior to prompting or direction.

The mediators for the second group, by virtue of their selection by the learners, were very probably more strongly associated with the stimulus terms by the members of the second group than they were by the members of the third group. It would be interesting to perform this study after controlling for the individual differences in associations. Bruner's dependent variable was initial learning of a list of paired-associates. Percentage learned in one trial is not a type of measure commonly used in studies of learning by discovery.

The study is reported very briefly near the end of his article. No specifics about method or analyses of results are presented. Bruner's study is important because it represents an attempt to apply mediation theory to the study of discovery. As a by-product one can see why self-selection of mediators may be an effective way to increase learning.

For the Future. The recent interest in the intervening variables has changed much from the early studies on connectionism–field theory and rote–meaningful processes. The intervening variables of recent interest include motivation, verbal mediation, and subverbal awareness.

As a description of an intervening process, discovery now competes with verbal mediators, concepts, and the competence motive. Discovery is now seen as an event which should mediate transfer—a theory of transfer. There is also interest in indexing discovery separately from the transfer it may mediate.

One reason why learning by discovery has created such a furor and interest among educators is that it poses an intervening variable, an event called discovery, while at the same time it is a theory of how and under what conditions associations and knowledge are acquired. There are not many theories of verbal learning which predict on theoretical bases, rather than on empirical bases, conditions for forming associations. For example, mediation theory (Osgood, 1953) predicts behavior after associations are formed. That is, if A is associated with B and B in turn with C, then there should be a tendency for C to be produced to the stimulus A. From the theory, one knows little about how to associate A to B and B to C.

One way for discovery to be useful is to lead to productive independent variables. For a useful discussion of functions of theories of instruction see Bruner (1964b).

For the future, one wonders if discovery has any merit as an intervening variable. If it does, the author suggests a behavioral emphasis for discovery as a mediating event. Mandler (1962) presents an important paper on association and structure. He discusses the distinction between cognitive and association theories in the use of the term response. From empirical evidence on the effect of overlearning on transfer and from the concept of learning set, he indicates that events which have been given structural and cognitive explanations are amenable, at least in part, to associative explanations. In research on discovery learning, the term response has little usefulness because the type or mode of response is often unimportant. If one chooses to use an associational theory to predict the results of learning by discovery, he must remember that the term response is deceptive and is narrow in its implication. A term such as answer might be more useful (Gagné, 1962).

The measurement of the behavioral results of mediating events is covered in a well known volume on the measurement of meaning (Osgood, Suci, & Tannenbaum, 1957). However, in this volume, the future researcher on discovery will find most attention given to the affective and connotative dimensions of mediating events. Little attention is given to denotative meaning and its transfer.

The second important part of this course for the future would be to relate discovery to its behavioral antecedents. Gagné (1964, pp. 310–317) discusses the nature of problem solving and presents paradigms to describe the hypothetical intervening events which occur in human learning and problem solving. He differentiates among the types of learning according to their complexity.

Increasing complexity is seen to reside not so much in what is learned, as in the nature of what has to be *preavailable* . . . in order for various types of learning to occur. Thus, verbal paired-associate learning in its pure form occurs when the responses (or response-connections) are already available (cf. Underwood and Schultz, 1960), originally made so presumably, by previous learning . . . And so on until the most complex form, problem solving is reached, which depends upon the preavailability of capabilities acquired in all the other forms of learning (pp. 311–312).

Although it may be too much to expect that a behavioristic approach will improve the usefulness of discovery, the attempt should be made. Unless the concept of discovery can be objectively indexed, it has little usefulness in behavioral research on learning and instruction.

The Independent Variables

The second major segment of research on learning by discovery is grouped under the heading of independent variables. These studies are focused on the functional relations between independent variables and dependent variables. Compared with the studies described under the Intervening Variables section above, there is relatively less attention given to indexing or theorizing about the hypothetical covert behavior of the subject. Instead, the researchers are primarily interested in discovery treatments and in comparing them with other treatments. In some of the latest studies, there are attempts to define operationally the independent variables separately from the dependent variables. The old rote–discovery labels are replaced gradually by names for treatments which imply little about the subjects' behavior, but describe the stimuli in more objective ways, e.g., answers given. The dependent variables are given less attention in these studies than are the independent variables.

The studies summarized below differ from one another in many ways: subject matter, age of learners, variety of treatments, and measures of the dependent variables. The reader is especially cautioned about the labels for the treatments and even for the tests. Quite different treatments are sometimes given the same name, and sometimes one research-er's rote treatment is highly similar to another's discovery treatment.

Principles and Answers. One of the earliest and best known of empirical studies on rules and principles, a precursor of studies on learn-ing by discovery, is by Judd (1908). He used transfer as a criterion and studied the teaching of a relationship between the depth of water and the refraction which results when one looks from a less dense medium (air) into a more dense medium (water) with an angle of incidence ap-propriate to produce a refraction. One group was taught, in verbal form, the principle of refraction. They then practiced throwing darts at a sub-merged target. Another group was given the same total instructional time, but the time was used to practice throwing darts without the teacher's verbalization or explanation of the principle. On a transfer test with a change in the depth of the water, the group given the prelimi-nary verbal training performed better.

Thorndike's admonition to avoid the practice of errors which may occur in discovery learning prompted a chain of studies on rules and principles. A type of task used by Thorndike was adopted in these studies. It involves eliminating the one word which does not belong among five. Craig (1953 and 1956), Kittell (1957), and Stacey (1949) used this task. Stacey studied information given before the learner made a response and also reinforcement and knowledge of results.

He divided 100 sixth grade pupils into five groups. Group A was told nothing about why a particular choice was correct. Group B was told only that there was a reason why one of the words did not belong with the other four. This group was also given three examples to work before they began the learning task. With the examples appeared the correct principles and the correct answers. Stacey called the above two groups his discovery groups. For the remaining three groups, correct answers were specified in advance for each item. Group C was given only the item and the correct answer. Group D was given the items, the correct answers, and the information and examples given to Group B, described above. Group E was given the same as Group D plus the correct reason for the answer to each item. Each subject was also given imme-diate feedback. The experimenter announced "right" and "wrong" as appropriate. A correction procedure was used, and S was allowed to continue until he selected the correct word.

Stacey found no interaction between amount of information given to the subjects and ability level. When gains from pretest to posttest were measured, there were no significant differences either among abil-ity levels or among the five treatments.

57

When the dependent variable was ability to give the proper reasons for the responses, the results indicated that those given the minimum amount of information (method A) or just about the minimum (method B) and just below the maximum (method D) gave the correct reasons in a higher proportion of cases than the subjects given the median (method C) amount of information. There were not any significant differences among methods A, B, and D. In other words, the two methods which Stacey thought involved discovery, methods A and B, produced greater ability to state reasons for correct responses. However, method D, which emphasized identification rather than self-discovery, produced similar mean scores.

Stacey's results indicate one danger of naming the stimuli in terms of behavior one hopes the stimuli will produce. Groups C and D might also be considered discovery groups if it is discovery of a generalization or principle rather than specific answers which is most important. Neither C nor D was given the correct principles. Stacey's results must be related to the dependent variables he sampled. The studies which follow often use other dependent variables.

Stacey's study influenced a series of later studies. Craig (1953, 1956) and Kittell (1957) used the same type of task. Craig (1953) reacted to the line of argument developed by Stacey. Craig felt that guidance could produce a positive effect on discovery. He described his independent variables as different types of stimuli. This description of variables represents an important step towards defining more precisely the learning by discovery issue and a step away from the rote-understanding issue and from the definition of treatments in terms of responses made by the learners.

He investigated the effects of cues about principles. There were four groups of 50 male college graduates. The task was the same as that used in the study by Stacey above: i.e., to determined the one word among the five of each item that did not belong. The first group was a minimum guidance group and was given no cues. For the second group, the items were arranged according to common principles. The third group received a blank space between the sets of items grouped by a common principle. This group was told that all items in a group were organized into a common principle. The fourth and final group, a maximum guidance group, was given the information described for the third group and also was given a short statement of each principle.

On initial learning, the amount of guidance was directly related to the number of correct responses. When transfer was a criterion, the same relationship held, that is, the more the cues, the greater the ability to discover.

In his second experiment, Craig (1956) divided 106 college sophomores into two groups, a No Help group and a Directed group. The No Help group was told only that one principle was used to answer all five items which were grouped together as a unit. The Directed group was given the same information as the No Help group, except that the principle was stated above each group of four items. Each item consisted of five words. The subject was to sort out the incorrect one of the five. He gave an immediate test, and retention tests 3, 17, and 31 days later. On the immediate test, the Directed group did better than the No Help group. Although there were no significant differences between the two groups on the 3- and 17-day retention tests, there was a significant difference between the two groups on the 31-day test. The Directed group did better than the No Help group. These tests all contained new examples of the rules previously learned. Another retention test, which consisted of new rules and examples of these new rules produced no differences between the groups. He interprets his study to indicate that external direction can help learners to make future discovery by providing them with an adequate background of information. Craig summarizes his experiment as follows:

> Many have advocated relatively independent problem-solving in the belief that learning situations should be similar to anticipated transfer situations. This point of view rests on the assumption that future discovery of principles will be through independent problem-solving, hence, more like pupil self-discovery than directed discovery. A different view is that problem-solving and discovery are never independent except in the sense that no one is physically present to prompt the learner. Principles previously learned in an area serve to direct discovery. Out-of-school discovery is not independent but directed by the knowledge gained under the direction of previous teachers. The more direction of this kind available to the learner, the more effective his discovery of new relations. The cumulative effect of greater learning through directed discovery over months or years may offset the effect of any lack of similarity between learning and transfer situations and prove to be the best preparation for new discoveries (Craig, 1956, p. 233).

Of course, it should be remembered that he found no effect upon transfer to new principles, a finding which has been often repeated by other researchers. He also found no differences on two of his three retention tests.

To study the effects of guidance upon problem solving, Corman (1957) used forms of Katona's match tasks which were presented to

255 twelfth grade students. He varied the information about the principle and about the method of solving problems. All possible combinations of these three factored variables (no information, some information, and much information) gave nine different treatments ranging from no information about either the principle or the method, to information about both the principle and the method. The dependent variables were initial learning, transfer to simple and complex problems, and ability to verbalize the principles.

His results are complicated. For the simple transfer problems, specific information about the rule, with explicit information about the method, was the best for the more capable students. On the test of complex transfer, the indirect clues (either to method or to the rule) produced for the more capable students performance worse than other combinations of information. But for students of less than average ability, performance on complex tasks was best when guidance, either specific or less explicit, was given about the method. When acquisition of the rule was a criterion, performance increased as the amount of information about the rule also increased. That is, explicit information about the rule was superior to no information about the rule.

When writing the rule was the criterion, the students who were given the most explicit information about the rule performed best, although their performance was better only than that of the No Information group. No statistically significant effect on this criterion was found for information about method. Corman concluded that appropriate guidance was beneficial for learning and transfer and that failure to provide it would delay rather than prevent solution; and that the effectiveness of the guidance may interact with student ability as described above.

One interesting part of this study was the attempt to define the independent variables in terms of two types of information (information about a principle and information about methods of solving problems) and three quantities of information (no, some, and much). His attempts to define the treatments in terms other than those which also describe the type of responses (rote or discovery) represent a step toward objectivity. However, the terms 'some' and 'much' leave much to be desired. At best they are on an ordinal scale. They still are defined in terms of assumptions about the learner's background, when these assumptions may not be valid. Another interesting part of the study was a dependent variable, ability to verbalize the principles, which he added to the usual dependent variables of initial learning and transfer to new problems. His study is of interest primarily because he elaborates the number and type of variables and studies all possible combinations of them.

The primary interest in dependent and independent variables rather than in intervening processes, characteristic of Corman's study and of the two Craig studies mentioned above, occurs again in a study by Kittell. He hypothesized that giving the underlying principles, in verbal form, was better for transfer and retention than not giving these principles. He used the same type of items as did Craig. He divided 132 sixth grade children into three groups. The Minimum Direction group was told that each group of three items had a principle in common and was told to look for the principle. The Intermediate Direction group was given the same direction as that given to the Minimum group plus a verbal statement of the principle. The principle was printed above the appropriate items and was also read twice, aloud, by the E. The Maximum Direction group was given not only the same information as the Intermediate group but was told the three correct responses to the three items in each group.

On a difficult test of transfer to new examples of previously learned principles, the Intermediate group did the best, the Maximum group next best, and the Minimum group did least well. The Intermediate group also retained more of the previously learned principles. On initial learning, the Intermediate and Maximum groups did not differ from each other significantly and each was better than the Minimum Direction group. His tests were difficult. The mean scores were less than five out of a possible 15.

Compared with Craig's two studies, Kittell increased the amount of direction by adding a group which was given both the relevant rules and the correct answers. Kittell's Intermediate group was probably more highly directed than was Craig's Directed group.

His results offer an interesting hypothesis about the relationship of direction to transfer. The hypothesis would be that when the material is most difficult the direction should match the population of items to which transfer is desired. For example, direction with specific rules produces transfer of these rules, even to situations where the rules do not apply.

That the most highly directed group would do as well as or better than any other group on initial learning of several specific responses agrees with much earlier research and is a surprise to no one. It is interesting that the group given the rules but not the correct answers produced the greatest transfer to new examples of the same rules. Perhaps the learner discovers how to apply the rules and receives extinction for incorrect attempts to apply these rules. The direction toward certain rules may make it likely that he will use these rules again in the future. One wonders what Kittell's results might have been had he used one transfer test which contained quite new and different items.

Craig and Kittell's studies also show that labels such as maximum and minimum are largely meaningless. Kittell's Intermediate Direction group was probably more highly directed than was Craig's (1956) Maximum group.

It was inevitable that the Craig and Kittell studies (which found that by giving rules transfer could be increased) would excite at least one rebuttal. Haslerud and Meyers (1958) used 100 college students as subjects, and 20 enciphering problems as the learning task. The two treatments consisted of either no directions or specific directions (including the rule) for deciphering the code printed above the problem. They used a treatment by subjects design; that is, each subject was given both treatments. There were 10 items for each treatment. On initial learning the specific directions produced the greatest mean performance on the test of transfer to new sentences, which involved the same 20 rules used during training. They found no statistically significant difference.

However, they give a dubious interpretation of the results and conclude that the No Directions Given treatment was the better of the two because the percentage of loss from the immediate to the test given one week later was less for this group than for the other group. Since each subject was given practice on each of the two experimental conditions, one might expect that the practice at discovering would generalize from one set of items to the other and that the treatments would then be contaminated. Again, the directed procedure was better on the original learning, even when there was no significant difference on a later transfer test.

Wittrock (1963) divided 292 college students into four experimental groups. The task was to decipher transpositional codes. To one group the rule as well as the answer to the specific item were given simultaneously with the encoded item. To a second group the rule was given but the answer was not given. To a third group the rule was not given but the answer was given. And to the fourth group, neither the rule nor the answer was given. It was hypothesized that with difficult materials (low association value also) direction toward the rules or specification of the rules enhances transfer to new examples of these same rules. It was also hypothesized that learning both rules and answers produces the greatest initial learning of a few correct answers, but would interfere with transfer, because S would not be practicing applying a rule or extinguishing his associated and incorrect answers. The results supported ($p < .01$) the hypotheses. An intermediate amount of direction produced the greatest retention and transfer but maximum direction produced the greatest initial learning. The minimum direction treatment was least effective on initial learning, retention, and transfer. This study exemplifies how the studies primarily interested in relationships between independent-dependent variables have recently tended to use materials which are simple, of low-association value, and somewhat foreign to the type commonly used in elementary and secondary schools. The use of coding or selection of one word from among five as tasks for experimentation is justified when one needs control over stimuli which he cannot get with sequenced materials. However, for the use of these materials one pays a price in ability to generalize.

These studies on rules and answers differ from one another in so many ways that no definite conclusions can be stated. However, some of them are better controlled than most of the studies described under the section on intervening variables. The learning by discovery hypothesis is being operationally defined better than before. Some of the complexities and oversimplifications of the earlier studies are being exposed. (See Grote, 1960; Moss, 1960; Ray, 1961; Rowlett, 1960; and Tomlinson, 1962 for further discussion of the effects of discovery treatments upon learning, retention, and transfer.)

Verbal Cues. One reaction against the complexity and diffuseness of the treatments common in learning by discovery is to design treatments that differ from one another by only one word or one sentence per problem and, in preliminary training, to teach a hierarchy of associations to these words or sentences.

In a series of experiments by Wittrock, Keislar, and Stern it was hypothesized if one knew the subjects' associations to these words, he could predict verbally mediated transfer, learning, and retention. One way to know many of the associations is to take unknown stimuli and associate a hierarchy to them. In the first study in the series (Wittrock, Keislar, and Stern, 1964), 52 kindergarten children were, over a period of three months, taught associations to the verbal cues used later in the experiment. By looking at pictures of 12 common objects and animals, and by hearing their French names pronounced aloud, each child was taught to say the French names whenever the appropriate picture was presented. Half of the 12 French names were masculine nouns and half were feminine nouns. After each child had learned to label the pictures, the next level of the hierarchy was taught. The children learned that each French name had an initial *la* or *le* sound. They were taught to say *la* or *le* and to discriminate *la* or *le* when a French name was spoken. Finally, they were taught to associate the words *la* and *le* with the word 'article.' During the experimental training all treatment groups were given a sequence of slides each of which showed three pictures—a model at the top and two alternatives below. The children were asked to select one of the two bottom pictures which matched the top picture in a certain way. The basis for matching was always the gender of the French name for the top picture. One of the alternatives at the bottom always had a masculine name and the other always had a feminine name. While they looked at each slide the verbal cues were presented. The children in Group I were told to press a button. In Group II the children were told the word 'article.' In Group III the children were told *la* or *le*, depending upon the correct basis for matching. In the fourth group the children were told the correct alternative.

The dependent variables were measured by learning and transfer tests given immediately and also three weeks later. The learning test consisted of items constructed from the six objects used during the experimental training. The transfer test used only the other six objects which had been named by the students during the preliminary training but had never been used during the experimental training. By analysis of variance and by a specific comparisons test, the mean of the group told *la* or *le* was statistically significantly greater $(p < .01)$ than any of the other three groups on the transfer test.

Apparently, after the preliminary associations were learned, transfer to new instances of the same concept was facilitated by explicit verbalization by E of the name for the correct concept, followed by practice and reinforcement for applying this label. The study indicated that kindergarten children may not learn and transfer if they are given only general or very specific cues or if they are left to discover answers on their own—at least when the stimuli are of common objects. It should be emphasized that all tests presented problems with no verbal cues. The child had to discover the correct basis for answering any set of ten or fifteen items. The study also indicated that whether or not discovery is effective may depend on the learner's history of associations to the items and the cues. A history of working with similar problems and similar materials may make discovery learning or reception learning a more effective way than the other to solve problems.

The second study in the series (Wittrock and Keislar, 1965) was performed with 160 second and third grade children and used the concepts color, size, shape, and number familiar to the children. The dependent variables were the same as those mentioned above, except that one which sampled transfer to new concepts was added.

By analysis of variance and covariance, both the group given the specific cue and the group given the concept cue did significantly better than the group given the most general cue. This was true on the tests of learning, transfer to new instances, retention, and the delayed test of transfer to new instances. None of the groups was any better than any other on the transfer to new concepts test. It seems that when the subject has a history of associations to cues, they help him eliminate many possible answers and mediate discovery on his own. At least he appears to be able to do this more readily with familiar materials of few dimensions than with comparable materials learned over a few days or months during an experiment. In both studies the group given the name for the concept did as well as, or better than, any of the groups.

In both studies, the most general cue was not effective on initial learning, retention, and transfer, including transfer to new concepts. This may simply mean that in order for the general members of a hierarchy to become effective cues in problem solving, some procedure other than what was used in this study must be attempted. With proper training, it may be possible to make these most general cues effective for transfer to quite different concepts than those learned in the experimental training.

From these two studies, it would appear that the subject's history and his associations to the terms E gives him are important variables. Certainly these associations plus those associations S has to the entire problem stimulus are variables which must be considered in future research.

Instructions. The studies grouped under the heading of Instructions differ from those under the Principles and Answers heading in two ways. First, they include among the independent variables vague or general cues. Second, they are taken from the literature on concept learning; but they are directly relevant to the learning by discovery hypothesis.

Maier (1930) studied the role of direction on reasoning and problem solving. His double pendulum problem was solved by eight of the 22 subjects in the Direction group. Only one of the 62 subjects solved the problem without the added cue ("Observe how easy the solution would be if you could only hang the pendulums from two nails on the ceiling"). Providing additional information here resulted in improving the problem solving process. Saugstad (1955) showed that performance on these problems can be improved if availability or prerequisite associations is induced.

Luchins (1942), in another well-known study, showed that a general cue, "Don't be blind," increased the problem-solving of the adult subjects, but not of school children. Here a very general cue changed negative transfer, which was produced by working six problems of one type, into positive transfer for problems seven and eight. However, the sentence was not effective with children.

Ewert and Lambert (1932) gave their subjects three cardboard disks, one in each of three circles drawn on a board. The three circles formed a triangular pattern. The cardboard disks were graduated in size and the object was to maintain the order of size within the stack and yet to transfer the disks one at a time, from one circle to another circle. One of the groups was given minimal instructions about the general rules of the game. A second group was told to try to find a general principle. A third group was given the principle in verbal form, while a fourth group was given the principle and a demonstration of how to solve a problem. The groups given the verbally stated principle did significantly better than the groups which were not given the principle.

Reed (1946a) investigated the effect of instructions on learning and retention of concepts. He found that instructions to learn the meaning of, as well as the name of, a stimulus produced a much higher rate of learning and degree of retention than did a set to learn only the names. The condition which produced the best learning did not involve giving the subjects detailed information about the meaning of the cards. However, the direction which he introduced did increase learning and retention. It seems that a minimal amount of direction improves performance over a situation which does not contain this type of verbal direction. Wittrock, in several experiments, found that with adolescents and with adults, a general cue which contains no information about the subject matter can still increase the learning of principles. This was true whether the subject matter was principles of economics (Wittrock, 1963b), Buddhism (Wittrock, 1963a), or history, American government, and English (Wittrock, 1962).

Underwood and Richardson (1956) studied concept learning as a function of instructions and of dominance level of concepts. Unrestricted instructions (UR) gave the subjects nothing about the nature of the concepts to be learned. They were told only that it would be a good idea to vary their responses from trial to trial. Partially restricted

(PR) instructions gave the subjects a class of responses needed to form the concepts. The experimenter probed the subjects about simple ways to describe common objects. Completely restricted (CR) instructions gave the subjects the six correct responses which they were allowed to keep before them and to study during the experiment. The results showed that the greater the amount of information given the subjects concerning the content or the nature of the concepts to be learned, the more rapid was the acquisition of concepts.

The above studies on instructions indicate that problem solving and concept learning can be facilitated by guidance upon discovery. In many instances, quite direct and specific guidance, which specifies the correct concepts, can also facilitate problem solving and concept learning. This is not to say that learning cannot occur incidentally or that it cannot occur without awareness or without instructions (Adams, 1957; Bugelski and Scharlock, 1952; Postman, 1964; Postman and Sassenrath, 1961; Sassenrath, 1962).

Verbalization by S. After reviewing Katona (1940) and Haslerud and Meyers (1958), Gagné and Smith (1962) studied the effects upon problem solving of two independent variables: Ss' verbalizations during practice, and instructions to find and to state a general principle. There were 28 ninth and tenth grade boys in the study. They were divided randomly into four groups which were composed from all possible combinations of the two, two factored independent variables (i.e., verbalizing versus nonverbalizing, solution set versus no solution set). The task was the three circle task used by Ewert and Lambert (1932). On transfer to new problems, the groups required to verbalize did significantly better than those who were not required to verbalize. This was true both in terms of number of moves and in terms of time. All other differences between pairs of groups were not statistically significant. They also found that the groups who were required to verbalize performed better than the nonverbalizing groups on a test of ability to state verbal principles. They summarize their results as follows: "The results appear to indicate that requiring Ss to verbalize during practice has the effect of making them think of new reasons for their moves, and thus facilitates both the discovery of general principles and their employment in solving successive problems" (Gagné and Smith, 1962, p. 18).

For the Future. The great variety of complex treatments, subject matter, students, and dependent variables used in the above studies on the independent variables makes it most difficult to compare results across studies. Any conclusions about learning by discovery are highly tenuous. However, several things can be learned from these studies and there are several possibilities for the future.

First, the results of a study should be generalized only to students, subject matter, and situations directly comparable to those sampled in the experiment. Although the future may show that broad general principles do encompass a variety of people and subject matter, the present state of the science warrants no such conclusion. Obviously, interactions among types of students, subject matter, and methods of instruction will not be found unless designs are used which will evidence them. With complex human behavior, we should expect these interactions to occur and measure them when they do occur.

The second thing to be learned from these studies is that future studies should give greater attention to individual differences and to the history of the learners. The effects of the treatments must be related to the learners' proactive influences. In a culture where children are customarily taught by reception rather than discovery, we should not be surprised if their histories are more influential than our brief treatments. Neither should we be surprised if a new discovery procedure is interesting and motivating, at least until the novelty wears thin.

The third thing to be learned is that considerable research on concept learning and problem solving is often relevant to the problems encountered in research on learning by discovery. For the future, researchers on discovery learning would do well to build on these results and procedures.

For example, Gagné (1962) has developed a model and a procedure that considers the history of the subjects, individual differences, knowledge and instructions, all important variables in learning by discovery. He reasoned that for the learner to perform on a dependent variable, certain knowledge is prerequisite and certain instructions from the experimenter are necessary. His term *knowledge* refers to information, ideas, etc., that are particular to a certain subject matter. His term *instructions* pertains to sentences which include information not peculiar to a certain subject matter. Instructions perform at least four functions. First, they help the learner to identify the required terminal performance. Second, they identify elements of the stimulus situation which are important. Third, they enhance recallability of learning sets. Fourth, they guide thinking. He introduces the history of the subject with the term *learning set*. Learning sets apply to subordinate classes of tasks necessary for the learner to be successful on the dependent variable, provided he is given instructions. These learning sets are hierarchically arranged. The lowest members of the hierarchy must all be present before more advanced members of the hierarchy can be performed. The lowest members mediate positive transfer to the higher levels. If one of the lower members cannot be recalled, transfer from one learning set to another would be zero. If the lower members can be recalled, transfer will range up to 100 per cent. Although one can question what Gagné means by one learning set being prerequisite to another, or being simpler than another, the results he obtains with this model are impressive.

For example, in the study by Gagné and Paradise (1961), they asked the question, "What would the individual have to be able to know how to do, in order to be able to perform this (new) task, being given only instructions?" (pp. 16–17). They studied the effects of mental ability factors and learning sets upon the solving of linear algebraic equations. Among the important findings were those which indicated that subordinate learnings sets mediate positive transfer to other members in the hierarchy. The proportion of transfer ranged from .91 to 1.00. They also predicted and found that while the correlation between relevant basic abilities and rates of attainment of learning sets progressively decreased at higher levels of the hierarchy, the correlation of basic abilities with achievement of learning sets increased at these higher levels. The correlation between rate of attainment and relevant basic abilities should decrease, according to Gagné and Paradise, because as one proceeds up the hierarchy, transfer depends increasingly upon the immediately subordinate learning sets or upon specific knowledge. The correlation between basic abilities and achievement of relevant learning sets should increase because, since the learning program is not perfect, high and low ability students will become more differentiated. This increase in the correlation indicates the ineffectiveness of the learning program.

Although again one could give other interpretations to these data and predictions, Gagné and his associates present an excellent model for much of the future research on learning by discovery. By analyzing complicated and hierarchically organized subject matter into its prerequisites and components, he has been able to produce impressive results on learning and transfer tests.

Stolurow and Bergum (1957) present a model which may also have usefulness in discovery learning. They tested the effects of different methods of training upon trouble shooting. They analyzed the symptom-cause and the cause-symptom relationships into their stimulus and response components. They described response sharing, that is, where one stimulus is associated with more than one response, and stimulus sharing, where several stimuli are associated with one response. Last, they described stimulus-response sharing, or many stimuli to many responses, where several stimuli are each associated with each of several responses. They argued that before one can learn new associations, such as symptom-cause relationships, he might have to engage in stimulus learning or response learning. Stimulus learning involves differentiating the occasion for one rather than another response. Response learning involves the acquisition of the response repertoire. By analyzing the complex problem of trouble shooting into its stimulus and response learning components, and by hypothesizing that learning would be more or less difficult in relation to the associations in the learner's repertoire, they predicted and found an interaction between the learner's experience with learning style and the direction of association, and the conditions under which he would acquire generalized habits of learning. This type of careful analysis of stimulus and response factors, as well as the analysis of the learner's history, is greatly needed in studies of learning by discovery. However, as discussed earlier, in discovery learning one probably should not think of particular responses. Instead, classes of responses or answers is probably a more useful term because the particular form of the overt response may not be crucial to learning.

Although many more lessons can be learned from the studies on the independent variables, only two more will be mentioned here. Treatments should be designed to vary one element at a time. If an experiment is performed, its treatments should differ from one another in a meaningful way. It does no good to know that a discovery treatment is more effective than a rote treatment if the two treatments are not systematically related to each other. This is more than a problem of labeling treatments. Perhaps standardized treatments, as suggested by Della-Piana and Eldredge (1964), are needed.

The last lesson to be mentioned here is that the rote versus discovery issue is a meaningless one and should be replaced by several, more useful issues. One way to rephrase part of the issue would be to look at the effects of the teacher's use of language. Discovery could be viewed as a condition to contrast with uses of different verbal stimuli. Another part of the issue is the use of language by the subject. Each of these fundamental issues could be studied as to the effects of the rate, variety, sequence, etc., of presenting stimuli in interaction with the subject's history. When supplemented with an analysis of the dependent variables discussed below, the result should be a substantial improvement in research, and should bring the study of the independent variables of learning by discovery into the areas of research on concept learning and problem solving.

However, the problems of studying the independent variables of discovery learning will not be solved simply by joining the ranks of researchers on problem solving. When Duncan (1959) reviewed the recent research on problem solving, and Schulz (1960), the research on transfer of training, they indicated a need for studies to relate stimulus events as antecedents to behavior as consequents. Duncan writes, "Problem solving particularly needs research to determine the simple laws between dimensionalized independent variables and performance" (1959, p. 426). Schulz writes:

> Until we know what the variables are that cause problem solving behavior to vary in predictable ways, our teaching is less likely to be as effective as it might be. Therefore, it is prerequisite to our success as educators that we discover the laws which describe the functional relations between various kinds of antecedent variables and later problem solving performance (1960, p. 62).

The problems of doing research on the independent variables of learning by discovery are not yet solved by researchers in problem solving.

The Dependent Variables

The lack of empirical research. Needless to say, the learning by discovery researchers have done almost no empirical work on the analysis or measurement of dependent variables *per se*. They have been interested in a few variables, described vaguely as transfer, motivation, and ability to solve problems. These variables tend to differ widely across studies. For example, Kersh (1958) was interested in the methods the students used to solve problems, not the number of correct answers. Some researchers are interested in the child's ability to solve examples of previously learned concepts. Others are interested in the child's ability to solve problems much different from those he encountered during the experiment. Gagné and Brown (1961) were interested in the child's ability to derive formulae, rather than in his ability to solve numerical problems. The identification and measurement of the results of discovery learning is a necessary prerequisite to improving research on the independent variables. There is no greater problem in the area today.

For the Future. A multi-dimensional analysis of the outcomes of learning is sorely needed. See Cronbach's chapter in this volume for his identification of important dependent variables. In addition to the common and overlapping dependent variables of transfer, motivation, and ability to solve problems, at least the dependent variables of savings and time should be included whenever possible. Savings can be quantified. It is important that a student be able to use the subject matter to further his learning in the same area and to avoid problems in that area.

The measurement of the dependent variables is also important. Della-Piana and Eldredge (1964) argue for standard types of treatments which could be used to compare one mode of presentation with another. One can argue for the development of standardized measures of dependent variables used in learning by discovery. At present there are very few of these types of measures of achievement available to researchers in learning by discovery.

Gagné, Foster, and Crowley (1948) reviewed the area of the measurement of transfer of training and summarized the methods which have been used to quantify transfer of training. Not much of a creative thrust has been made in the measurement and evaluation of the differences among groups of learners after they have been exposed to complex instructional treatments. Glaser (1963) has written about this problem. Criterion referenced tests and measures designed to discriminate among treatments should be developed. These would be useful in experiments on learning by discovery.

DISCUSSION

At the beginning of this chapter it was stated that the independent–intervening–dependent variable framework helps one to explicate some of the complexities and inconsistencies in research on learning by discovery, and it helps one to develop suggestions for the future. Throughout the chapter, the framework has been applied and has been used to suggest improvements for the future. There is no reason to repeat all those suggestions here. Instead, an evaluation of the learning by discovery hypothesis will now be made.

The early simple conception of the hypothesis carried much surplus meaning. The early field theory-versus-connectionism controversy involved far more than discovery. In fact, one could argue that Thorndike's treatments which specified correct answers but not explanations left much room for student discovery. Field theory, which sometimes injected explanations and verbalizations of generalizations, left reduced opportunity to discover these verbalizations. The early conception of the hypothesis is no longer useful. It injected serious oversimplifications and ignored distinctions made later.

Since the early conception of the problem, confusion has existed among researchers about the complex nature of the issues in the hypothesis. The framework for this chapter has helped to expose some of those issues. Induction-deduction is a variable commonly confused with the discovery hypothesis. The learner can discover from either very general or very specific cues, one presented before the other. When applied to independent variables, induction-deduction pertains to the order in which general and specific cues are presented. When applied to hypothetical, logical processes, the learner can still discover a principle or generalization by either procedure. It depends upon where he starts and what he is asked to discover.

Whether he succeeds or fails in the process is not only a function of the treatment he is given, but it is also a function of his individual history. Proaction and individual differences have complicated the simple, early hypothesis.

Discovery as a Way to Learn

Perhaps the most useful distinction which the framework helps one to make is that learning by discovery denotes both a way to learn and an objective of learning. As a way to learn or to teach, discovery may not be an effective treatment when measured by the criteria of learning, retention, transfer, affectivity, and time. It depends upon what is meant by learning by discovery as a treatment. The treatment may refer to the way a teacher uses verbal stimuli—their sequence, nature, and variety. It may also refer to the learner's use of verbal stimuli. The result also depends upon the dependent variable sample, e.g., learning or transfer.

For example, as a way to learn a few specific associations, discovery may be inferior to more highly directed procedures. When the criterion is the learning of concepts and hierarchically ordered subject matter, discovery may fare better. If the criteria are transfer to new concepts, originality, and learning by discovery, learning by discovery as a treatment may fare well. There are no carefully gathered experimental data on this last issue. As Bruner stated the hypothesis quoted above, it has not been given a fair test. In no experiment has anyone carefully studied learning by discovery both as a treatment and as a dependent variable. Both conditions are necessary to test the practice hypothesis.

As a way to learn, discovery may also produce definite, positive or negative affectivity, and may not produce an affective loading near zero. Along with the other above mentioned tenuous hypotheses, this last one depends upon the individual learners and upon the subject matter.

From the above analysis of discovery as a way to learn (a treatment), there emerge several learning by discovery hypotheses, not just one. Research is needed upon each of them and upon the fundamental psycholinguistic variables relevant to discovery learning. Many of the discovery enthusiasts have quickly rejected or disparaged E's use of verbal statements of rules and principles. These variables should be studied. The literature on concept learning and problem solving indicates they are important for many outcomes.

Discovery as an Objective of Learning

As an objective, ability to discover is important in its own right; this is a value judgment. As an agreed-upon objective for teaching and learning, we can still ask whether learning by discovery as a treatment is as effective at producing learning by discovery as are other treatments. In other words, is practice an important independent variable? Many researchers feel that it is. Many others, including the author, feel that alternatives to practicing the terminal behavior deserve study. Perhaps a sequence of verbal materials, given with some practice at discovering would be better than an equal amount of time devoted exclusively to practice at discovering. Again it probably depends on many subject and subject matter factors. One can scarcely do better than to agree with Bruner that the practice hypothesis is an important one, and it should be tested—in the schools.

Summary

The aging but still elusive learning by discovery hypothesis has outlived its usefulness to researchers. It has not been one hypothesis but a set of several hypotheses. The practice hypothesis, discussed in detail above, is only one of this set of hypotheses. Embedded within the discovery hypothesis were other issues, such as: (1) rote versus discovery learning; (2) student control versus teacher control of the rate and order of presenting stimuli; (3) inductive versus deductive learning; (4) interaction of methods of learning with individual differences among students; (5) the order of presenting to students rules, principles and more specific information and problems; (6) the teacher's classroom use of verbal abstractions; (7) the separation of independent and dependent variables; (8) the operational definition of terms, especially of the dependent variables such as transfer and savings; and (9) the teaching of rules and generalizations.

We have progressed beyond the rote versus discovery issue. We should be directing our energies to operationally defined issues and hypotheses, such as number 9 above. Let's take one important objective now commonly cited in research on discovery but amenable to research on the teaching of rules. It is the ability to go beyond the data or to go beyond the specifics.

In more mundane terms, this is usually called positive transfer. One issue immediately follows: How can a student be taught rules, principles, and problem solving strategies which will transfer positively to new problems or show a savings in further learning? Now theories of transfer and of teaching can be applied to this operationally definable problem. We might investigate the savings and transfer obtained from hierarchically organized verbal stimuli and sequences taught to students. Instead of disparaging the teacher's use of verbal abstractions, we could now analyze them and study their effects upon learning as these effects interact with individual differences among students and among ways to learn. For example, one interesting conjecture is that there is an interaction between the specificity of the information taught to students and the amount of transfer obtained. A method which produces sizable results upon the learning of a few specific associations may produce only a limited amount of transfer. Methods which produce transfer may be slow at producing learning of a large number of specific associations.

The problems involved in the teaching of rules and principles are basic to the study of education. The area of rule and principle learning is open and ready for creative, theoretical and empirical research.

It remains to be seen whether the above conceptualization of discovery learning as one issue in the teaching of rules and principles will be more productive for research than was the discovery hypothesis. But we should have learned not to repeat two mistakes of the researchers on learning by discovery. When we state an hypothesis we should make explicit its independent, intervening, and dependent variables. When we begin our research, it would be better to start with the problem, the teaching of rules and generalizations, rather than to begin with a ready made solution to the problem, learning by discovery.

Chapter V

The Logic of Experiments on Discovery

LEE J. CRONBACH

IN SPITE OF THE CONFIDENT ENDORSEMENTS OF TEACHING THROUGH discovery that we read in semi-popular discourses on improving education, there is precious little substantiated knowledge about what advantages it offers, and under what conditions these advantages accrue. We badly need research in which the right questions are asked and trustworthy answers obtained. When the research is in it will tell us, I suspect, that inductive teaching has value in nearly every area of the curriculum, and also that its function is specialized and limited (Cronbach, 1963, pp. 378–382). The task of research is to define that proper place and function.

Honest research is hard to do, when learning by discovery is the battlecry of one side in the ardent combat between educational philosophies. We have, on the one hand, the view of education as cultural transmission, which hints strongly that it is the teacher's job to know the answers and to put them before the pupil. On the other, we have the view of education as growth, arguing that the only real and valuable knowledge is that formulated by the pupil out of his own experience. The second position, which appeals to liberal, humanitarian, and instrumentalist biases, has a long history. In the last thirty-odd years the bias favoring do-it-yourself learning has been very strong, as educators and psychologists have united in attacks on teacher dominance and pupil conformity. Consequently, we have had almost none of the cut-and-thrust debate needed to define issues and to expose implications or fallacies of the evidence.

It is time to put aside the polemic question, Is teaching through discovery better than didactic teaching? (*Didactic* is perhaps not the ideal brief label for the pedagogy in which the teacher sets forth knowledge, but among the words that come to mind it has the advantage of being least value-loaded.) We shall have to ask subtle questions and exhibit both patience and ingenuity in unravelling them. How to frame research studies to get the right information is not at all clear; sometimes we can meet one of the supposed requirements of research design only at the expense of another, and if all my recommendations were to be followed, research would become impossibly elaborate. One of the hopes is that discussion among investigators and educational innovators can generate some agreement as to which subquestions and which improvements in research design should have priority in the next stages of investigation.

I propose that we search for limited generalizations of the following form:

> With subject matter of this nature,
> inductive experience of this type,
> in this amount,
> produces this pattern of responses,
> in pupils at this level of development.

Since this sentence constitutes an outline of the remainder of my paper, let me clarify each segment of it before I proceed.

First, the subject matter. Surely we cannot generalize over all educational content indiscriminately, yet the literature on discovery reads as if a general conclusion is sought. Moreover, unless learning tasks are comparable to those of the classroom, they are unserviceable as a basis for educational recommendations.

Second, the type of training. I can amplify this sufficiently for the moment by referring to type and amount of guidance as a significant aspect of the training.

Third, the amount of inductive experience. I have no faith in any generalization upholding one teaching technique against another, whether that preferred method be audiovisual aids, programmed instruction, learning by doing, inductive teaching, or whatever. A particular educational tactic is part of an instrumental system; a proper educational design calls upon that tactic at a certain point in the sequence, for a certain period of time, following and preceding certain other tactics. No conclusion can be drawn about the tactic considered by itself.

Fourth, the pattern of outcomes. Education has many purposes, and any learning experience must be judged in terms of all those goals. To take a simple example, there must exist some method of teaching arithmetic that produces graduates who compute brilliantly—and who hate all work involving numbers. It would be improper to advocate this method on the basis of research that considers only its effect on computational skill. It is no defense for the advocate to say that computation is the only objective that concerns *him*. If he recommends an educational change, it is his responsibility to consider how that change will affect all the outcomes that reasonable men consider important.

Fifth, the pupils. I suspect that inductive teaching is more valuable for some learners than others, and that we should not generalize over all pupils.

As I go on to illustrate wise and unwise research decisions, I am restricted by the content of past, studies. In these studies the learner is nearly always to discover some simple connection or, at best, a formula or inductive generalization. When a writer argues that discovery is a thrilling personal experience he seems to have in mind the sort of startling reorganization of interpretation illustrated on the grand scale by Kepler, and on a lesser scale by Kekulé. These "retroductions" (Hanson, 1958) are Discoveries that appear to be quite different psychologically from discoveries of simple regularities. Big-D discoveries are infrequent even in the life of the scientist. I doubt that the pupils in today's innovative classroom are having many big-D experiences, and I doubt that the psychologist will be able to arrange conditions so that Discovery will occur while the subject is under his eyes. Hence my account is limited to research on little-d discovery. We should not, however, allow ourselves to think that in these studies we are learning about the effect of retroductive discovery. (E. R. Hilgard draws my attention to the fact that we are equally without research on a "really fine kind of discovery: discovering problems rather than discovering solutions" [Mackworth, 1965]).

SELECTION OF LEARNING TASKS

Since the question before us is educational, experimental tasks ought to have psychological properties closely similar to those of educational subject matter. Discovery surely becomes more valuable as the linkage between the stimulus and the correct response becomes more rational. Rationality is at a maximum in tasks where the correct response can be deduced from the givens of the problem or from a network of established ideas. For example: finding the number of diagonals from any vertex in a polygon of n sides. Once a child understands the question, he can confirm or infirm any rule he proposes, with no help from an instructor. While the younger child confirms empirically, the older child can see that the rule is a logical necessity. There is a natural (but not necessarily a logical) linkage in tasks where the response has a readily discerned consequence. Do apples taste good? The answer might in principle be deduced from the chemistry of plants and the physiology of taste, but in practice the discovery is made through a provisional try followed by natural reinforcement. At the opposite extreme from rationality are those tasks where the S-R linkage is arbitrary, so that the person can know what is correct only because the experimenter tells him so. An example is Duncan's experiment (1964), where a digit is presented along with three adjectives and the learner has to guess which adjective has been selected randomly as correct. Discovery at this point has been reduced to sheer trial and error.

Learning by discovery is said to teach a sort of intellectual self-reliance. The child who understands the structure of the number system believes that he can work out subtraction combinations for himself, believes that he can check his own answers, believes that the answer to an arithmetic problem is always the same, believes (more broadly) that any new quantitative problem has a discoverable solution. Piaget and Smedslund (Ripple and Rockcastle, 1964) consider intellectual self-regulation—checking the consistency among one's beliefs before converting a belief into action—to be the chief ingredient in operational thought. Where inductive teaching is to promote intellectual self-reliance, is it not obvious that it must use tasks whose answers are rationally determined? Where we want to teach an experimental attitude, must we not use tasks whose solutions are empirically confirmable? Arbitrary tasks cannot possibly generate the important attitudes sought in serious inductive teaching of educational content.

Many experimental tasks that have value for other problems seem too lacking in rationality for the proper study of discovery. The task of Wittrock et al. (1964) where the child selects a picture representing a *la* or *le* French noun is arbitrary; the child's task is primarily to discover what the experimenter has in mind. The rules and codes used by Stacey (1949), Haslerud and Meyers (1958), and others are likewise arbitrary. The subject has to detect a pattern or regularity, but the patterns change from example to example. The patterns are not 'principles' (even though mistakenly given that name), and they do not fit into any system of mutually supporting propositions.

If we are concerned with the implications of discovery for understanding a discipline, the task should be part of a whole system of subject matter. The summation-of-series task of Gagné and Brown (1961) is well chosen. A solution called correct is correct in the eyes of God as well as of the experimenters. The training tasks are representative of series problems and, insofar as one task can be representative, of all mathematics. But we should not generalize from mathematics to other school subjects. If it is proposed, for example, to apply inductive methods in history by requiring pupils to draw conclusions from source documents, then there had better be experiments with such lessons. We might learn, for example, that the pupil who forms his own historical generalizations becomes much too confident of the dependability of his inferences, since social data cannot be counted on to contradict an error unequivocally.

Type of Teaching

With regard to experimental treatment, the first requirement is that each treatment be given a fair chance to show what it can do; by and large, educational innovators have violated this rule. What usually happens is something like this: John Doe contends that programmed presentation of college geology is better than conventional lectures. He assembles a writing team and spends two years drafting material, editing every sentence, trying it on pilot classes, and revising. Then Doe runs a grand experiment in which 10 classes are taught with his material, while 10 classes take the regular lecture course. Unless his writers were painfully inept the test scores favor the new method, and unless Doe is a very saint of an experimenter, he concludes that programmed instruction is more effective than the lecture method. Doe *has* shown that his programs give better results than the lectures in their casual, unedited, tired old form, but the outcome would very likely to have been reversed if he had put the same two-year effort into tuning up the lectures. Nothing of explanatory value has been learned from his study.

Studies of discovery have rarely given didactic instruction a fair shake. The control group suffers from one or another of the following impediments in nearly every study:

1. **Shorter training time.** In the Hilgard-Irvine-Whipple (1953) study with Katona's card tricks, the students who developed the rule for themselves worked with the material two to four times as long as those given the rule; they had to, to reach the criterion. In such a case, differences in transfer scores are interpretable only if the discovery group, with its greater opportunity to learn, *fails* to surpass the contrast group.

2. **Limited goals.** The nondiscovery group is often led to think that manipulation of a formula is the only goal of instruction. Any insight into the nature of the formula is incidental rather than inten-

tional learning for them, whereas the discovery group is oriented toward the meaning of the formula. Consider the Gagné-Brown experiment. The rule-and-example group practiced substituting numbers in the formulas for summation of various series, and was trained to criterion on that limited decoding skill. The guided-discovery group was taught to look for a pattern relating the terms of a particular series and the corresponding sums, to use a symbolic code for term number, term value, and sum, to translate the pattern into a symbolic formula, and then to substitute numbers into the formula. These students met a four-fold criterion. Gagné and Brown are right in asserting that instructional effectiveness depends more on what is learned than on method of instruction, but their study is interpreted by them and others as supporting the *method* of guided discovery. For a fair test of the value of discovery, their rule-and-example program should have explicated the structural relationships that the discovery group was led to find for itself, and these relationships should have entered the end-of-training criterion for the rule-and-example group. (Note that my comments on this aspect of the Gagné-Brown study do not agree with those in Wittrock's paper (pp. 52–54).)

Mental set is an important variable in the training, as we see in the Hilgard experiment. One of his treatment groups was shown how to find the rule in one card-trick problem after another, but often the student who found a rule set about at once to memorize it. Because no one had conveyed to him that he was supposed to learn the rationale and the rule-finding technique, he put them out of his mind. Rarely is the experimental subject told, even in general terms, what transfer tasks constitute the objectives of instruction. Keeping the objectives of instruction secret from the learner is pedagogically unsound, and an experiment where this is done is an improper base for educational generalizations.

3. **Rote instruction.** The McConnell (1934) studies of arithmetic and others like it allegedly compare discovery with didactic teaching—but note these excerpts from McConnell's description of the second method: "The [number fact] is identified by the teacher dogmatically and autocratically. There is a studious effort to keep the child from verifying the answers. He will not know why $8 + 5$ is 13. [The method] does not tolerate concrete teaching, discovery, or insightful manipulation." Thiele (1938) shows a similar exaggeration; his nondiscovery group was given "isolated facts as though each fact had no relation to any other fact taught." Such experiments with nonrational drill may once have been justified by the challenge of Gestalt theory to that of

Thorndike (as it stood before he introduced "belongingness" as a principle in 1932), but they are not pertinent today.

Didactic teaching can and should develop meaning out of concrete experience and lay bare the mathematical structure behind an algorithm. Only comparing that kind of didactic teaching with discovery methods tells us anything of value today. We may note that Forgus and Schwartz (1957) found no difference at all between discovery and meaningful didactic teaching.

4. **Prejudicial data analysis.** As Olson (1965) points out, one of the studies most often cited as supporting discovery attains this result by illogical analysis of the data. Haslerud and Meyers (1958) had the student work with codes, each sentence requiring a different encoding rule. For any one person ten sentences were in this G form:

> Write each word backwards.
> (A) THEY NEED MORE TIME
>   YEHT DEEN EROM EMIT
> (B) GIVE THEM FIVE MORE

On the G rules the subject merely practiced encoding. The D form for the other ten sentences was the same except that the rule was omitted and had to be inferred from the A example. The G and D sentences were presented alternately in a single list. The G_1 score was the number of sentences correctly encoded from the G list; the D_1 score was the number of D sentences for which the code was found and applied. The transfer measure presented multiple-choice items like this:

> THEY CAME AND WENT   a. MNEN ECTE
>   ATA HWYD
>   b. DOBM RGHO
>   CKF DEIN
>   c. YEHT EMAC
>   DNA TNEW
>   d. HPZC OHAT
>   RRS FSHZ

One of the four alternatives is a transformation of the given sentence by a rule that was in either the G or D list during training. The G_2 score was the number of items based on G rules where the subject chose the correct alternative, and the D_2 score was similarly based on the ten items involving D rules. The score means were as follows:

G_1	8.6	G_2	7.8	Difference	—0.9
D_1	5.4	D_2	8.0	Difference	2.7

The Haslerud-Meyers report gives these facts, but puts all the emphasis on the difference scores. The authors first run a significance test to show that the mean difference for the discovery group departs from zero. This is wrong for many reasons, not the least of which is that with a free-response first test and a multiple-choice second test, one would expect a gain of 2.5 points among persons performing entirely at random. But the more fundamental error is to use difference scores at all. Test 2 is the only measure that is operationally the same for both groups and therefore the only fair basis for comparison. The difference of 0.2 points is trivial and nonsignificant. The much-cited conclusion, based on the difference in difference scores, arises simply because the D_1 task was much harder than the G_1 task, and so there was lots of room for an increase from D_1 to D_2.

I turn now to a pervasive dilemma in experimental design and analysis. Shall we train every subject to criterion under both D and G methods, in which case the D training ordinarily gets more time to produce its effect? Or shall we equate time, and if so, how shall we treat the nondiscoverers? In the latter design an average over the whole D group, while assessing the net utility of the treatment, has no explanatory value. Using a principle one has discovered is one thing; performing on a problem whose principle was not discovered during training is another. We might discard those who fail to discover, but that biases the experiment by throwing out the weaker members of the experimental group. To pair experimental and control subjects and to discard every nondiscoverer along with his opposite number in the control group is better, but places too much faith in our imperfect matching. I am inclined to think that transfer data for all subjects have to be analyzed in a way that takes initial scores into account. One possibility is to treat separately the discoverers in the D group and the nondiscoverers, since their transfer scores have different meanings. I am not content with this resolution of the difficulty, however, since there are probably degrees of discovery and nondiscovery (cf. Travers, 1964, p. 498).

One further complication. Surely it is good pedagogy to apply a further treatment to the child who fails to discover. In most studies prior to 1960, the subject who could not discover the answer simply left the problem unsolved. We may contrast this with Baddeley's little study (1963), where, after a minute of effort to unscramble an anagram, the unsuccessful subject was given the answer and went on to another anagram. Interestingly, his subjects later recalled more of the answers given to them than of the answers they had worked out for themselves. The finding, like Kersh's (1958), begins to make a case for learning by trying to discover and failing! Or, at the very least, suggests an aspect of the discovery treatment that has been given very little attention.

The fact that experiments are often loaded against the nondiscovery group leads naturally to a recommendation to make the discovery and didactic treatments alike in every respect but one, but this is too facile a recommendation, as can be seen if we think further about duration of training. Suppose we agree that the discovery instruction is to continue until nearly all the pupils pass a criterion test. Then there is no way to make the treatment uniform even for members of that treatment group. A certain child reaches the criterion early: if we terminate his training we allow him less training time than others; if we have him work on additional relevant problems, he encounters content others in his group do not. It is even less possible to hold constant the experience of different groups. The didactic group can be expected on the average to master the solution earlier. Do we shorten their instruction? Give them more problems on the same rule at the risk of boring them? Take them on to additional rules? Whatever we do, it is clearly impossible to give desirable instruction for each group while keeping all variables constant save one.

I doubt that any recommendation will fit all studies, but my inclination is to fall back on optimization within a fixed time. In education, a certain amount of time is allocated to a particular course, and experimentation should tell us how to use that time (cf. Lawrence, 1954). I would fix a certain period of instruction, say, 400 minutes, and compare two styles of instruction by arranging the two best instructional plans we can within that time limit. For style A, then, we have to select subject matter suited to that style, arrange whatever length and spacing of instruction fits that style, and similarly adjust explanations, reinforcements, etc. Likewise for style B. In the Gagné-Brown summation task, for example, I can imagine that the series problems used to develop insight by a rule-and-example style would differ from the set of problems best suited to the discovery style. If so, not even the content studied would be held constant.

Have I now completely contradicted my criticism of experimenters who confound other variables with discovery? I think not. An educational procedure is a system in which the materials chosen and the rules governing what the teacher does should be in harmony with each other and with the pupil's qualities. If we want to compare the camel with the horse, we compare a good horse and a good camel; we don't take two camels and saw the hump off one of them. My objection is to didactic treatments that do not use sound didactic pedagogy. Wherever we can reasonably predict that giving a concrete experience or explaining clearly or stating the aims of instruction will make the didactic teaching more potent, we should adopt that good procedure. We should likewise optimize the discovery treatment in *its* own terms, though it is impossible to adjust all the parameters experimentally. When the study is finished, and style A produces the better result, a colleague can always argue that a change in one another parameter would have reversed the result. That trouble we can never escape. Even after the most highly controlled experiment, our colleague can contend that style B would have been superior if one of the controlled parameters had been held constant at a different level.

On the whole, I would favor more attention to comparisons of different inductive procedures than to further studies with a didactic contrast group. Experiments have shown a good deal about how to optimize didactic procedures, but there has been little analytic work on discovery methods. The study of Hilgard, Edgren, and Irvine (1954) where different groups were led to the solution in different ways is, I think, unique. We have seen useful studies on degree of guidance, but there has been less attention to the character of the guidance. We have some studies where the instructor gives hints about solution of the problem at hand (e.g., Gagné and Brown), others where the instructor gives hints about information-processing technique for solutions (Corman, 1957; Wickelgren, 1964), and, in the Hilgard studies, didactic teaching of an algorithm for generating (discovering?) a solution to a certain type of problem.

An important aspect of the treatment is the extent to which the pupil puts what he discovers into words. The instructor may or may not urge the learner to formulate his generalization in words and may or may not monitor the formulation for correctness. Closely related is the choice of criterion for deciding that a pupil has reached the solution and can go on to new work. A discovery emerges through several stages, and one can solve quite a few similar problems before he consolidates the intellectual basis for the solution. It is hard to say which decision on these points would make for the best inductive teaching; right now the need is to make an explicit decision in the experimental plan and to report it clearly. The Gagné-Smith (1962) study is a model in this respect. It puts considerable substance behind George Stoddard's famous remark that we learn not by doing but by thinking about what we are doing.

I shall draw attention to just one more of the variations in teaching procedure that must be studied. The experimental psychologist has invariably studied discovery by the isolated learner. He arranges conditions so that the learner cannot profit—or be handicapped—by what other members of the class do and say. Educators, however, are concerned with group instruction in which many pupils face a problem together and all of them throw their partial insights into the discussion. The teacher may lead out one pupil Socratically; if so, are the others discovering vicariously or are they learning a solution given to them? Studies of isolated learners tell us nothing about the effect on bystanders or those who share a discussion. There have been some controlled studies of group problem-solving (Lorge et al., 1958) and team-learning (Glaser, Klaus, and Egerman, 1962), but they are rather remote from our present topic. I have seen no studies of inductive teaching that analyze the group process and its effects on pupils who play different roles.

EXTENT OF INDUCTIVE TEACHING

Educational recommendations seek to optimize the student's development over a long time span. The educator is not nearly so concerned with the mastery of a single principle as with the student's cumulative development of insight and skill. Studies of inductive teaching have generally employed very brief instruction, yet the recommendations apply to whole courses or whole curricula. I am dubious about such extrapolation, and join Carroll (1963) in urging studies of instruction continued over a substantial time span.

Even as small experiments, the discovery studies have been too miniature. Typically, there is an hour of training and one delayed transfer test. But consider the moral of Duncan's study (1964) with five consecutive days of work and a new learning task each day. He found negative transfer from Day 1 to Day 2, and positive transfer thereafter. A study confined to two days would have given a false conclusion. Something like a minimum length for an educational experiment is seen in Kersh's 1964 study with 16 hours of instruction and McConnell's with 35–40 hours (1934).

I am impressed by the possibility that some experience in discovering principles in a field of knowledge will radically alter the relation the learner perceives between himself and the knowledge, and his way of behaving when he forgets a solution or encounters an unprecedented problem. I offer the hypothesis, however, that this can be accomplished by devoting only a small fraction of the instructional time to inductive procedures.

To illustrate, let me offer a hypothetical plan for teaching cooking; if nothing else, this will provide relief from too much talk of mathematics and physics. Although recipes can be discovered or invented, I would start by giving experience in following recipes, along with reasons for measuring exactly and following directions. This is didactic teaching. The pudding scorches if not stirred according to directions, and the girl discovers that authority was right in its warnings—but that surely is not what we mean by a discovery approach. Around, perhaps, age 12, my class would experiment. The most elementary experiment might be to vary the amount of water added to one cup of pancake flour and observe the product under standard baking conditions. Trivial as this is, it can float profound enough notions in its wake: optimization, control of experimental conditions, interaction of variables, variation in criterion with the purpose or artistic taste of the judge, etc. While these simple experiments would initiate new thinking about recipes and cooking, I'd guess that six such parametric inquiries could teach nearly as much as six dozen. We might well shift back to prescription and demonstration when we teach the girl to make pie crust. Once she has some experimental background, she should have no difficulty in accepting the teacher's statement about what chilling the crust before rolling does to the texture, particularly if the teacher supports the statement with photographs and samples. We had her make discoveries to establish an attitude. This attitude, once established, can be sustained in subsequent didactic teaching. Later exposition can and should continually hold in view the experimental base of recipes, the legitimacy of adapting them to fit personal criteria, and other such concepts. From time to time there will need to be further experimentation, in inventing recipes, for example. When I propose that some small fraction of the course use discovery methods, I am not saying 'and let the rest of the course remain as it was.' On the contrary, I want didactic teaching modified to capitalize on the meanings and attitudes that were established through discovery.

Now there may be those who argue that a girl simply cannot fully understand the technique for making piecrust if she is told how to do it. Then what is the right experiment to determine how much discovery is needed? No short-term treatment can provide any evidence. Instead, we need experiments lasting at least a semester, and ultimately extending into studies of long-term growth.

Some of the advantages claimed for discovery in past experiments may arise from its novelty, and would vanish in a long-term treatment. Kersh (1958) had students learn or discover rules for summation of series and found a sleeper effect. Many in the discovery group had not mastered the rules at the end of the training hour, but a month later they outperformed an instructed group. Their side comments at the time of retest convinced Kersh that the discovery method had aroused such interest that they puzzled over the problem on their own time or looked up the answer in the library. Something similar was found in Kersh's 1962 experiment. I have long felt that this result can be attributed to novelty. I doubt that a discovery approach causes typical pupils to work on math for their own satisfaction when further problems are put before them day after day. I was therefore somewhat gratified by Kersh's 1964 experiment. After sixteen training sessions there was no difference between didactic and inductive groups in tendency to use the information outside of class. This supports my argument for reasonably extended studies.

Outcome Variables

Although in general writings we preach that education has many outcomes, this view is not much honored in planning research on educational learning. Only gradually are we moving away from the experimental paradigm in which amount or rate of learning is the sole dependent variable, and into a timid attempt to appraise educational development multidimensionally. Recent studies on discovery usually include both retention and transfer tasks, but even so the dependent variables are few compared to the outcomes that spokesmen claim for discovery methods. If we put together these various claims, we have a list somewhat like the following. To facilitate discussion I have offered a neat label for each class of outcomes, but I do not take the labels as constituting a taxonomy. I make no attempt to list all available illustrations of studies that assess a given outcome.

1. **Time to criterion.** Ordinarily, a criterion of performance on the tasks on which the subject is trained. May require ability to verbalize principle. (E.g., Gagné and Brown, 1961; Corman, 1957).

2. **Application.** Ability to solve problems where the discovered rule is relevant, for example, applying the formula for the sum of an arithmetic series to a set of numbers not encountered in training (e.g., Kersh, 1958).

3. **Retention.** Ability to recall a rule or to rediscover or reconstruct the rule (e.g., Ray, 1961). While delayed tests calling for verbal statement or application are common, the experimenter rarely finds out which mode of retention the subject is using.

4. **Conviction.** Adherence to a principle in a confusing stimulus situation where perceptual cues support an answer contrary to the principle. This type of resistance to extinction is best represented in Smedslund's study (1961) of the Piaget plasticine problem, where the tester palms a bit of material and so it seems that the conservation principle has been violated. Evaluation of conviction is also illustrated by the social psychologists' studies of propaganda and counterpropaganda.

5. **Rationale.** Understanding of the consistency between this principle and other concepts in the discipline. This might be exemplified by the child's explaining the equal-angle reflection of a billiard ball in terms of vectors. Interviews used by McConnell to obtain data on how pupils account for number facts are also pertinent.

6. **Epistemology.** Concept of the logic of the field of study, of the criteria of truth in the field; knowing, for example, the relative weight in judicial decisions of *stare decisis*, the election returns, and the judge's digestion.

The foregoing all represent different levels of knowledge of the subject matter.

7. **Specific rule-finding technique.** Ability to find rules for closely similar problems. Gagné and Brown develop this, for sum-of-series problems, by teaching the subject to line up in a table the term number, the term, and the sum to that point, and then to look for patterns. (See also Hilgard *et al.*, 1953.)

8. **Heuristics.** Ability to solve diverse problems in the discipline by having acquired general search and information-processing behaviors. E.g., Kersh's (1964) observations of attack on new problems.

9. **Aptitude.** Ability to learn subject matter in the field, whether by improved motivation or tendency to look for meaning or to criticize preliminary solutions. The changes that increase aptitude for learning from one type of instruction may not be helpful under other instruction. McConnell (1934) had taught number facts; as one measure of effect he presented a silent-reading lesson on two-digit subtraction and tested how well pupils could perform after that instruction. Since the operation took just twenty minutes, it is not a very adequate measure of learning ability. (Cf. Carroll, 1963, and Cronbach, 1965).

10. **Interest.** Concentration or voluntary effort at the time of training. Represented in Kersh's studies and in an attitude questionnaire of McConnell.

11. **Valuation.** Enduring interest, desire to study in the field, appreciation of the value of knowledge in the field.

12. **Creative urge.** Finding gratification in coping with problems, making efforts to construct knowledge for oneself, being less dependent on authority.

If, in referring to one of these objectives, I have cited no illustrative measurement of that objective, it is because no example in the literature on discovery is known to me. Hence our first conclusion is that many possible consequences of discovery have not been investigated. It seems to me that our interest should concentrate on those wide-ranging objectives that have to do with the pupil's broad educational development, rather than on his mastery of the particular lesson. I believe that inductive teaching is rarely superior to other meaningful teaching for putting across single generalizations, but I share the hope that it has special power to make a practicing intellectual out of the student. I want to see a heightened effort to collect data on theoretical understanding, heuristics, aptitude, valuation, creative urge, and epistemology. These are the variables least considered in the past research, and not surprisingly, since it is scarcely credible that a 50-minute experimental treatment will confer any of these benefits on the learner. Educational development comes through continued instruction with intellectually significant subject matter and that is what we should investigate.

Individual Differences

Discovery surely has more value for some pupils than for others. We should expect an interaction between the discovery variable and pupil characteristics, such that among pupils classified at the same level some respond better to inductive teaching and some better to didactic teaching. Perhaps the simplest question to begin with is the matching of instructional technique to age, or to some subtler measure of general development such as mental age, along the lines suggested by Osler's studies (Osler and Fivel, 1961: Osler and Trautman, 1961).

The interacting variables may have more to do with personality than with ability; I am tempted by the notion that pupils who are negativistic may blossom under discovery training, whereas pupils who are anxiously dependent may be paralyzed by demands for self-reliance. If that were to be found, however, it might imply that those of the latter group especially need training in intellectual independence rather than that they should be allowed to learn passively.

Ultimately, enough knowledge should permit us to say that a

fourth-grader with one profile of attainment needs discovery experience, whereas another will move ahead more rapidly on all fronts if teaching is didactic. A pupil who already accepts the meaningfulness of the number system and who has the confidence to look for generalizations on his own will only be delayed, I suspect, by having to figure out his own rules for multiplying decimals. Conversely, for the pupil who has plenty of arithmetic skill and very little understanding of the origin of the rules, nothing could be more important than some experience in discovering such rules.

Conclusions

The educational psychologist is torn between two responsibilities. His responsibility as educational specialist is to give schools advice on matters where the evidence is pitifully limited. His responsibility as scientist is to insist on careful substantiation of claims for each educational innovation. In education, unfortunately, there is great furore about whatever is announced as the latest trend, and the schools seem to career erratically after each Pied Piper in turn. This giddy chase keeps them almost beyond earshot of the researcher standing on his tiny, laboriously tamped patch of solid ground, crying in a pathetic voice, "Wait for me! Wait for me!"

Knowing that panacea-mongers always have the last word (even though the word changes from year to year), knowing that it will take decades at best for research to catch up with the claims, what stance are we to take? I suggest a judicious blend of these not-incompatible attitudes:

Hospitality to new ideas.

Skepticism about slogans and ill-defined terms, and about doctrines that promise to cure dozens of educational ills out of the same bottle.

Resolution to make research incisive rather than polemic, to clarify what about the new proposal is valid and why, rather than to score points for or against the innovation.

Willingness to advise educators along whatever path we can extrapolate from what we know, but to make clear that this advice is extrapolation and nothing more.

I have indicated a number of reasons why the existing research on inductive teaching has not begun to give the answers needed for firm recommendations to the schools. I have suggested that there will need to be more complex experiments, planned along quite different lines from those of the past literature. We have to explore a five-fold interaction—subject matter, with type of instruction, with timing of instruction, with type of pupil, with outcome. Understanding will be advanced by each experiment, so long as the investigator is open-mindedly curious, and keeps the whole problem in mind while interpreting his exploration of one small corner of it.

Chapter VI

Educational Objectives

THE SECOND SESSION OF THE CONFERENCE WAS CLEARLY THE ONE IN which the questions concerning dependent variables became paramount, sparked primarily by Cronbach's list of suggested outcomes. The discussion began with the suggestion that, in Piaget's terms, our profession is at the stage of concrete operations, while our educational criteria, our discussions, and our research are at the stage of formal operations. This is an enormous gap which we must bridge; and it is difficult enough to describe in some meaningful sense what we are doing in any particular teaching effort, much less try to contrast two different approaches to educating children. Furthermore, what we are teaching is an important variable in these discussions. The organization of one subject matter is different from that of others. We are in great need of some system of classification.

Following a lengthy and heated discussion about the role of the psychologist in the determination of educational goals, the extent to which consensus might be obtained on the desirability of each of Cronbach's outcome variables, and the relationship between individual differences and educational objectives, the group turned to consider the nature of goal-setting in teaching.

A distinction was made between seeing a 'shaping' process as the instructional approach most adequate for attaining the objectives of education, and seeing an 'opening-up' process as the appropriate technique for achieving those objectives. A shaping process is an attempt to elicit progressively from a child a complex of behaviors that sequentially approximate more and more closely a desired set of terminal behaviors. This is quite different from an opening-up process. The latter is an attempt to teach the child to match his own cognitive structures with what is 'out there' in the environment in order to provide greater meaning for him in what is around him. The instructional strategy is one of making it possible for the child to have experience in this match-making process. Part of the secret here is letting the child take a natural course: Let the child try whatever he has. Let the child go, see how what he has operates and where he must run up against a wall. Let him collect data and accommodate. The role of the teacher here is to suggest alternative models for the child to try out and to elicit from the learner his own hypotheses. A plea was made for opening up the learning process instead of focussing on the method and the objectives, whether discovery-like or not; we should simply watch the process.

The position just described was characterized by another discussant as the mind-unfolding approach, which leads to the dangerous notion that one is teaching for nothing. In reality, it would be quite possible to formulate in behavioral or operational terms the educational goals implicit in the opening-up process.

The first participant responded that the important concept here is that of openness. The child must negotiate this match-making between his internal structure and the external world for himself. It is not the same if someone else decides the sequence. If our goal is to get him to make this match, we will get more cues from the learner himself than we can from our theories. He knows what is bothering him. Just open up the situation and in effect let the learner be free to write his own program. Put him in what we might call a responsive environment. Let the teacher be sensitive to the ideas that are shaping up in the child's mind and reflect them back to the pupil, as it were, Socratically. Have him reexamine his position and then let him move on. The notion of education as engineering is severely limited; it ultimately leaves the child dependent on someone else. This participant wanted the child to know two things: (1) knowledge is a transient thing, and (2) he can participate in the process of creating knowledge and testing its validity for himself.

A second participant agreed. He too would leave substantive goals open. He preferred more abstract or stylistic kinds of goals. For example, the real pay-off for the student is the ability to evolve his goals as he goes along. In this sense, the goals are stated in terms of operating styles of students.

In rebuttal to this position it was suggested that there are different meanings to the term 'opening up.' One can open up the classroom situation in order better to observe what is going on. A very different meaning, however, refers to the process itself, that process called match-making by one participant. Such an inference about the kind of process that is going on may in turn be adopted as an indication of what ought to go on. Here, we dangerously leave the level of observation and enter the realm of the polemic. If our goal is, in fact, to study the process, we must close it up someway by means of some controls. Too much respect for style gets one into the position of the Chinese where style becomes everything. We must identify, however broadly, the changes in behavior desired and then train teachers to change behavior in this direction. The alternative is a romantic position of simply watching the kids and believing they will show us where they ought to go. It was pointed out that research on clinical versus actuarial judgments had pretty much shown that the more you put human judgment into the system, the more noise you get. We cannot attempt to adapt to every child from moment to moment without getting wild oscillations in the system—and poor education. The romantics have to recognize the kinds of teachers we actually have today, not the kind they would like to create. We have no alternative but to standardize.

Another participant denied that this position was romantic. It was the very antithesis of an undisciplined approach to education. This discovery approach to teaching requires preparatory work that is so detailed and so complex that neither most teachers nor most children can do it themselves. We must make provisions ('we' in the sense of those who developed curricula) for them in the form of the indexing of materials and the like. If this constitutes romanticism, then let it be considered a good word.

It was then suggested that we need not place all our trust on the ability of the teacher to diagnose what is happening inside the student. We must provide for both the teachers and the students a range of exemplars of what is to be learned, so that if the student falls off one track he can climb back on another. The point is not to avoid the stating of objectives, but to state them in a sufficiently broad sense and in a sufficiently general manner that different styles of learning are anticipated and hence planned for. One major advantage of the new curricula is that they do not provide one route, e.g., discovery, but rather are replete with multiple alternatives for different kinds of students, and, for that matter, teachers.

There are certain terminal behaviors which all agree must be mastered. It is important to distinguish between these kinds of goals, which Schwab calls *axiomatic*, and those goals which are not axiomatic. Critical evaluation of one's own thought processes is not generally seen by society as one of the axiomatic skills. If we see this as a goal, we then must make attempts to produce cultural change in order to make such objectives axiomatic. If teachers uncritically reinforce the dominant values of the present culture, they may unwittingly undermine the innovative features of new educational programs.

Since Glaser's definition of discovery implied the inevitability of mistakes, the group now turned to a consideration of the use of the term 'error.' The discussion began with an examination of the differences between correct and incorrect responses. One participant maintained that the desirable response to be elicited by the educational process is not necessarily the specific behavior of writing or speaking a given response, but rather internal changes of the concept or of the total linguistic structure of the child. He thus raised the issue of whether, in the programmed learning approach, what is being changed is a specific response, a particular conception, or the full linguistic structure of the child.

It was countered that we never teach a specific response, but rather a response class. That is, we intend to teach a general conception of which any specific response is but an instance, even though the shaping process in programmed instruction in fact forces one response. Unless the experimenter uses a transfer design, which is not in the typical program, he never knows whether it is the specific response or a response class which has been learned. Yet, the response is always seen by the experimenter as an instance of a response class. The idea of teaching a single response is a sterile one. This position was buttressed by a quote from Bradley that "associations marry only universals."

Error is also a function of the subject matter with which one is dealing. In some subject matter you can define quite easily and dichotomously the difference between right and wrong. In other subject areas, error points out simply the necessity for revision and emendation of a concept to be acquired. When there is no clear-cut correct response, error becomes a process of constant correction.

In the context of correction, the relationship between language and discovery becomes somewhat clearer. Because animals do not have language, there is in most experiments a finite set of contingencies, such as withholding reinforcement, when an incorrect response is made. Hence, in the language-free animal learning situation, you get either positive or negative instances, reinforcement or extinction. In contrast, with language comes correction, for the experimenter (teacher) can now say, not only Don't do that, but also Do this, instead!

There are circumstances in which the concept of error may become quite meaningless. These occur when the consequences of different courses of action are rendered equivalent, as in a setting where all behaviors are equally rewarded or unrewarded. For example, in Tolman's latent learning experiments, the rats have no sharp criterion of error when they are in their Platonic (unrewarded) state. Hence, they do not regard a blind alley as a wrong place to be. Error is the wrong word, until the individual is given or develops a specific sense of where he *ought* to be going. Thus, by loosening up the objectives, we lower the probability of nonreinforcing error, while increasing the likelihood of profitable, nonthreatening exploratory behavior. The error concept is irrelevant when the goal is exploration. There are 'goodies' at every turn. Here was another way of contrasting the implications of the shaping and opening-up positions.

PART THREE

THE CURRICULUM

Chapter VII

Some Elements of Discovery

JEROME S. BRUNER

I FIND THE TOPIC OF THE CONFERENCE A LITTLE BIT PUZZLING. I AM NOT quite sure I understand anymore what discovery is and I don't think it matters very much. But a few things can be said about how people can be helped to discover things for themselves.

A word of caution first. You cannot consider education without taking into account how a culture gets passed on. It seems to me highly unlikely that given the centrality of culture in man's adaptation to his environment—the fact that culture serves him in the same way as changes in morphology served earlier in the evolutionary scale—that, biologically speaking, one would expect each organism to rediscover the totality of its culture—this would seem most unlikely. Moreover, it seems equally unlikely, given the nature of man's dependency as a creature, that this long period of dependency characteristic of our species was designed entirely for the most inefficient technique possible for regaining what has been gathered over a long period of time, i.e., discovery.

Assume, for example, that man continues to adjust when he learns a language and certain ways of using tools. At that particular point, evolution becomes Lamarckian in the sense of involving the passing on of acquired characteristics, not through the genes, but through the medium of culture. On the other hand, it becomes reversible in that one can lose parts of culture in the way that Easter Islanders or the Incas of Peru seem to have lost some of their techniques. Culture, thus, is not discovered; it is passed on or forgotten. All this suggests to me that we had better be cautious in talking about the method of discovery, or discovery as the principal vehicle of education. Simply from a biological point of view, it does not seem to be the case at all. We ought to be extremely careful, therefore, to think about the range of possible techniques used for guaranteeing that we produce competent adults within a society that the educational process supports. Thus, in order to train these adults, education must program their development of skills, and provide them with models, if you will, of the environment. All of these things must be taken into account, rather than just taking it for granted that discovery is a principal way in which the individual finds out about his environment.

You make no mistake if you take the phenomenon of language-learning as a paradigm. Language-learning is very close to invention and has very little in common with what we normally speak of as discovery. There are several things about language-learning that strike me as being of particular interest. For example, in language-learning, the child finds himself in a linguistic environment in which he comes forth with utterances. Take the first syntactic utterances. They usually have the form of a pivotal class and an open class, like 'All gone, Mommy,' 'All gone, Daddy,' and 'All gone this; all done that.' The child, exposed linguistically to an adult world, comes forth not with a discovery but with an invention that makes you believe somewhat in innate ideas, in a linguistic form that simply is not present in the adult repertoire. Such language learning consists of invention or coming forth with grammar, possibly innately, that then becomes modified in contact with the world. The parent takes the child's utterances which do not conform to adult grammar. He then idealizes and expands them, not permitting the child to discover haphazardly but rather providing a model which is there all the time. It is the very earliest forms of language learning.

Thus, within the culture the earliest form of learning essential to the person becoming human is not so much discovery as it is having a model. The constant provision of a model, the constant response to the individual's response after response, back and forth between two people, constitute discovery learning guided by an accessible model.

If you want to talk about invention, perhaps the most primitive form of uniquely human learning is the invention of certain patterns that probably come out of deep-grooved characteristics of the human nervous system, with a lot of shaping taking place on the part of an adult. Consequently, wherever you look, you cannot really come away with a strong general consensus that discovery is a principal means of educating the young. Yet, the one thing that is apparent is that there seems to be a necessary component in human learning that is like discovery, namely, the opportunity to go about exploring a situation.

It seems to be imperative for the child to develop an approach to further learning that is more effective in nature—an approach to learning that allows the child not only to learn the material that is presented in a school setting, but to learn it in such a way that he can use the information in problem-solving. To me, this is the critical thing: How do you teach something to a child? I am going to say teach even though I know that the word teaching is not very fashionable anymore. We talk about the child learning, or about programming the environment so that he can learn, but I want to raise the following question: How do you teach something to a child, arrange a child's environment, if you will, in such a way that he can learn something with some assurance that he will use the material that he has learned appropriately in a variety of situations. This problem of learning by discovery is the kind that guarantees a child will use what he has learned effectively.

We know perfectly well that there are the good rote techniques whereby you can get the child to come back with a long list of information. This list is no good, however, because the child will use it in a single situation and possibly not even effectively then. There must be some other way of teaching so that the child will have a high likelihood of transfer. This problem of how to teach a child in such a way that he will use the material appropriately breaks down, for me, into six subproblems.

First, is the attitude problem. How do you arrange learning in such a way that the child recognizes that when he has information he can go beyond it, that there is connectedness between the facts he has learned with other data and situations. He must have the attitude that he can use his head effectively to solve a problem, that when he has a little bit of information he can extrapolate information; and that he can interpolate when he has unconnected material. Basically, this is an attitudinal problem—something that will counteract inertness in that he will recognize the material that he has learned as an occasion for moving beyond it.

Second is the compatibility problem. How do you get the child to approach new material that he is learning in such a fashion that he fits it into his own system of associations, subdivisions, categories, and frames of reference, in order that he can make it his own and thus be able to use the information in a fashion compatible with what he already knows.

Third involves getting the child activated so that he can experience his own capacity to solve problems and have enough success so that he can feel rewarded for the exercise of thinking.

Fourth is giving the child practice in the skills related to the use of information and problem solving. This is a highly technical problem that has to do not only with psychology but with learning those valuable short cuts within any field that we speak of as heuristics. I do not think that psychology stops at the level of psychological terminology, by any means, when we talk about learning in this particular context. But it is a feature of the thought process when a child learns some basic principles in mathematics he can use. Essentially, the tools of the mind are not only certain kinds of response patterns, but also organized, powerful tool concepts that come out of the field he is studying. There is no such thing, to be sure, as the psychology of arithmetic, but the great concepts of arithmetic are parts of the tool kit for thinking. They contain heuristics and skills that the child has to master and the great problem here is how do you give the child practice in the utilization of these skills, because it turns out that however often you may set forth general ideas, unless the student has an opportunity to use them, he is not going to be very effective in their use.

Fifth is a special kind of problem that I want to speak of as 'the self-loop problem.' The child, in learning in school settings, will very frequently do kinds of things which he is not able to describe to himself. We see this all the time in our new studies—namely, children who are able to do many kinds of things, for example, to handle a balance beam quite adequately by putting rings on nails on both sides of a fulcrum and getting quite interesting balances, but are not able to say it to themselves and convert this fact into a compact notation which they could hold in mind and push around. They can't, to use some barbarous computer language for a moment, develop adequate subroutines until they can get the responses right and describe them to themselves. Phil Rizzuto, playing baseball, does not field a grounder in a certain way because he understands the differential equation of how the ball will move. Rather he is combining one act with another; using a sensori-motor skill fitted to the situation. But there is also self-loop, a turning around on your own behavior, a chance for reflection. One goes from this skill at action to a deeper cognitive understanding. Various people have talked about this idea in different ways. I see it as a separate and special problem in discovery—discovering what it is that you've been doing and discovering it in a way that has productive power to it.

The sixth factor involves the nature of our capacity for handling information flow manageably so that it can be used in problem solving.

Let me spell out these six problems in more detail, giving examples from a curriculum on which we are now working.

First is the matter of attitude. We have talked about being corrupted by the vanity of teaching something oneself. I am going to illustrate some of that corruption not only because I am full of my own ideas but also because I have been teaching children, and one's little successes corrupt in a most intoxicating way. Discovery teaching generally involves not so much the process of leading students to discover what is 'out there,' but, rather, their discovering what is in their own heads. It involves encouraging them to say, Let me stop and think about that; Let me use my head; Let me have some vicarious trial-and-error. There is a vast amount more in most heads (children's heads included) than we are usually aware of, or that we are willing to try to use. You have got to convince students (or exemplify for them, which is a much better way of putting it) of the fact that there are implicit models in their heads which are useful.

Let me give you some cases, though you will have to forgive me while I tell you a little bit about the course that we are putting together. We are a group of anthropologists, psychologists, linguists, and so forth. This elementary-school course is one which we are at the moment trying out with children in the fifth grade, children who are 10 years old, taught in small groups of 10 children at a time. The course is on the emergence of man as a species. It deals with the kinds of things that lead to the humanization of the species *Homo*. It is based on a great quantity of powerful work that has been done in the last decade and a half, by linguists, by archaeologists, by physical anthropologists, and so on. It centers on four humanizing factors in man's history: tool-using, language, social organization, and the uniquely human child-rearing practices. We are operating on the assumption that in order for the children to understand what role these factors played in man's evolution, they have got to understand the nature of each one of the functions. We are, therefore, teaching them a good deal of anthropological linguistics, structural linguistics, with a main emphasis on the design features of the languages as you get it from Hockett, as well as on linguistic productivity. They get some idea of what a flexible tool system language is, and what it has done in the way of opening up the range for man coping with his environment. With respect to tool-using, what we are trying to do is to give them some sense of what a tool is, how a tool fits into a program of skill. I will tell you something about this particular thing later on. Social organization is the hardest part to teach. We are using a variety of techniques. We have some very high-brow game-makers who work mostly with generals in the Pentagon when they are not working with us. They have devised some games, one of them called Hunters. It is based on the way in which Bushmen operate in the Kalahari Basin in Southwest Africa. Their social organization has to do with hunting; therefore the game deals with social organization. The child-rearing section starts off with our making a census of the kids' skills, and analyzing when they learn certain kinds of things. It is centrally concerned with the idea of the human life cycle.

The course is based on a fair amount of contrasted material; we try to give them the sense of comparison of human languages with other forms of communication. We use also the social organization of modern Western man as compared to the traditional Eskimo to give them some sense of recognition of their own culture. We have a store of material on Bushmen as well. We also look at free-ranging baboons in East Africa. That is enough about the course for a moment.

Let me just say one thing about the attitude problem, to give you an example of how we try to have the children recognize that they can use their own heads in their own education. We wanted the children to learn that, generally speaking, one can reduce a language into what is called *type* and *order*. I, therefore, used a trick that I got from an experiment by my colleague, George Miller, which consists of the following. First write a sentence on the board. Then get the children to form similar sentences as follows:

The	man	ate	his	lunch.
A	boy	stole	a	bike.
The	dog	chased	my	cat.
My	father	skidded	the	car.
A	wind	blew	his	hat.

At this particular point, we have the children provide other sentences *ad libitum*. And they provide them. Sometimes they are wrong. Usually not. We then shift them to the following puzzle: How is it that one can go from left to right across the sentences in practically any row and still come out with a sentence: The boy chased the cat; A father chased a lunch; The man stole my bike; A father stole his hat. Some of the sentences are rather silly, but clearly sentences. Soon they will say things like, There are five places and you can put lots of things in each place. But which kinds of words will fit into each column? Type and token begin to emerge as ideas. Now we reach a very critical point. Ask, for example, whether they can make up some more columns. One child proposed the following, something that put the class on a new level of attitude toward the use of mind. He said that there is a 'zero' column that could contain the word 'did.' I asked what other particular words this column could contain. The children said, 'did,' 'can,' 'has.' This was the zero column. Then one of the pupils said that this did not quite fit and that you would have to change the word in the third column too but it would not be very much of a change. They were ready and willing now to get into the syntax of the language, to invent it afresh. They talked about the family of words that would fit and that two columns affected the families each could carry. Only then did we introduce some terminology. We talked about *type* and *order*, and that in sentences there were words that were types and they appeared in a certain permissible order. One of the children said of types, "They're called parts of speech. A noun, for example, is a 'person, place or thing.'" To produce a pause, we asked about 'dying' and 'courage.' They were quick to grasp the syntactic distinction of 'privilege of occurrence' in a certain position, in contrast to the semantic criterion of 'person, place or thing' and found the idea interesting. They soon began on the alternative ways a sentence could be said and have the same meaning. We were soon building up the idea of productivity.

We were struck by the fact that once the children break into an idea in language, once they get a sense of a distinction, they quickly 'turn around' on their own usage and make remarkable strides toward linguistic understanding. The only point I would make is that you must wait until *they* are willing reflectively to turn around before you begin operating with the abstractions. Otherwise they will become obedient and noncomprehending. In time, the habit of or attitude toward reflecting on what you habitually do or say becomes well established. I put this matter first for I feel that it is the one thing that children most rarely encounter in school—that it is a good practice to use their heads to solve a problem by reflecting on what they already know or have already learned. Are college students so different from fifth graders?

Consider activation now. I do not want to say much about this. I think that the reward that comes from using materials, discovering regularities, extrapolating, etc. is intrinsic to the activity. It probably goes beyond the satisfaction of curiosity. It has more to do with the form of motivation that Robert White speaks of as effectance or competence. Extrinsic rewards may mask this pleasure. When children expect a payoff from somebody, they tend to be drawn away from or distracted from the behavior that provides intrinsic rewards. You can corrupt them all too easily into seeking your favor, your rewards, your grades. But enough of this subject.

The compatibility problem is next in our list and it is interesting. Let me describe it in terms of the behavior of some of our pupils. We were treating tool-using as a problem. I would remind you that our children were suburban. They had not used many tools, nor thought much about what a tool is. A tool was something to get at the hardware store. Could we relate tools to something that they themselves knew about? Our aim was to present tools as amplifiers of human sensory, motor, and reflective powers—which includes mathematics in the range of tools.

To get the children away from their parochial notions about tools, we prepared a set of drawings of all kinds of tools and devised an exercise whose object was to restore some manner of awareness about tools. We would present a hammer. What is its use? One child said it is used for beating in nails. What do you want to drive in nails for? You drive nails in because you want to have the nail in the board. Why do you want to have the nail in the board? To hold two boards together. Why would you want two boards together? Well, to make a building steady or to support something like a table. Any other way to do it aside from hammer and nails? Yes, you could use string. String and nails do the same thing? Etc., etc., etc. Along the way, it was quite apparent that when you got the pupils to rephrase uses in their own terms and kept pushing them as to how something could be used, eventually they would find some place where it connected with a structured body of knowledge they already had. This is what I mean by the 'compatibility problem'— finding the connection with something they do know.

Frequently, you came upon some very striking surprises. Let me give you a couple of examples of this. One of the pictures was of a compass—the kind that is used for drawing circles. One child, a particularly interesting one, was asked about it. What is that for? It's a steadying tool. What do you mean, a steadying tool? She went to the board and took a piece of chalk. You see, if you try to draw a circle, you're not steady enough to make a real circle, so a compass steadies you. The other children thought the idea was great and came forth with a stream of suggestions for other steadying tools. One suggested a tripod for a camera. Another said a stick could be a steadying tool. He had seen a sign painter the other day, resting his arm on a stick.

I was struck by the fact that they were doing something very much like Wittgenstein's description of concept formation. Recall his description of a game. What is a game? There is no obvious hierarchical concept that joins tennis and tag. What these children were doing with steadying tools was forming a concept in which neighboring elements were joined by "family resemblance," to use Wittgenstein's phrase. The concept that emerges is like a rope in which no single fiber runs all the way through. The children are getting connections that allow them to travel from one part of the system to the other and when something new comes in, they find compatible connections. You can, at your peril, call it association. By calling it that you forget the systematic or syntactic nature of their behavior, as when they dealt with the idea of type and order in language. They were dealing with tools as governed by a rule of filling certain requirements—the different ways of getting steady or of holding things together. But the rules are not as simple as formal concepts. It is this kind of binding, this kind of exercise, that helps solve the compatibility problem, the problem of how to get a new piece of knowledge connected with an established domain so that the new knowledge can help retrieve what is likely to be appropriate to it as needed.

The compatibility problem turns out to have some surprising features. Let me illustrate by reference to a junior high school course which I will not tell you about except for one particular unit. In this unit we deal with an episode in which Julius Caesar must decide whether to cross the Rubicon, leave Cisalpine Gaul to penetrate Italy and try for Rome. The children have the commentaries of Caesar, nothing from Pompey who was Caesar's opponent, and letters from Cicero to various characters around Italy. The data are insufficient. The pupils must pull all the shreds together. Amusingly enough, the class divided into Caesarians and Pompeyans, comparing their heroes to people they knew about. The discussion was dramatic; they reasoned like politicians! Caesar must have had friends along there. He'd never have taken his army through a narrow valley like that if he hadn't some friends in there to count on! As a result, one group of pupils set off looking through Cicero's gossipy letters to find out whether Caesar might possibly have friends who had been passing information to him about the people along his narrow valley. The connections they were making were with their knowledge of the human condition and how people got on with each other. We did not care whether they made connections through the imagery of unsavory Boston politicians (with whom they at once equated Roman politicians). The interesting thing is that they connected. We tried out the Caesar unit in a 'problem' class in Melbourne, Florida—a group of leather-jacket motorcycle kids. They went completely for Caesar! They were exquisite analysts of the corrupt Roman system. Pompey just could not hold them. He was a fink without guts. The transcripts of these lessons are marvelous! It was only when they found the connection between Caesar and their strong-arm fantasies (and not always fantasies) that Rome and Melbourne came together. Forgive me for going on about something so obvious. It is just that it was not so obvious to us when we started.

Consider next the skill problem. It has had fewer surprises to it, but let me say a few things about it anyway. One of the skills is pushing an idea to its limit. Let me give you an example. A question came up in one of our classes of how to get information from one generation to another. One fifth-grader said that you did it by "tradition" and this empty formula satisfied most of the pupils. They were ready to go on to the next thing. I said that I did not quite understand what they meant by tradition. One child said that a tradition is that dogs chase cats. The others laughed. Well, the laughed-at boy responded, some people say it is an instinct, but he had a dog who did not chase cats until he saw another dog do it. There was a long silence. The children picked the issue up from there, reinvented the idea of culture, destroyed the idea of instinct (even what is good about it), ended up with most of their presuppositions rakishly out in the open. Had I stopped the discussion earlier, we would have been contributing to the creation of passive minds. What the children needed were opportunities to test the limits of their concepts. It often requires a hurly-burly that fits poorly the decorum of a schoolroom. It is for this reason that I single it out.

Training in the skill of hypothesis making has a comparable problem. Let me give you an example of what I mean. We got into a discussion in one of our classes of what language might have been for the first speaking humans. We had already had a similar session with one other class so I knew what was likely to happen. Sure enough, one child said that we should go out and find some "ape men" who were first learning how to speak and then you would know. It is direct confrontation of a problem, and children of 10 like this directness. I was teaching the class. I told the children that there were various people in the 19th century who had travelled all over Africa on just such a quest, and to no avail. Wherever people spoke, the language seemed about the same in sophistication. They were crestfallen. How could one find out if such ape men existed no longer? I thought I should take drastic measures and present them with two alternative hypotheses, both indirect. It is usually a fine way of losing a 10-year-old audience! They had the week before been working on Von Frisch's bee-dance 'language' so they knew a little about other than human forms of communication. I proposed, as a first hypothesis, that to study the origin of *human* language they look at some animal language like bees and then at present human language, and perhaps *original* human language would be somewhere in between. That was one hypothesis. I saw some frowns. They were not happy about the idea. The other way, I proposed, was to take what was simplest and most common about human language and guess that those things made up the language man first started speaking.

This discussion, weighing the worth of the two hypotheses took the whole period. What struck me was that in the course of the discussion the children were learning more how to *frame* hypotheses than how to test them, which is a great step forward. One child asked whether what would be simple in one language would necessarily be simple about another. They were trying to invent a hypothesis about language universals. Or another pupil suggested that the way babies speak is probably the way in which man first spoke. They enjoyed discussing not only whether the hypotheses were 'true' but also whether they were testable. I told them finally that the Cercle Linguistique de Paris in the 1880s had voted that nobody should be permitted to give a paper on the origin of human language, and that they were not doing badly, all things considered. They took a dim view of Paris as a result! I was struck by the avidity of the children for the opportunity to make hypotheses. I believe children need more such practice and rarely get it.

Training in being concise is, like limits testing and hypotheses making, a neglected though crucial area of skill-training. I heard one fifth-grader answer another who asked about a movie by starting off to recount it from the beginning. He was prepared to give a blow-by-blow account. They have little training in condensing information. I feel reasonably convinced that we could take a lesson from a game that Ford Maddox Ford and Joseph Conrad are alleged to have played on Sunday outings. Who could describe a landscape before them in the smallest number of words? I do not have much experience with this kind of training. All I do have is a sense of the overwhelming prolixity that gets in the way of the children I have observed.

Consider now the fifth or 'self-loop' problem. Edward Sapir once made the remark that language is a dynamo that we use principally for lighting little name plates, for labelling and categorizing things. When human beings some day learn how to use language effectively, we will probably spend much more time grasping the logical implications of how we say things. Let me start the discussion of the self-loop with that thought. When the child becomes aware of what he is saying, when he turns around on himself, he will gain a special advantage from his language.

Let me give you some examples. One child said to the class that all they were doing that day was saying the same thing over and over in different ways. Another child responded that the things in question being talked about did not say the same thing. Still another argued that they were the same thing. Now, the distinction between the syntactic and the semantic mode is an extremely difficult one. The children sensed, though, that the word 'same' needed to be decomposed into different kinds of sameness—a sameness of words and of things. This is an example of turning around on your own language, the self-loop that permits you to recognize what you are up to.

Another instance happened quite by accident. A child, smitten by the intersubstitutable sentences, put down a list of two-word expletives:

jeepers	creepers
leaping	lizards
aw	gee
good	grief
my	goodness

I asked how they were alike. The children suggested you could substitute in each column as with the sentences: 'gee creepers,' and 'oh lizards,' etc. It is an interesting kind of substitutivity. But the more interesting thing is that some children said that these phrases are the same though they do not stand for a thing that is the same. If you speak of this as discovery, I would agree. But it is discovery via self-consciousness, and these I esteem as of particular importance.

Let me move on to the last point: How one engineer's discovery so that it takes place in a context of problem solving—so that one can retrieve and combine information in an appropriate setting rather than under the spell of 'inspiration.'

One of the most powerful tools we have for searching is contrast. Contrast can be engineered or self-engineered. Indeed, it can become an acquired taste. We have gone out of our way to present material to children in contrastive form—film of baboon juveniles playing followed by human children playing in an identical 'habitat.' The children discover quite readily that little baboons play mostly with little baboons and do not play with things, that human children play with things and with each other. This is engineering a situation. It provides a start for a discussion of tool use, free hands, and so on. Later, give them kittens (who play with things) and then have them deal anew with the problem. They will very quickly understand that cats play with things, but not by holding them.

We believe that by getting the child to explore contrasts, he is more likely to organize his knowledge in a fashion that helps discovery in particular situations where discovery is needed. I need not go into an elaborate justification of the method of contrast here, and will only note that its efficacy stems from the fact that a concept requires for its definition a choice of a negative case. Man is a different concept contrasted to standing bears, to angels, to devil. Readiness to explore contrasts provides a choice among the alternatives that might be relevant.

In conclusion, let me take a very pragmatic position. Develop the best pedagogy you can. See how well you can do. Then analyze the nature of what you did that worked. We do not yet have enough good principles at this point to design an adequate experiment in which this group gets this 'treatment' and that group another 'treatment.' The experiments of this type have been grossly disappointing. The best things that you can do at any given point, I would urge, is to design a pedagogical 'treatment' that works extremely well, and then work your way back. Later on, design hypotheses to determine what you did. But for the moment, can we not declare a moratorium on little experiments that produce miniscule effects? Instead, use contrast, use different kinds of representations, use such formalisms as you can, develop self-consciousness. With a mixture of psychology, common sense, and luck you may produce an effect on learning that is worth studying. Then purify and experiment. But first invent and observe. That seems to me to be the pragmatic strategy. It is not in the grand experimental tradition of physics. But is experimental pedagogy in the grand tradition of physics at this point in history? It may very well be that it is more like economics, a mixture of models and pragmatics. It is in this spirit that I have suggested six ways of possibly aiding a child to discover something for himself. The formal experiments can wait until we have shown that some 'treatment' is worth the trouble.

Chapter VIII

Discovery in the Teaching of Mathematics

ROBERT B. DAVIS

WHETHER ONE THINKS OF THE AERONAUTICAL ENGINEER VERSUS THE pilot, or of the pure mathematician versus the engineer, or of the economist versus the businessman, virtually every major field of human endeavor is split between a group of theorists and a group of practitioners. It seems to me that it is a sign of health when the two groups are able to communicate, and when they attempt to work closely together. Speaking as one of the clinical people or practitioners, I want to thank the theorists for their efforts at bridging the gap which sometimes seems to separate us.

My remarks are made from the practitioner's point of view, which is the only one I can legitimately claim. Based on the Madison Project work of the past eight years, I want to cite a few examples and a few ideas related to them.

Specifically, I have three goals: first, I want to give examples of what we have regarded as discovery experience for children, in the hope that some of you will be able to suggest a few of the ways in which these experiences differ from exposition, and even differ from one another. This last remark deserves emphasizing, for it is my present notion that there are many different kinds of discovery experience, and we confuse the issue badly when we treat discovery as a single well-defined kind of experience.

My second goal is to offer a few remarks attempting to interpret or describe some of the things we mean by discovery, and to explain why some of us believe in its importance.

Finally, I shall list a few things that might be called objectives of Madison Project teaching, for this, too, may clarify why we think we believe in 'discovery.'

SOME EXAMPLES AND SOME INTERPRETATIONS

The students in my first example were some low-IQ culturally-deprived children in the seventh grade, some of whom were older than normal for grade seven. The topic was the matter of finding pairs of whole numbers that would satisfy linear equations of the form

$$(\square \times 3) + 2 = \triangle$$

Although we found that $\square$, $\triangle$ notation useful, and consequently did use it with these children, what I have written above could be translated into traditional x, y notation as

$$y = 3x + 2$$

We passed out graph paper and suggested that suitable pairs of whole numbers be recorded according to the usual Cartesian use of coordinates.

Very nearly all of the students made the obvious discovery that there is a simple linear pattern to the resulting dots. A considerable number of them actually applied this discovery, by extrapolating according to the pattern, then checking to see if their new points gave numbers that satisfied the equation.

It is these students who used the discovery this way whom I wish to discuss. Some of them spent several days working with various linear equations, using the patterns to find points, then checking by substituting into the equation. This was one of the earliest things the project ever did that seemed to fascinate children far beyond their normal degree of involvement with school.

My conjecture is that the important aspect of this was perhaps a combination of achievement in making their own discovery, competitive gratification vis-a-vis those classmates who did not make the discovery, autonomy of having set the task for themselves, some intrinsic esthetic or closure reward, and the existence of a verification that did not depend upon the teacher.

These were culturally deprived children, with a middle-class teacher and a middle-class curriculum. Previous observation had already convinced us that these children were at best *tolerant* of a schoolish learning that was wrong in every important respect. The children were always checking up, between school and social realities outside of school, and invariably found the school to be wanting.

The school taught you to speak the language incorrectly—for example, the school taught, 'It is I' in a world where the social reality was, 'It's me'—the school taught personal economics incorrectly, the school taught civics incorrectly, and so on. Nothing ever checked when you tried it out against actual reality. (For example, if a majority of people in the county don't like the sheriff, he won't be reelected—according to what they teach in school. But in reality, perhaps a majority of the people are not even allowed to vote—to use an example that is in our newspapers at the present moment.)

Here, in their *own* discovery, they had found something that *really worked!* If you tried it out, it checked out perfectly!

In any event, some of the children were captivated, and spent several days on the matter, asking to take graph paper home and so on.

(Incidentally, in the long run—i.e., over the year that we worked with this class—truancy decreased markedly, and parents reported their children taking an unprecedented interest in school—for example, by discussing it at mealtime.)

My second example is perhaps somewhat similar. We wanted to give children in grades 3–9 some experience with *variables* and with *the arithmetic of signed numbers*. It is one of our principles that such experience should always be provided *in a sensible mathematical context*, and (if at all possible) in a form which would permit a student to make one or more interesting discoveries. We believe that this procedure helps get the children in a frame of mind where they are always poking around looking for interesting patterns that may be lurking just beneath the surface.

I should emphasize that the discoveries in question will usually not be part of the basic purpose of the lesson, and it is not essential for a child to discover them. They are primarily a bonus for those who do discover them.

In the present instance, remember, we wanted the children to get some experience using *variables*, and working with the *arithmetic of signed numbers*. We consequently gave them quadratic equations to solve, beginning with

$$(\Box \times \Box) - (5 \times \Box) + 6 = O$$

and gradually progressing to harder problems, such as

$$(\Box \times \Box) - (20 \times \Box) + 96 = O$$

Now, at first the only method available to the student was, of course, trial and error. If he makes no discoveries, the student continues with this method, and gets full benefit from the basic part of the lesson; that is, he gets a great deal of experience using variables and signed numbers, and in a situation where he does *not* regard this as drill.

But—if the student discovers the so-called coefficient rules for quadratic equations, his use of trial-and-error can be guided to maximum efficiency. He has discovered a secret—and one which many of his classmates don't know. They may *never* know!

Torpedoing

In both of the previous examples, we make use of a technique which we call 'torpedoing.' After a student has discovered what he believes is the pattern for linear equations from working with

$$(\square \times 1) + 3 = \triangle$$
$$(\square \times 1) + 5 = \triangle$$
$$(\square \times 1) + 2 = \triangle$$

and so forth—*after* he is confident of his mastery, we unobtrusively slip in a problem like

$$(\square \times 2) + 3 = \triangle$$

He uses his pattern, he checks—and the numbers don't work!

What shall he do?

With a little thought, he discovers there is a pattern here, also—indeed, there is a more general pattern of which he had discovered only a special case.

In a similar way, with the quadratic equations, we begin by using only unequal prime roots, so that one of the two coefficient rules (the product rule) is extremely obvious. Using it alone leads to easy solution of the equations, such as

$$(\square \times \square) - (5 \times \square) + 6 = 0$$
$$(\square \times \square) - (12 \times \square) + 35 = 0$$
$$(\square \times \square) - (13 \times \square) + 22 = 0$$
$$(\square \times \square) - (7 \times \square) + 10 = 0$$

and so on.

Here also, once the student is really pleased with his discovery, and with the new power it has given him, we confront him—unobtrusively and unexpectedly—with a variant problem which will tend to confound his theory.

In this instance, we slip in a problem having composite roots, instead of the prime roots the student had previously dealt with.

The product rule now seems to indicate more than two roots: for example, with

$$(\square \times \square) - (9 \times \square) + 20 = 0$$

many students will say the roots are

$$\{2, \quad 10, \quad 4, \quad 3,\}$$

Trial by substitution shows that this is wrong. Again, by persevering, the student finds that there is a broader theory, of which he had found only a narrower part.

Why do we like Torpedoing?

It may seem that what I have described is simple sadism, or How to Be One Up on Your Students Without Really Teaching. We *feel* that it is not so (although, unfortunately, it *can* be in the hands of a teacher who really *is* a sadist.)

Why do we use this technique of torpedoing some of our students' best theories?

It is important to realize that, at the outset, we don't know. We use the technique because, intuitively, it feels right.

But, in the years while we have been using this technique, we have, of course, discussed it often, and even made some analytic attempts at constructing an abstract rationalization for it.

Perhaps we like the technique because:

i) It gives the brightest students something to work on while the others catch up on more basic work;

ii) It is a friendly challenge from teacher to student, and students rise to such bait better than fresh-water fish do to flies;

iii) Perhaps Piaget's processes of 'assimilation' and 'accommodation' need to be practiced, and this is where you practice them;

iv) Or, to put point iii in less technical language, perhaps the security of a friendly classroom is the best place to gain experience in fixing up theories that used to work, but somehow don't seem to work any more—the classroom is a better place to learn this than, say, the political meetings of anti-integrationists or the radical right;

v) Then, too, it is worth learning that science does not deal in absolute truth. Sufficient unto each day are the theories thereof—and an irreconcilable contradiction may be discovered tomorrow! (Or, for that matter, a better theory!) If your theories work, make the most of them —but keep a wary eye out, just the same.

vi) Finally, this is one of the ways that we go about bringing *history* into the classroom. If one wishes to *understand* history, one must have some background of relevant experience. Since the history of mathematics is an unending story of trials, failures, break-throughs, temporary successes, new points of view, and so on, it is unintelligible to the person who has no background experience in trials, failures, break-throughs, temporary successes, revised points of view, and so on. Torpedoing theories in the classroom provided background experience that parallels important historical phenomena. Can you *realize* what the discovery of irrationals meant to the Greeks if you, yourself, start out with the sophisticated viewpoint of the 20th century?

The 'Crisis' dilemma: seeking the unit matrix

This next example involves a different kind of discovery situation. In the previous examples, the discoveries were merely optional bonuses added to the meat of the lesson; moreover, students discovering any secret patterns kept the secret to themselves, revealing their knowledge only indirectly, by using the secrets to solve difficult problems easily and quickly.

In the present example, all eyes are focussed upon a central problem which we wish to solve, if possible—or to recognize as unsolvable, if a logical argument shows that no solution can exist. If anyone finds an answer, he will announce his discovery at once.

Specifically, we look at the system of 2-by-2 matrices and ask how this new mathematical system compares with the familiar old system of rational numbers. One question is this: is there a 2-by-2 matrix which plays a role analogous to that of the rational number zero? The answer turns out to be that there is, and it is the matrix

$$\begin{pmatrix} 0 & 0 \\ 0 & 0 \end{pmatrix}$$

So far so good. Now—is there a matrix that plays a role analogous to the rational number *one?* Students invariably—and wisely, on the available evidence—guess

$$\begin{pmatrix} 1 & 1 \\ 1 & 1 \end{pmatrix}$$

but a quick computation shows that this is *not* satisfactory.

Here we have the dilemma: *IS* there any matrix that behaves like the integer one? Has our failure to find one been a symptom of the impossibility of the task, or have we merely failed due to personal reasons, not reasons of fundamental impossibility. Is it worth-while trying any longer? If so, how shall we proceed?

This has proved to be a consistently exciting lesson for fifth-graders, or anyone older who doesn't already know the answer.

Going Beyond the Data or the Task

In the filmed lesson entitled, "Graphing an Ellipse," at the end of a lesson on graphing

$$x^2 + ky^2 = 25, \qquad 0 \leq k,$$

a seventh-grade student (Debbie H., according to her nametag) asks: "Why couldn't you use matrices, and make a graph for k less than zero?"

Since these students have previously used matrices to introduce complex numbers, this is an ingenious and appropriate suggestion. The teacher does not immediately respond, but another student (whose nametag reads Lex) answers: "No, you can't, because you won't be able to graph matrices." This answer is essentially correct—but both of these remarks go beyond anything the teacher had planned or anticipated.

The teacher's contribution to this is mainly a genuine appreciation of the students' contributions—but we believe this is important. Children somehow act far cleverer when their cleverness is welcome and appreciated.

Do It Your Own Way: Kye's Arithmetic

Somewhat similar is this example. A third-grade teacher was introducing subtraction, with borrowing and carrying:

$$\begin{array}{r} 64 \\ -28 \\ \hline \end{array}$$

She said: "You can't subtract 8 from 4, so you take 10 from the 60 . . ."

A third-grade boy named Kye interrupted: "Oh, yes you can!

$$4 - 8 = -4$$

$$\begin{array}{r} 64 \\ -28 \\ \hline -4 \end{array}$$

and $60 - 20 = 40$

$$\begin{array}{r} 64 \\ -28 \\ \hline -4 \\ 40 \\ \hline \end{array}$$

and $40 - 4 = 36$

$$
\begin{array}{r}
64 \\
-28 \\
\hline
-4 \\
\hline
40 \\
\hline
36
\end{array} \text{."}
$$

The teacher did nothing here to *solicit* originality, but when she was confronted with it, she *listened* to the student, tried to understand, and *welcomed* and appreciated his contribution.

This was an unusual, but actual, occurrence. The more common, 'traditional' response would have been to say: "No, Kye, that's not the way you do it. Now watch carefully and I'll show you . . ."

Where does this traditional rejection of his contribution leave Kye? He is given the feeling that mathematics is a stupid subject that never works out the way you'd expect it would . . . Given enough experiences of this sort—and in a traditional situation he will be—Kye will probably transfer his interest and his energy to some other field of endeavor.

This example has always seemed to me to suggest the essence of good 'modern' teaching in mathematics, as opposed to 'traditional' teaching. In a phrase: *listen* to the student, and be prepared for him to suggest a better answer than any you know. The 'modern' teacher *actually learns from his students!*

Kye's algorithm for subtracting was an original contribution of a third grade boy. It is in many ways the nicest algorithm for subtracting that I have ever seen—and it was invented by a boy in the third grade.

The traditional teacher assumes from the outset that such a thing is impossible. Is it any wonder that the traditional teacher somehow never encounters such clever behavior from students? Like the spirits that move Oui-ja boards, such clever student behavior rarely appears before the eyes of those who don't believe in its existence.

Autonomy and Proliferation

In introducing graphical integration and differentiation to an eighth-grade class, we proceeded as follows: We obtained a print of the PSSC film "Straight Line Kinematics" which is an *expositional* treatment of these topics in relation to velocity and acceleration. The students could view this film whenever they wished—and as often as they wished. They were then given a shoebox full of simple equipment—the PSSC ticker-tape equipment—to take home if they wished, and were asked to devise their own experiments and work up their own data. They later performed their experiments in school, at a session which has been recorded on film.

The effort and ingenuity that some students put into this went far beyond their normal effort for 'schoolwork.'

What Questions

In one instance, we give physical apparatus to students and ask them *what questions* might be worth studying about this apparatus. The point here is for the student to identify appropriate *questions*. An eminent mathematician, Professor McShane of the University of Virginia, has said that his favorite mathematics problem is stated in a textbook as follows:

A pile of coal catches on fire.

These seven words are the *entire* statement of the problem—in a *mathematics* book!

Now—what *mathematics* questions does this pose?

Leaving Things Open-Ended

Many mathematics problems occur at a stage in the child's life when he is not yet prepared to answer them. An honest use of logic seems to compel us to leave these questions open for the time being. The alternative would be to 'answer' them on the basis of authority—but we believe this would tend to make the child think that mathematics is based upon the pronouncements of authorities. We prefer to leave the question open—after all, aren't most scientific questions open at the present time? Or, perhaps, *always* open?

Example: Is

$$\square \times O = O$$

an *axiom* or a *theorem?* Ultimately the child will learn that it is a theorem:

$$\square + O = \square$$
$$O + O = O$$
$$\square \times (O + O) = \square \times O$$
$$(\square \times O) + (\square \times O) = \square \times O$$
$$\therefore \square \times O = O$$

This proof, however, involves some subtle and awkward points, so that the child cannot settle the question when it first occurs to him, and we leave the question open. The child knows that if he is ever able to *prove* the result, he will be able to classify it as a theorem. In the meantime . . . Who knows which it is?

Where Does It Come From?

The Madison Project approach to *logic* is, so far as we know, completely unique and unprecedented. Virtually every existing book on logic *tells* you what *modus ponens* is, *tells* you what the truth-table is for 'and,' 'or,' 'if . . . then,' and so on.

But why? Where does all of this come from, anyhow?

Given the transitory nature of scientific knowledge, we can hardly settle for facts which are static pieces torn out of the fabric of time past, time present, and time future.

Where does all of this logic come from? How would we go about making up our own logic if we wished to do so?

In order to answer these questions—at least, according to our own view of the answer—the Madison Project proceeds like this:

First, we ask children (grades 7, 8, 9, or older) to analyze statements of their friends, and to classify them as true or false. They realize that this is a vast oversimplification, for most ordinary statements in the ordinary world are neither true nor false; there's some truth in them, but one still has some possible doubts or reservations.

We then ask the children to focus on actual usages of 'and' and 'or', and to record *as many different uses of 'and' and 'or' as they can find* by means of truth tables.

Ordinary language has a great many different uses of both words. One of my favorites—we might label it 'and$_1$', in order to distinguish it from *other* uses, which can be labelled 'and$_2$', 'and$_3$' and so forth—is this one:

Keep driving like that and you'll kill somebody.

A somewhat similar use of 'and' occurred prior to the 1964 election, in the radio admonition: Vote, and the choice is yours, Don't vote, and the choice is theirs. If you fail to register, you have no choice. Consider, also, the poem: "Laugh, and the world laughs with you, Weep, and you weep alone." The result of this activity is an extensive truth table with many different columns, headed 'and$_1$', 'and$_2$', 'and$_3$', etc, and 'or$_1$', 'or$_2$', 'or$_3$', and so on. Usually some students insist on moving into a more-than-two-valued logic, in order better to reflect nuances of meaning which seem to them to be present. Once we have collected together this large truth table, we have completed stage one, which might be labelled Observing the Behavior of the Natives.

We move next to the Legislative stage: In order to gain clarity, we agree on one single meaning for the word 'and,' we pick one column in the truth table to define this meaning, and we legislate that 'and' shall henceforth be used in that single sense only.

The study of logic proceeds further: after the Sociological stage, and the Legislative stage, we move on to the Abstract stage, and so forth—but the point is that these children have made up their own systems of logic. As a result, they know where logic comes from. In the same way, you understand Beethoven differently after you, yourself, have written some music of your own composition.

An Active Role, and Focussing Attention. Discovery of another sort is perhaps involved in teaching students (second-graders, say) to plot points on Cartesian coordinates. The teacher plots a few points, but the students learn more by imitation than by following a careful exposition. Learning by imitation of course involves a kind of discovery, since you must figure out how the teacher is doing it.

As David Page has pointed out, the best mathematics students have always learned by discovery—even when listening to a lecture, they are *actively thinking*: asking Why? Why not? How about doing it this way? Now what do you suppose he meant by that? Why can't you do it *this* way? and so on.

Games Using Clues. One of our most successful lessons goes like this:

Three students, working together, make up a rule. For example, Whatever number we tell them, they'll double it and add twenty. They do *not* tell us their rule; instead, we tell them numbers. They apply their rule to each number we tell them, and tell us each answer. It's our job to guess their rule.

There is a great deal of mathematics involved in this lesson— for example, the distinction between formula and function, and such properties of functions as linearity, oddness, evenness, rate of growth, and so on. But perhaps the main *discovery* aspect resembles closely Suchman's (1964) work on inquiry: By choosing wisely the numbers we tell them, we can get *clues* as to the nature of the function they are using. No single clue will usually be decisive, but a suitable combination will be.

A somewhat similar format has been used by David Page in his lessons on Hidden Numbers. A few numbers are written on a piece of paper, and the students are to guess the numbers from a set of clues. To make matters harder, *some of the clues are false*, so that the students must recognize *and make use of the contradictions* which are contained in the set of clues (grades 4, 5, 6, 7, 8, or 9).

Two Theoretical Interpretations

An extremely valuable approach to analyzing communications in class has been developed by Professor J. Richard Suchman. The data inside a student's mind at an instant in time can be classified (as an oversimplification, of course) into three categories: facts, unifying mental constructs (roughly, 'theories'), and applications. The possible communications can be diagrammed as follows:

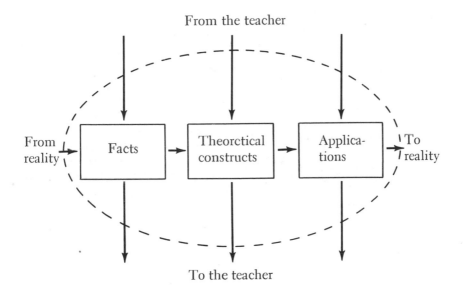

Using this analytical approach in interpreting classroom lessons can be very exciting and gratifying—which, as J. Robert Oppenheimer has remarked, is perhaps the most valid test of a theoretical approach.

Because of limitations of time and space, I shall not attempt to illustrate the use of Suchman's diagrams, beyond remarking that on a Suchman diagram, discovery communications seem to appear as conspicuously horizontal channels, whereas expositional and rote communications appear as conspicuously vertical channels. Particularly in connection with the work of Piaget, Tolman, Lewin, Kohler, White, and Bruner, Suchman diagrams are a powerful analytical tool for the practitioner seeking a rationale for understanding what goes on in the classroom.

Another aspect of discovery experiences is being emphasized in the motivation studies by Richard de Charms (in press) in relation to the analytical dichotomy of the learner's perception of his role, which de Charms polarizes as 'origin' versus 'pawn.'

THE GOALS OF EDUCATION

It is worth remembering that the life of a human being, or the inter-related lives of many human beings, are in reality unified wholes, not separated into pieces in any way whatsoever. When, in order to analyze life abstractly, we break off pieces by invoking *categories*, we do a violence to the reality whole that can impede comprehension as easily as it may, hopefully, facilitate it.

In particular, motivation is not separate *in reality* from perception, personality, learning, social interactions, or communication. Still more specifically, *reality* does not begin with a statement of *explicit goals*. If a teacher begins with an attempted statement of explicit goals, he does so by choice, and may easily do so in error, for his subsequent behavior may not reveal the same goals as his initial words did.

In our own Madison Project teaching, our original conscious goals were general and nonspecific: we wanted to find some of the best experiences with mathematics that children could have. To choose among alternatives we relied upon our intuitive assessments.

From this highly general purpose we spun out a sequence of specific activities in the classroom. In order to *discuss* these experiences, *after they were created*, we have attempted to work out some suitable analytical categories. In particular, we have identified what appear to be some of our probable goals. Here is a tentative list, surely somewhat incomplete:

i. We want to give students experience *in discovering patterns in abstract situations;*

ii. We want students to have experience in *recognizing potentially open-ended situations, and in extending open-ended situations by original creative work;*

iii. We want the students to be familiar with the basic concepts of mathematics, such as *variable, open sentence, truth set, function, Cartesian coordinates, mapping, isomorphism, linearity, matrices, implication, contradiction, axiom,* etc.

iv. We want the students to build up, in their own minds, suitable *mental* imagery (in the sense of Lewin, Tolman, Piaget, Leibnitz,

Polya, et al) to permit them to perform mental manipulations involving the basic ideas of mathematics (such as *function, linearity, isomorphism, mapping,* etc., as mentioned above);

v. We want the students to acquire a modest mastery of the *basic techniques* of mathematics;

vi. We want the students to know the basic facts of mathematics, such as $7 + 3 = 10$, $-1 \times -1 = +1$, and so on;

vii. We want the students to possess considerable facility *in relating the various parts of mathematics one to another*—for example, using algebra as a tool in studying geometry, or recognizing the structure of the algebra of linear transformations of the plane into itself, and so on;

viii. We want the students to possess an easy skill in *relating mathematics to the applications of mathematics* in physics and elsewhere;

ix. We want the students *to have a real feeling for the history of mathematics,* derived partly from having been eye-witness observers (or participants) on the occasion of mathematical discoveries.

We regard the preceding nine points as intellectual matters; but they must be accompanied by some emotional or value goals, namely:

x. We want the student to know that mathematics *really and truly is discoverable* (something few people believe);

xi. We want each student, as part of the task of knowing himself, to get *a realistic assessment of his own personal ability* in discovering mathematics;

xii. We want the students to come *to value 'educated intuition'* in its proper place;

xiii. We want the students *to value abstract rational analysis* in its proper place;

xiv. We want the students—as much as possible—*to know when to persevere, and when to be flexible;*

xv. We want the students to have a feeling that *mathematics is fun or exciting, or worthwhile.*

The preceding goals do not sound like the goals of a traditional arithmetic or algebra program. They are not.

Space and time do not permit us to pursue the matter, but implicit beneath all Madison Project work is the notion that *education* and *training* are different, that education is for people, and training is for electronic machinery (which usually doesn't need it anyhow)— indeed, all repetitious routine tasks are basically nonhuman.

One example of the distinction—a tragic and highly suggestive example—will have to serve where many might be cited:

A few years ago in a hospital nursery in Binghamton, N.Y., the formula for new-born babies was made with salt instead of sugar. By the time the error was discovered, a dozen or so babies had either died or suffered severe and irreparable brain damage.

Now,—who or what was at fault? Many babies—indeed, virtually all of them—*simultaneously* developed feeding problems. Some of the *mothers*—but none of the nurses!—tasted the formula and complained that it was unusually salty.

No nurse heeded either clue. The nurses had been trained to soothe a new mother's anxieties, lest they be passed on to the infant and create feeding problems.

Those of us who have children of our own know how much this episode meant to the parents of the babies involved.

New York State has responded by passing a new law, which, I believe, makes it illegal for a hospital to store salt in a room in which nursery formulas are prepared.

This is a significant step in the wrong direction.

Every time we attempt to by-pass human resourcefulness—by laws, rote training, or otherwise—we move toward, and not away from, the unintelligent behavior of the nurses who were trained but not educated. The response of the *mothers* was more appropriate than that of the nurses, but the nonadaptive blind weight of authority decided the outcome in favor of the 'trained' nurses.

I think it important for every teacher always to remember that *he, the teacher, does not know the right answer or the right response*—he can only hope that, when the time comes, his former students will respond appropriately.

Those theorists who study education are on shaky ground indeed if their analysis assumes that they can separate right answers from wrong answers. If the matter in question is trivial, perhaps they can; but if it is important, they surely cannot.

The present emphasis on creativity and divergent thinking would never have occurred—and should never have occurred—but for the fact that we had gone all too far down the road labelled training, and had, surprisingly, lost sight of education.

Chapter IX

Teaching and Discovery

WHAT ARE THE RELATIONSHIPS AMONG THE ACT OF TEACHING, THE content of the curriculum, and the concept of discovery? The conference group turned to this set of questions in their third meeting. The starting point for discussion in this third session of the conference was a film of Dr. Robert Davis teaching a junior high school mathematics class a unit on the multiplication of matrices. This was the first concrete example of a teaching sequence which purported to be learning by discovery that the members of the conference had had the opportunity jointly to observe. In the film, Davis repeatedly provided a series of cues for the students and then led them to appropriate generalizations by using a sequence of leading questions or prompts. As in most recitation or discussion situations, not all the children participated equally. A small number of students seemed to dominate the discussion. After the showing of the film was completed, Davis turned to the participants and asked, "All right, gentlemen. You saw the film. What did I do?"

One participant suggested that the term which best characterized Davis' instructional tactics was "commando teaching," genuinely eliciting responses from the students, rather than telling them the answers. You may lecture, but you leave 'empty boxes' for the students themselves to fill in, which is quite different from a straight, didactic presentation of materials. It differs from a pure discovery approach in that the students are not at all just "messing around," in Hawkins' terms. It is like a discovery approach in that they are called upon to discover or invent material to fill in gaps.

There appeared to be two independent axes operating in this definition of teaching by discovery. One was the extent to which 'messing around' was characteristic of the behavior of the students. The second was the extent to which students were called upon to invent or discover facts or generalizations in the subject matter, in contrast to being told the given statements directly. In messing around, the students may generate a wide variety of possible gap-fillers, all of which may be equally acceptable to the teacher. In Davis' approach, the students, though inventing or discovering constantly, were essentially seeking those responses which filled the gaps in the same way Davis wanted them filled. Thus, in contrast to messing around, the object of discovery was to come up with one right answer.

Another relevant distinction is whether it is the teacher or the student who selects the order in which questions or materials are examined. When the children themselves are selecting the order in which the materials are handled, the consequences for learning might be quite different than when the teacher is making these decisions.

One participant now protested that the argument over whether a piece of teaching behavior was discovery or not, was quite unnecessary. Why must there be such hard and fast distinctions? Why can there not be a continuum for looking at discovery, just as there is for looking at many other variables such as *intelligence* or *rigidity?* There was no question that the film was full of kids making discoveries.

Another participant agreed with this position. He went so far as to maintain that not only was a 'pure discovery' approach absent in the film, but that no educator would ever suggest using one. The *pure discovery* notion is *pure nonsense*, he asserted.

In further analyzing teacher and pupil behavior in the film, and the relative purity of the discoveries, it became clear that the teacher was not the sole guide to the student's exploration. Several kinds of things guide individuals in this kind of instructional situation. First, in mathematics, a student checks his discovery against reality. That is, the student has alternative means of checking the response he has generated and of determining whether or not it is accurate. The students are constantly called upon to check their findings against an incontrovertible reality.

Second, the other students in the group can guide the individual. In the case of the film which the group had observed, the students were constantly monitoring each other and correcting each other's responses. Finally, there is the kind of guidance with which we are most familiar, in which it is the teacher who is the primary corrector of the behavior of the student. A major criticism of the individual exploratory 'messing-around' approach to teaching is that, under these conditions, children are deprived of all except the first kind of guidance. They work individually and can thus only check their results against reality.

With this in mind, the group now shifted the focus of discussion to the differences inherent in teaching individuals and teaching in a group. One participant raised the possibility that, in the film shown by Davis, it was unnecessary for the teacher to state whether a response was right or wrong because the children themselves played this role for each other. Thus, the students acted as teacher-surrogates. What happens if you try to work with only one child utilizing this same method?

There was a good deal of consensus here that working with one child using this form of discovery technique was not at all as successful as using it with a group. The reasons for this were now examined. One suggestion was that in a group situation, you simply have more teachers. Another suggestion was that the group situation is superior because it supplies either competition or simply an appreciative audience. A third suggestion was that in an individual teaching situation there is too much of a work or information overload for the individual child. In a class situation he can sit back and relax for a moment, while others carry the ball. Conversely, a classroom atmosphere can sometimes be so tense or competitive that no one can relax, because each student feels called upon to come up with a new and brighter idea than his classmate. When the overall atmosphere is this tense, the level at which the class operates is often rather 'surfacy' and banal.

Most research in human learning, however, takes place under conditions where individual subjects cannot communicate with others. If the discovery techniques are so much more effective in a group situation, much more research is needed in investigating the process of learning in a group. For example, is the learning of the individual who offers an insight during a discussion qualitatively different from that of other individuals who are just listening to it? One way we could test the discovery principle is by checking the differential abilities to transfer their training of those who actively provide insights during a discussion and those who more passively sit back and listen.

A participant now observed that the group had been focusing almost exclusively on problems of understanding, and subsequently manipulating, the child and his environment in such a way as to elicit the learning desired. Equally important is the question of how to prepare the teacher so that she in turn may affect the child in a given way. Unlike the former problem, this is a topic which has not been explored very fully. It is quite apparent, though, that for purposes of dealing with problems of instruction, an understanding of the processes of learning alone is not sufficient.

Is it possible to enumerate a range of instructional strategies which reflect the concept of discovery? It became apparent that even in the heuristic sense of generating descriptions of teaching tactics, discovery was not a sufficiently precise term. We must be able to outline specific discovery-type strategies which are distinctive and amenable to systematic examination. In this way, we can discuss with teachers the kinds of things they now do, and more effectively categorize and evaluate instructional procedures.

For this kind of task, we need a meta-language of education which will allow psychologists to communicate with educators in the same language. We need a theory of instruction stated in these same terms. That is, we need ways to bring our knowledge of perception, storage and retrieval, mediating processes, motivation and the like within the framework of the classroom in some meaningful sense. To fulfill this function the teaching of psychology may need to be improved.

College students of psychology perceive this discipline at a pre-operational level, in Piaget's terms, while the instruction proceeds at a formal level. Then, when these students become teachers, we find, to our surprise, that their perceptions are not very refined. They seem only to recognize the primitive extremes of differences and cannot even associate these with the terms we have taught them to use. One strategy may be to infiltrate the training of these youngsters at an earlier age and begin teaching them to think about their own mental processes and those of others when they are much younger. This kind of learning can possibly grow out of courses like that which Bruner, for example, describes in this volume. Thus, the long-range key to preparing teachers adequately to function in the 'discovery-oriented' classroom, may lie in the introduction of behavioral science concepts to potential teachers in their own elementary school experiences.

PART FOUR

PSYCHOLOGICAL INSIGHTS

Chapter X

Varieties of Learning and the Concept of Discovery

ROBERT M. GAGNÉ

IN VIEW OF WHAT HAS BEEN SAID IN THE OTHER PAPERS, IT IS UN-necessary to point out that *discovery* is a word tending to call forth distinctly positive reactions in the world of education. Discovery is a 'good' word for describing one aspect of the educational process and, on the whole, this state of affairs is probably a good thing in itself. One effect is that the consideration of the nature of *instruction* as a central part of the educative process increasingly emphasizes student behavior, as opposed to teacher behavior, classroom conditions, and so on. Discovery is something that the student does, beyond merely sitting in his seat and paying attention. What the student does, or to say it another way, the events that transpire within the student, are bound to be of crucial importance for learning.

These processes that take place within the student are traditionally of interest to the psychologist. He wishes to study them, not primarily because they are good or bad, but in order to determine how they can be employed to account for instances of actual learning. He is interested in constructing a useful model, or theory of learning, which will incorporate such constructs as 'discovery,' if this is possible. Some theories of learning have not made use of a construct like discovery, to be sure. The reason may be either (1) that the theory actually rejects such a construct as unnecessary, or (2) that the varieties of learning situation to which the theory of learning is applicable are restricted to those which do not, in fact, involve such a process as discovery.

In any case, if the psychologist is to use a construct like discovery, he must seek to define it in terms of observable events. This is what I shall try to do in this paper. At the very outset, it seems highly likely that discovery will turn out to have more than a single meaning. When Gibson (1941) examined the concept of mental set, a number of years ago, he found it to have a bewildering variety of meanings. I hope this will not be true of discovery. But if discovery is to be useful as a scientific term, the search for its meaning or meanings must be made, whatever the outcome may be.

LEARNING: EXTERNAL AND INTERNAL EVENTS

It is obvious that the change in performance potential that is called learning involves phenomena that are directly observable, located outside the organism, as well as other phenomena that are inferred as taking place inside the learner, that is, in his nervous system. One would not expect the learner to discover the external events, since these are the 'givens' in bringing about the act of learning. In contrast, certain internal events or states are said to be 'discovered' because they are not supplied by the learning experimenter as a part of the situation which he controls. The implication is that discovery of these internal events must involve (1) a process of *search*, and (2) a process of *selection*, each of which takes place within the learner's nervous system, and each of which may be idiosyncratic to the individual learner.

What is it that must be searched for and selected in this activity called discovery? In attempting to answer this question, we are soon led to realize that the object of the search is not always the same kind of thing. And if this is a possibility, we then can ask, What kinds of entities can be searched for and selected within an act of learning? Since what is sought must be internal events or states, we must presumably look for them inside the learner. The tools to be used are inference and reasoning from external observations; and these, of course, are fairly good tools. Using them, I shall attempt to answer the question, What is discovery? for several types of learning situations.

Simple Associative Learning

As nearly everyone will agree, there *is* a type of learning which may be called simple associative learning, or connection learning. In a dog, an example is learning to raise his paw when his master says, Shake hands. In a human child, it is learning to imitate saying a previously unfamiliar word. In a human adult, it may be such a thing as learning to pronounce *ch* in German. As each of these examples illustrates, there is often a motor component in connection learning. In fact, it is doubtful whether the prototype of connection learning can be considered truly typical unless this motor component is present. This, however, is a subject too complex to consider here, and I must leave it with a reference to Mowrer (1960).

Can it be that there is discovery in connection learning? Many investigators have said there is. For example, consider some of Thorndike's results (1898) concerning the behavior of cats in getting out of "problem boxes." I need not show you a slide to illustrate the difference exhibited by Cat No. 10 in getting out of Box D, and the same cat in getting out of Box C. The first of these problems required him to pull a short string, and showed a decrease in time from seven minutes to 25 seconds following the first trial, with a small reduction thereafter. The second required the cat to rotate a button, and showed variable times of release from seven minutes to two minutes to four minutes to 40 seconds to three minutes, and so on and on, for 30 trials. Thorndike interpreted the gradual reduction in time as a gradual strengthening of the connection. This, however, will not begin to explain why there should be such a difference between the two boxes. Apparently, one connection was strengthened right away, whereas the other showed great variability over many trials.

It seems simpler and more reasonable to interpret the cat's variable fumbling around as indicative of a process of search and selection. At least, nothing in the cat's behavior contradicts such an interpretation. Why was the string-pulling performance established rapidly? It was because the motor-feedback aspect of the stimulus (that is, the kinesthetic part of the stimulation) was quickly discovered. Why did it take so long to establish the button-turning performance? It was because the kinesthetic parts of the stimulus were not quickly discovered. The difference no doubt has something to do with the native constitution of cats, as the Brelands (1961) point out. This analysis suggests, therefore, that connection learning does indeed involve discovery, and that what is being discovered is the internal (kinesthetic) part of the stimulus. It also suggests that much, if not all, of the 'gradualness' of learning motor acts is an indication of the process of discovery, of internal search and selection. It will be evident that such an interpretation is most consistent with modern learning theories that emphasize stimulus selection (e. g., Estes, 1959).

This interpretation is also quite compatible with what is known about human motor learning. Learning a motor act *does* seem to be a process in which there is discovery of the proper kinesthetic stimuli. As the lady golfer said when she holed a ball from the edge of the green, I wish I knew what I did right. Practical methods of establishing human motor acts are almost entirely concerned with facilitating the process of discovery. Sometimes they do it by getting the learner to take the proper stance, sometimes by means of verbal or pictorial instructions. But always there appears to be the necessity for repeating the action over and over again in the attempt to discover the proper response-generated stimuli.

It is worth pointing out, perhaps, that this is not a novel view of the process of simple associative learning; the occurrence of discovery in such learning has been recognized for many years by those investigators whose thinking is not hindered by rigid theory. Melton (1950, p. 671) has written:

> Problem situations may also be described in terms of the extent to which they require the discovery and/or fixation of responses which are *available* in the repertoire of the individual . . . [Thus] in motor learning, learning to wiggle one's ears is different, in terms of this dimension, from learning to push the proper switch (an already available response) on a certain signal.

The function of practice in this kind of learning may be conceived to be that of providing repeated occasions on which the discovery process can take place. If the German word *ich* does not come out quite right the first time, the individual practices some more. Over several trials, it may be supposed that the kinesthetic stimuli become more and more precisely selected so that the performance meets some established criterion. In this meaning of the term, it is fair to say that if we want discovery to occur, we must provide practice, or repetition of the learning situation.

Discovery in Verbal Associate Learning

Learning psychologists have been fond of studying the learning of associations between pairs of verbal terms, like GUZ-FIV, or 22-Green, and the like. While one may reasonably deprecate the idea that such learning forms a large part of what is learned in school, it nevertheless seems true that verbal associations do have to be learned, on occasion. There are many kinds of codes or translations that must be acquired in the course of learning academic subject-matter. Perhaps the clearest example is learning the translations of foreign words into English, and vice versa.

Does discovery play a part in this paired-associate kind of learning? Is there a process of search and selection which can be identified in connection with such learning? There certainly seems to be mounting evidence that paired-associate learning is a far more complex thing than the connection of a stimulus with a response. Let me mention here some of the evidence that supports this view, and attempt to point out what this shows about the occurrence of a discovery process.

The evidence marshalled by Underwood and Shulz (1960) adds up to a pretty clear indication that much of the gradualness of the typical paired-associate learning task must be attributed to the process of becoming familiar with the response members (nonsense syllables or words). There is also evidence that the paired-associate task diminishes in difficulty when the learner is more highly familiar with the stimulus terms (Noble, 1963). While the question of the nature of the process underlying familiarity has not yet been answered fully, it seems clear that the process is not one that involves discovery. Familiarity seems to be graded in amount, but not to involve search and selection.

Undoubtedly, the major event which dominates the learning of sets of paired associates is *interference*, as Underwood (1964), Postman (1961), and others have emphasized in summarizing the experimental findings in this area. Interference may be an extinction-like phenomenon, as the study of Barnes and Underwood (1959) suggests. But again, one can find little evidence of a discovery process here.

It is when one asks the question, How does a *single* pair of verbal associates get connected? that the possibilities of discovery reveal themselves. The occurrence of mediation in such learning is by this time a well-established fact. For example, Jenkins (1963, p. 213) reports a study by Sacks and Russell which had the following procedure: First, learn verbal associations of the sort ZUG-Table, BOP-King; then, learn a second set of associations of the sort ZUG-Chair, BOP-Queen. The subjects learned the second set in virtually one trial.

Taken as a whole, the evidence on mediated verbal learning makes it fairly clear that verbal associates are increasingly more easily learned to the degree that there already exists in the learner a readily available mediating link (cf. Jenkins, 1963; Russell, 1963; Staats & Staats, 1963). Some writers (e.g. Gagné, 1965) consider verbal association to be typically a process of mediation, while others (e.g. Underwood, 1964) caution that a mediation process need not necessarily be involved. It is noteworthy, though, that when subjects are asked how they form associations, in a very high proportion of instances they report what Underwood (1963) has called a "functional" stimulus, which is usually not the same as the "nominal" stimulus. The events of association, as distinguished from those of word-familiarity and interference, do appear to provide the conditions for a search-and-selection process—in other words, for a process of discovery.

If the possibility of discovery exists in verbal association, how does it come about? It is a reasonable hypothesis, perhaps not yet fully established, that the words or syllables to be associated generate a process of recall in which the learner discovers a link between them. In the Sacks and Russell experiment, the discovery is easy, because the links between *table* and *chair*, and between *king* and *queen* are highly available. In contrast, links between such words as *cheese* and *river* may be less readily available, while the discovery of a link between GUZ and RYK may be a relatively difficult task. Is there an advantage to reducing the need for discovery by actually supplying a link (as is typically done in experiments on mediation), or is it better for learning and retention if the learner discovers his own link? According to Bruner (1961), the latter procedure has the advantage: in one study, 95 per cent of the associations were recalled when the learner had to supply his own mediator, whereas less than 50 per cent were recalled when the mediator was supplied for him.

In learning verbal associates, then, there is evidence that a process of discovery enters into the learning activity in an important way, as *discovery of mediating links*. There is an important difference to note between this kind of learning and the simple connection learning previously described. In the former case, it was notable that practice provided the opportunity for discovery. But practice does not appear to have this function in verbal learning. It does not take repetition of the verbal associates to bring about discovery of the mediator. Rather, what it takes is a rich store of mediators, established by *previous* learning. Learning facility will be increased to the extent that mediators are readily available, and this in turn will be determined by the previous learning of word associations. The individual who has earlier acquired a great store of verbal associations will presumably have the advantage in learning new verbal associates. This is also the reason for the advantage to meaningfulness (in one of its meanings) in verbal learning: discovery is easier when many associates are available (cf. Deese, 1961).

Concept Learning

Another typical variety of learning, bearing some relation to verbal associates, is called concept learning. As a result of this kind of learning, the individual becomes able to perform identically toward stimuli which may differ markedly in their physical appearance, but which are responded to as a class. A fairly clear and simple example of a concept is provided by Harlow's (1949) "oddity problem." The individual, whether animal or human being, presented with stimuli which may be varied in their physical appearance, responds by choosing the odd one: if there are two triangles and a circle, he chooses the circle; if there are two books and a pencil, he chooses the pencil. In related studies of an earlier period, Hunter (1913), in studies of delayed reaction, showed that raccoons and children could learn to choose the middle one, or the left one, or the right one of three stimuli. The point of these techniques used to study concept learning is to set up a situation in which it can be shown that the learner's behavior is not controlled by specific external stimuli. Instead, the learner himself must supply an internal "symbolic" stimulus (as Hunter called it) that represents the class of stimuli being presented to him. He must somehow represent to himself 'odd,' or 'middle,' or 'left,' or whatever, and be able to transfer this capability to new situations of the same class.

Experimental controversies generated by these basic studies of concept learning have centered around the question of how logically tight is the demonstration that a self-generated mediating process must be inferred, as opposed to the idea that behavior is controlled by some sort of external cue. Techniques to insure the soundness of this inference are still being invented. Besides those previously mentioned methods of Harlow and Hunter, there are the transposition experiments of Spence (1937) and Kuenne (1946), and the reversal technique of the Kendlers (1961). However thorny the arguments against them, it is really quite difficult to believe that all these instances can somehow be 'reduced' to simple associative learning; and, accordingly, it is not difficult to believe that both human beings and many animals can learn concepts.

Is there evidence of a mediational process in concept learning? Yes, indeed there is; in fact, this is what most of the evidence is all about. If it can be demonstrated that consistent responses can be made in the face of widely varying external stimulation, then one is forced to infer that there must be a consistent *internal* process supplied by the individual's own nervous system. Hunter's raccoons generated an internal symbolic cue. Harlow's monkeys acquired learning sets. When an individual is able to respond to 'stimulus relationships' in some transposition problems, this is taken as evidence that some mediational process must have guided the behavior. Seven-year-old children are able to switch rapidly from choosing the black card to choosing the opposite (or white) card, because they are able to represent 'opposite' to themselves, whereas four-year-olds cannot.

Mediation, then, is characteristic of concept learning. Some internal process must be searched for and selected which makes it possible for a great variety of specific stimuli to be represented as a class. It is an interesting question, though, as to how such a discovery process might be affected by a greater or lesser amount of guidance, particularly verbal guidance.

Guidance in Concept Discovery. One can certainly set up a learning situation to require that concepts be learned by discovery with a minimum of external guidance. In fact, this is the procedure that Harlow did use, in having his monkeys learn to choose 'the odd one,' or to acquire the other concepts he required of them. They solved one particular problem, went on to the next, and the next, and so on, until they reached a point at which the new problem (involving the same concept) was solved almost immediately. The animals *had to discover* the concept; Harlow gave them no help, only practice.

It is of some importance to note that a learning situation can readily be set up to require human beings to discover concepts with almost no guidance. Goldstein and Weber (1965) arranged a learning situation in which learners of high school age were asked to make a choice on successive exposures of two nonsense figures. Confirmation of correct responses was provided in such a way that in one group of learners 'position' was the correct choice (i.e., the one on the right), and in another group, a particular appearance was correct. The subjects were asked simply to indicate choices, and minimal verbal directions were provided. The positional concept turned out to be much more difficult for these human subjects to discover than was the appearance concept. But in either case, it took a relatively large number of trials before the discovery was actually made.

If one examines these kinds of situations dispassionately, they lead naturally to the following conclusion: Discovery without guidance makes the learning of concepts a terribly slow process. It is quite evident that adult human beings do not typically learn concepts by this method. If one wants an adult to learn to choose the one on the right, he says, 'on the right,' and the concept is attained in a single trial. If one wants efficient behavior in a reversal problem by seven-year-olds, he says 'opposite,' and the concept is available for use at once. Examples from school learning situations are not different in principle. The student does not start to learn what a *cell* is by discovering that this is its name; he is *told* what it is. The child does not begin the process of discovering what a circle is by searching for a drawn circle; he is told what it is. That is to say, when the mediators have been previously learned, as verbal responses or some other kind, it is considerably easier to arouse their recall by means of some verbal instruction than it is to expect them to be discovered. If the monkey or ape could respond to verbal instructions as a human being can, he too would probably be able to acquire concepts in a small number of trials. To expect a human being to engage in a trial-and-error procedure in discovering a concept appears to be a matter of asking him to behave like an ape. It is of psychological interest to do this, of course, but possibly not of much educational interest.

It is true that there must be a difference between the use of a previously learned concept by an adult in a new situation, on the one hand, and the absolutely brand-new learning of a concept by a young child, on the other. Perhaps the latter is not and cannot be done simply by transferring a previously learned verbal label, acting as a mediator, to a novel situation. The young child must have to respond to a certain number of instances of a given class before he is able to respond conceptually to any member of the class; and in addition, he must have differentiated negative from positive instances. Unfortunately, we seem to have too little evidence on this point. We know that the four-year-old learners in the Kendlers' study could learn to reverse by means of a period of trial-and-error learning. But could they have learned the concept 'opposite'? And how might they have learned such a concept most efficiently? These are the questions which seem to me to be unanswered at present.

As a hypothesis concerning how a child might learn a concept, the following is offered (cf. Gagné, 1965):

(a) Show the child one instance of the concept (e.g., edge, as the edge of a piece of paper), and say, This is an edge.

(b) Show him another instance, such as the edge of a swimming pool, and say, This is an edge.

(c) Show him a negative instance, such as the side or top of a cylinder, and say, This is not an edge.

(d) Show him still another object, such as a cup, and pointing appropriately, say, This is an edge, and, This is not an edge.

(e) As a test, give the child a box and say, Show me the edge.

I think this method might work, although I have not tried it. More examples, both negative and positive, might be needed for some children than for others. A teacher might prefer to use a questioning form of statement in most cases, rather than the declarative form. But it is most important to note that this is a highly guided procedure, which requires communication through language for its success. There may be an internal process of discovery in the attainment of the concept, but the external learning situation is one which uses extensive guidance.

Discovery in the Learning of Principles

A still more complex kind of learning pertains to the learning of principles or rules. This sort of learning constitutes a very large part of what is accomplished in school situations. Principles, in their ideal form, are combinations of concepts. They range from such a relatively simple set of ideas as Birds fly, to considerably more sophisticated combinations such as that represented by $F = ma$.

It should be clear that when I speak of principles I do not refer to the simple expression of the principle as a verbal sequence, such as Birds fly. Learning this as a verbal sequence is quite a different matter, already described in terms of learning verbal associates. If one wants to determine whether the individual has acquired the principle, he must ask him to *apply* it, or *supply* an instance of it. Often the person can also say it, but this is not directly relevant. Brown and Fraser (1963) make this point vividly in their discussion of the learning of syntactic rules by children.

A different and equally important point about the learning of principles is that what is learned is the *combination*, and not the concepts of which it is composed. If a learner is to acquire the principle, $F = ma$, in an efficient manner, he must previously have learned the concepts of *force* (as push or pull), of *mass*, of *acceleration*, of *equality*, and of *multiplication*. Only if he already knows these concepts can he learn the principle in the most straightforward and efficient manner.

Again let us consider the question, Is there opportunity for search and selection, for discovery, in the learning of principles? The answer is Yes, there seems to be. The reason appears to be quite simple, and perhaps it is deceptively so. When one has two or more concepts in mind, that is, in the status of ready recall, there are many possible *kinds* of combinations that may be made, and then selected or rejected. The concept 'birds' may be combined with a number of possible concepts, including fly, walk, flutter, soar, peck, and so on, whereas there are others it cannot be legitimately combined with, such as frown, bark, growl, and so on. Similarly, there are many ways that the concepts of force and mass and acceleration *might* be combined, but only a few valid ways. It is not unreasonable to suppose that a search and selection process may occur in the learning of principles. This would be a sort of 'internal trial-and-error' activity, or, as some writers might prefer to call it, a 'hypothesis selection' process. Of course, any such process must be followed by feedback, or verification, in order for the learner to complete the acquisition of the principle.

Probably everyone would agree that it is possible to learn a principle without discovery. Many examples come to mind. A scientist who is reading a technical article in his field learns a great deal from it, that is, he acquires a number of principles that are new to him. Of course, he must already know the concepts which enter into these principles in order to learn anything at all. But he does *not* discover these principles. He is told them. He engages in what Ausubel (1963) calls reception learning. If, in fact, a scientist can learn this way, and learn a tremendous number of new principles in reading his professional journals, surely a student can learn this way too. There seems to be little doubt about it—students *do* learn this way, without discovery. It is doubtless incorrect, too, as Ausubel also points out, to equate reception learning with rote learning.

There is, however, the interesting question as to whether learning principles via a discovery process is somehow better than learning them by reception. Most probably, one cannot maintain that discovery learning will be faster, since it may involve a greater number of internal trials in which hypotheses are rejected until the right one is found. How else could discovery learning of principles be 'better'? One possibility is that retention may be better, another that transferability may be greater.

There are a number of studies that bear upon this question of the value of discovery learning of principles to retention and transfer (McConnell, 1934; Thiele, 1938; Swenson, 1949; Anderson, 1949; Craig, 1956). It is not possible to review them in detail here. What may be said, though, is that it is somewhat difficult in all of these studies to be sure that only a single independent variable was being manipulated in each case. I refer again to that thoughtful critic of discovery, Ausubel (1961b), who makes a similar point. It is surely highly suggestive that advantages in retention and transfer have been found in a number of instances in which discovery was at least one of the variables being manipulated. But it is my impression that there is a strong need for a really well-controlled laboratory experiment in this area. Such an experiment should include at least the following features: (1) insure that the learners have already acquired the concepts to be combined into principles; (2) require the learning of principles, not verbal associates, or something else; (3) compare discovery with reception (that is, no discovery); and (4) apply well-designed measures of retention, transfer, or both. Surely such an experiment can be done!

There would appear to be some theoretical reasons for predicting that discovery of principles might be a more effective means of learning than the sheer reception method, if the criterion of effectiveness is either retention or transferability. First, in the process by which a second concept gets combined with a first, the selected concept is likely to be highly available in the learner's repertoire. It is recallable in all of its idiosyncratic characteristics. Such a concept, if it turns out to be the correct one, is likely to have an advantage at the very outset for both recall and for transfer. And the combination of one highly available concept with another, in the formation of a principle, is accordingly likely to possess a comparably high degree of prepotency in its retention and its transferability.

A second reason to expect advantages for discovery learning of principles derives from the nature of the process itself. As emphasized previously, it is a search-and-selection process, which means it is a *discriminative* kind of process, in which unsatisfactory combinations are rejected and successful ones confirmed. Such a process may have the effect of reducing interference with other concepts and combinations of concepts. Reduction of interference from conflicting principles may be expected to produce a result favorable to both retention and transfer.

Guidance in Learning Principles. Even after the well-designed experiment on discovery in principle learning is done, this will still leave the problem of the effects of various amounts of *guidance*. It is evident that a discovery method can be contrasted not only with a reception (or no discovery) method, but also with methods falling in between the two with respect to the degree of *independent search* they demand. The discovery of a principle defining an unknown object is progressively guided in the game of Twenty Questions, by exclusion of categories like 'animal, vegetable, or mineral.' The discovery of the principles involved in the anagram CNABO may be guided, that is, the search may be simplified, by instructions which furnish the category 'food.' One of the most carefully designed experimental studies in this field, that by Craig (1953), demonstrated large differences in transfer of a method of guided discovery versus nonguided discovery used during the original learning. A number of other studies, concerned with the learning of different principles, appear to support these findings (Kittell, 1957; and Kersh, 1958).

In the case of guided discovery, too, there is a theoretical reason why this method might be expected to be superior to unguided discovery. So far as initial learning is concerned, providing guidance should have the effect of cutting down the search time, and thus speeding up the act of learning. Giving the learner guidance instructions may, as

Gagné and Brown (1961) noted, make it possible for some of the wilder hypotheses to be eliminated immediately. At the same time, it may be noted, the *selection* part of the process can still occur. The learner is not told the principle, as in reception learning; the combination of concepts still takes place internally. If this is true, it may also be that the most important aspect of the discovery process is preserved, insofar as retention and transfer are concerned. Under these circumstances, highly recallable concepts are favored as the rejection of the most confusable combinations takes place. In summary, the technique of guided discovery may be successful because it cuts down the necessity for search, eliminates the most extreme wrong hypotheses, while at the same time it provides the opportunity for selection of correct combinations of concepts to occur.

Discovery in Problem Solving

A still more complex kind of learning situation within which it is appropriate to suppose that discovery may occur is called *problem solving*. In order to define this kind of learning, it is necessary to distinguish two things. First is the fact that problem solving typically requires the learner to acquire what may be called a higher-order principle, formed by putting together two or more simpler principles. In some formal sense, the drawing of conclusions in logic may represent this process. The individual already has learned the elementary principles, Birds fly, and Flying requires wings. He goes on to formulate the new higher-order principle, Birds have wings for flying. Surely this example is too simple; yet I think it is a prototype for problem solving.

The second characteristic of the problem-solving situation is a matter of method, rather than content. Problem-solving situations are usually designed to *require* discovery on the part of the learner. This is an inevitable part of their makeup; otherwise, they would probably not be called problem-solving. If I ask an individual to supply the next two numbers in the number series

$$1 \quad 2 \quad 5 \quad 14 \quad - \quad -,$$

he has a problem. If I tell him the principles, Multiply by three, and Subtract one, there is no problem. There would almost certainly be learning in this situation, but it would not be called problem solving.

By definition, then, learning which results from a situation of the sort usually considered to represent problem solving involves discovery. There is search, some of which may take place overtly, and there is selection of a higher-order principle. These features seem clearly to characterize some of the most interesting studies of problem solving, such as those of Maier (1930) and Katona (1940). In Maier's pendulum problem, for example, college students were expected to learn a complex principle involving the use of a vertical pole to wedge a horizontal stick against a ceiling, holding up two pendulums constructed from string and a weighted object. In Katona's matchstick problems, the students were learning a principle about how to open up a matchstick figure to produce fewer squares with a given number of matches.

Correct solutions to such problems as these were best achieved in both cases with considerable amounts of 'guidance.' This was delivered, in the case of Maier's study, by verbal instructions, and in the case of Katona's, by means of a blackboard demonstration. When such guidance was given, a significantly greater number of solutions was achieved than when it was omitted. Learning was thus made more probable. In Katona's study there is also the suggestion that the demonstration produced greater transfer to new matchstick problems than occurred when learners were told the higher-order principle. More evidence on this point would be welcome.

Learning to Discover

Can individuals learn how to discover the solutions of problems? The evidence just cited from Katona (1940) suggests that they can learn how to solve matchstick problems. Gagné and Brown (1961) showed that high school students were able to learn how to discover the solution to number-series problems. The work of Bruner, Goodnow, and Austin (1956) demonstrated that strategies of discovery were learned which transferred to a variety of card-coding problems. There would seem to be reasonable evidence that there is some reality to the notion of learning how to discover. But there are some extremly important limitations to this statement, which need to be carefully noted:

The strategies of discovery, the heuristics of discovery, as Bruner (1961) has called them, apparently do not have to be *learned* by discovery. Gagné and Brown's (1961) subjects learned how to discover solutions to number-series problems by several methods, and the pure discovery method was not the best. Many of Katona's subjects learned how to discover the solutions to matchstick problems when they were *told* the principles involved. Maier's subjects discovered the solutions to problems with a good deal of verbal guidance. That the criterion performance involves discovery does not automatically prove that learning this performance requires the method of discovery.

The heuristics of discovery have not been shown to be highly generalizable. People can learn to discover strategies of solving particular kinds of problems, but it is a long way from this fact to the idea that they have learned how to discover in some general sense. Critical thinking ability, as Ausubel (1961b, p. 54) avers, "can only be enhanced within the context of a specific discipline."

Summary and Conclusions

Here I have attempted to review the functions that the process of discovery might reasonably be expected to have in learning. The issues which seem to me to be in need of precise definition in relation to this question are these:

Within an act of learning, discovery may be said to occur when the performance change that is observed requires the inference of an internal process of search and selection. What is sought for and selected varies with the kind of learning that is taking place.

Discovery processes may occur as a part of most kinds of learning acts, from the relatively simple to the relatively complex. In this sense, discovery may be considered a "dimension" of learning, to use Melton's (1950) term. Usually, discovery processes occupy more time in learning than do the processes of acquiring and storing. Accordingly, methods of learning which emphasize discovery are not self-evidently more efficient than other methods.

Analyzing the role of discovery in learning requires that the kind of learning, as determined by learning conditions, be specified first. The analysis then reveals different functions of discovery for different varieties of learning. Some salient points are as follows:

The learning of simple connections (like pronouncing a strange foreign word) typically involves a process of discovery in searching for and selecting the kinesthetic part of the stimulus complex. This gives rise to a need for practice.

The learning of verbal associates may involve discovery of a mediating link between the two verbal members. Some evidence suggests that a self-generated link may be more favorable to learning and retention than a link which is externally supplied.

The learning of concepts appears to require a process of discovery in the sense that an internally generated process of representation is involved. In adults, who have available suitable verbal mediators, concept formation in a novel situation appears to be a most rapid kind of learning. Laboratory studies of effective conditions for concept learning in children seem to be singularly lacking. But the employment of a high degree of guidance, verbal or otherwise, seems to be a necessity for efficient learning.

149

Principle learning can be done with or without discovery. When discovery is introduced as a requirement, there is some evidence to suggest that the learned principle may be better retained and more readily transferable. Guided discovery may serve to cut down the time of search while maintaining the advantages of internal selection.

Problem solving, when considered as a form of learning, requires discovery, since the learner is expected to generate a novel combination of previously learned principles. In this case, too, guidance appears to have its familiar role of decreasing the time for search.

Learning to discover, or learning the heuristics of discovery, appears to be possible, according to the evidence, in an importantly restricted sense: People can learn strategies of solving particular classes of problems. How large these classes may be remains to be demonstrated. It does not, however, seem likely that this generality of content can be very great. There is no convincing evidence that one can learn to be a discoverer, in a general sense; but the question remains an open one.

What implications do these conclusions have for educational practice? First is the idea that discovery is an integral process for several varieties of learning. It is not a panacea for learning effectiveness, nor is it an essential condition for all kinds of learning. But it can be identified widely in school learning situations. Second, when discovery does occur, it is obviously dependent upon internal events generated within the learner. This means that if one is interested in promoting the occurrence of discovery to achieve some educational objective, he must somehow see to it that prerequisite capabilities have been established. In other words, there must certainly be a lot of attention to the preparation phase of instruction, if discovery is going to take place.

Chapter XI

Learning, Attention and the Issue of Discovery[1]

JEROME KAGAN

HAPPILY THIS ESSAY IS A LOGICAL CONTINUATION OF CRONBACH'S URG-
ing that we search for limited generalizations of the form "content
area [by] child [by] form of presentation." It is assumed, first, that we
agree that the issue of discovery versus didactic form in teaching is
too simple and overgeneralized to be discussed with profit. But it is
profitable to talk about variation in presentation of specific academic
contents to specific children at specific stages of development. Consider
a third-grade child learning the essence of multiplication. Should you
let him discover the insight that multiplication is no more than a
series of successive additions, or should you tell him this blessed idea
and let him brood about it. The core of this paper considers some issues
that must be resolved before that question can be answered. We shall
consider, first, those personological variables that affect learning in general, and then summarize the arguments pro and con the discovery
strategy.

A useful and vivid analogical model for learning in children is
the biological process of fertilization. Learning involves a change in
cognitive structures, as fertilization leads to its unique structural changes.
There are two ways to facilitate these changes. The fertilization model
implies that the sperm be made sharper or the ovum made more per-
meable. I acknowledge the advantage of each of these strategies but
vote for the latter, for altering the child's receptivity to the communication from a teacher should have a more permanent effect on future
conceptions.

The basic premise of this paper is that learning and performance
require an understanding of the interaction between cognitive skills and
motivational variables, a proposition offered by Hull over a generation

[1] This research was supported by research grant MH–8792 from the National Institute of Mental Health, U.S.P.H.S.

ago. If the child has minimal motivation to learn, manipulation of external stimulus materials may have little effect on new acquisition. There are many analogies from the natural sciences to support this view of the importance of a catalyst in creating new structures. Without the presence of an enzyme, no sugar is formed from a combination of starch and water. No structural changes occur in the starch without the proper catalyst, and motivational variables are to be viewed as catalysts. A child can be exposed to the richest possible set of material and the most exquisitely architectured schools, and experience no substantial structural changes in his cognitive life.

What are these personological variables that influence the ease of acquisition of new information? The issues are complicated, and dogmatic statements are probably not too helpful. But the advantage of this type of meeting is the license to speak with more conviction than is prudent; to make suggestions that are a bit more extreme than one believes.

The puzzlement that envelops the twin issues, What is learning? and How does it occur, is clarified by assuming that if a child attends to information he is likely to learn something about it. If attention is guaranteed, some learning is likely to occur. Many of the manipulations performed by curriculum builders begin to acquire a superstitious air, for the manipulations often become deified without realizing that the child's attention is the central process being manipulated, and there are many ways to accomplish this goal. Once this theme is assimilated, the problem of learning loses some of its mysticism. Put aside any temporary complaints to this presumptuously simple-sounding proposition, and consider the major directives suggested by the following hypothesis: inquire into the psychological variables that promote or obstruct attention to symbolic material. Let us consider some examples of the general usefulness of the concept of attention.

Many investigators have devoted much effort during the last decade to demonstrate conditioning and learning in the young infant, and many experiments came to the conclusion that the infant was not capable of learning anything during the opening weeks of life. Examination of the character of the conditioned stimulus used in these studies revealed that it was often a continuous tone of short duration. We now realize that in order to capture the young infant's attention, we must present either a tone of long duration or an intermittent tone. When these changes are made in the conditioned stimulus, learning is demonstrated with ease. When one considers the quality of the stimulus that evokes maximum attention, and shifts away from a fetish for a particular manipulation, progress is made in larger leaps. Similar examples could be found in other literatures. Elliott (1964), for example, found no relationship between a host of biological variables and performance in a reaction time task in six-year-olds. Elliott concluded that this was because the child's level of attentiveness and involvement fluctuated markedly during the experiment and influenced his heart rate, respiration, EEG, and performance in different ways.

THE CATALYSTS IN LEARNING

The learning of a new rule or a new word or a new bond between two previously unrelated elements requires, first, a certain level of prior knowledge and, second, a particular constellation of intrapsychic processes that lead to sustained attention to the material to be learned. These psychological processes, which include motives, expectancies, sources of anxiety and standards, exert primary control over the child's distribution of attention in a classroom situation. These processes lead to the initiation of mental work, and determine how long the child will persist at the learning of a new task, how difficult a task he will attempt, and how he will interpret success or failure on that task. A brief description of some of the relevant variables follows:

The motive for acceptance and positive valuation by parents and parent-surrogates. The child's desire for signs of positive evaluation from selected adults leads him to work at the learning process. Most adults issue these signs when the child invests effort in academic mastery. The child wants to obtain and retain adult praise, acceptance, nurturance and recognition, for these responses signify to the 10 year old that he is positively valued. For many preadolescent children, academic tasks are intrinsically boring. The learning of multiplication and division operations is, on the face of it, a meaningless and often monotonous procedure, but one that becomes interesting and important if it is associated with the most significant objects in the child's world—people. For most seven-year-olds, learning is primarily a socially motivated enterprise.

This conclusion may jar those who have read reports of young children enthusiastically working alone at machines to learn various skills. The writer has seen these children, and it appears that subtle social rewards are the fuel that keeps the children at work. Attractive female teachers are often present in the laboratory, and visions of accelerating mothers at home are present in the child's head. Moreover, the child's behavior is often much different when the teacher leaves the training booth and the child is working alone.

There are, of course, significant individual differences in the incentive value of adult praise and recognition. For example, praise and recognition are usually more important for girls than boys, for younger children (age five to eight) than for preadolescents and adolescents, and more relevant when the task is not directly related, in the child's purview, to previously valued instrumental skills. That is, the fuzzier the link between the task to be mastered and the skills the child values, the greater the incentive value of adult praise and recognition for task mastery.

The motivation to maximize similarity to a desirable model. A common motive among children and adults is the desire to maximize similarity to certain models who are perceived to command power, status, instrumental competence, and affection. The child wishes to be like these models who seem to possess these highly desirable resources. If these models display an active interest in intellectual mastery, the child is likely to attempt to mimic them in order to increase behavioral similarity to the model. The reward for this behavior is the strengthening of the belief that the child *is* like the model, and therefore capable of sharing vicariously in the model's more desirable attributes of power, competence and affection. Many people are prone to interpret the poor school performance of lower-class children as a result of their parents' indifference. Lower-class parents presumably do not punish poor report cards, or they fail to urge the child to do well. This belief is stereotypic and not completely valid. The writer has been in many lower-class homes where children were punished severely if they came home with poor grades. Moreover, the child is often told, "Now you'd better do good in school this week." These children perform poorly, in part, because the models to whom they are exposed daily do not reveal that intellectual mastery is a desirable activity for adults. The middle-class child learns the desirability of learning because his models convey this message directly in their behavior.

The motive for differentiation. It is a general human tendency, present in the child from six or seven years of age on, to seek to acquire attributes that differentiate him from his peers and siblings. The child attempts to acquire skills and attributes that allow him to label himself in some unique way. I recall my eight-year-old daughter pointing to the telephone book with great delight and squealing, "We're the only Kagan in the telephone book." This delight in certain kinds of uniqueness can be seen in most children, and the gratification appears to be related to a need for some degree of differentiation.

The need for differentiation is obviously important for creativity. Professor MacKinnon's (1965) work on creative architects and mathematicians indicates that a salient difference between the creative and noncreative professional is the desire of the former group to be creative, to be different from their peers. This motivation is a primary incentive for the product that society regards as creative.

Expectancy of success or failure. Children develop different degrees of expectancy of success or failure on particular intellectual tasks as early as kindergarten. The most frequent reaction to expectancy of failure in a young child is decreased involvement and subsequent withdrawal. At a stronger level of conjecture, expectancy of failure or success has a determining role in guiding preferences and motives. It is more likely that expectancies of goal attainment guide the growth of motives rather than the other way around. Children in extremely progressive school atmospheres, especially in grades one through three, may suffer from too much permissiveness in their intellectual diet. The young child is often reluctant to attempt tasks he thinks he may fail. He wants to learn to read, but questions his competence and his expectancy of failure may push him to the crayons and paints. The assumption that a six-year old is a blossom who, if left alone, will seek the proper academic delicacies is an ingenuous and romantic view of the child. The superb school environment has the power to minimize the potential of painful humiliation that accompanies failure, but this goal is to be reached and has not been attained by most classrooms.

It is important to recognize, incidentally, that *anxiety over possible failure* is to be distinguished from *expectancy of failure*. These variables are different in meaning, although the literature speaks of 'fear of failure' as if expectancy of failure and anxiety over failure were the same constructs. It is likely that there is a curvilinear relation between these two variables. The child with extremely high or low expectancy of failure is less anxious over the possibility of failure than children who are uncertain, and where expectancies are firm (as in extreme confidence or surety of failure) anxiety should be less intense. We have tested many second- and third-grade children from lower-class homes who have been exposed to chronic failure and who behaved as if they expected failure in intellectual tasks. Nothing in their behavior reflected anxiety. There was no apprehension, and when they were incorrect and were told so, they appeared unperturbed.

Conflicts over learning. There are some specific conflicts that can obstruct the child's receptivity to learning, and we shall consider a few of them. One of the most important conflicts operative in the primary grades is related to sex-typing and sex-role values. Many young children label the school situation as a feminine activity. The reasons for this labeling are not mysterious. A child decides that objects are masculine or feminine depending on the contingencies that link these objects with either males or females in his life experience. A sailboat is masculine, a refrigerator feminine, a hammer is masculine, and a sewing machine feminine, because of the frequency with which these objects are used by males or females in the culture. The typical first-grade is led by a woman who promotes and reinforces activities like cutting, pasting, singing songs, obedience, and quiescence. These values are most congruent with the sex-role standards for girls. This double standard in the classroom may be responsible, in part, for the greater proportion of conduct and academic problems among boys than among girls. There are some data to support this conclusion. We did an experiment to demonstrate that young children label the school situation as feminine (Kagan, 1964). You cannot ask a child if a piece of chalk is more appropriate for boys or for girls. The child will laugh at the nonsensical quality of the question. But a moderate disguise seems to work. Second- and third-grade children were shown some pictures and were told, "We have some pictures here that belong to one of three groups, and we're going to call them three different crazy names. These pictures are DEP pictures, these pictures are ROV pictures, and these pictures are FAM pictures. Now you've got to guess whether the picture is a DEP, a ROV, or a FAM (the DEP pictures were masculine, the ROV pictures feminine and the FAM pictures were farm-like scenes)." The child was then shown obviously masculine, feminine, or farm-like pictures in order to teach him quickly the association between the three nonsense syllables and the three concepts. The picture contained trousers, baseballs, footballs, hammers, nails, purses, sewing machines, lipstick and so on. In five to 10 minutes the children were performing with no errors. We then inserted pictures involving academic objects, such as a blackboard, a book, and a page of arithmetic, but there were no people illustrated on these pictures. Most of the children labeled these academic objects as feminine, with one exception, and that was a picture of a map that was labeled masculine. On reflection, the map resembled those used by navigators and ship captains. However, books, pages of arthmetic, and blackboards were labeled predominantly feminine. Among third graders, the boys began to label some of these objects as masculine, because they had begun to see the link between knowledge and a masculine vocation they might choose some time in the future.

A second source of data is cross-cultural. In the United States and Western Europe, where women teach the elementary grades, the ratio of boys to girls with reading problems varies from three to one, to six to one. In Japan, the island of Hokkaido in particular, there is no excess of boys with reading problems, and half of the teachers in the elementary grades are men. Thus the link between sex-typing and school mastery is an important variable that should be attended to by psychologists and teachers.

A second conflict concerns anxiety over competitiveness, and it usually becomes intense during junior-high and high-school. Most public-school classrooms set up an implicit competitive atmosphere in which children who want very good grades must compete with their rivals in the rank-order world in which they live. It is not unlikely, therefore, that children with strong motivation to do well entertain hostile impulses toward the rivals who are competing with them for top honors. Children who have strong conflict and guilt potential over hostile motives may inhibit intense academic effort in order to attenuate the anxiety that surrounds the hostility that surrounds competitive feelings. This is one reason why preadolescent girls suddenly begin to inhibit intense motivation in school. Guilt over hostility is more intensely felt among girls than among boys, and the girl is less free to enter into intense competitive rivalry in the academic situation.

Finally, there is a special conflict, usually more intense in boys, involving assumption of a passive posture with teachers. Boys are encouraged, both by role-models and the general social environment, to be independent and autonomous, especially with respect to women. The traditional school situation, especially in the primary grades, places the young boy in a situation in which he must conform passively to the demands and requests of the female teacher. For boys for whom this is conflictful, there will be rebellion and withdrawal of involvement from the academic enterprise.

These constructs deal with some of the major motivational variables that exert control over the degree of attention and involvement in the learning of new cognitive structures. This essay continues by addressing itself to the issue of discovery. Recall the example given in the introduction: Which method of presentation is more effective in producing learning of multiplication; present the rule first and allow the child to explore the instances, or permit the child to infer the rule? The answer to that question must involve an appreciation of individual differences, not because this represents an evasion of the writer's responsibility to be specific, but because it appears to be the most valid posture to assume on this issue. It would be a mistake to promote or urge one method of presentation for all children. Individual differences in behavior are the rule rather than the exception, and there are few environmental intrusions that have the same effect on all children, regardless of the simplicity of the intrusion. Behavioral geneticists came to this conclusion years ago, and Harlow, in a personal communication, reaffirmed this view. Harlow placed rhesus monkeys individually in homogeneous black boxes for over six months. These monkeys had as homogeneous an environment as one could create. And yet, when they were placed in the Wisconsin General Test apparatus, their performances were palpably different. If individual differences in problem solving remain after this degree of environmental homogeneity, it is certainly not foolhardy to argue for interaction between method of presentation and the psychology of the school-age child. Let us consider, therefore, the pros and cons of a didactic-versus-discovery approach to the presentation of arithmetic problems.

Arguments for Discovery Learning

The discovery approach requires more involvement on the part of the child and, therefore, greater attention to the component materials being presented. Studies of both animals and young children indicate that the more active involvement required of the organism, the greater the likelihood of learning. This principle is even applied to help interpret the phenomenon of imprinting. If the young chicken has to follow the decoy, imprinting is more effective, for the active following presumably leads to increased arousal and greater attention to the decoy. A major advantage of the discovery strategy is that it creates arousal, and as a result, maximal attention.

Because the discovery approach requires extra intellectual effort, the value of the task is increased. This principle is different from the first one stated above, which assumes that effort increases arousal, and subsequent involvement. This second principle is a more subtle psychological variable concerned with the value the child places upon the task. It is reasonable to assume that activities become valuable to the degree to which effort is expended in their mastery. The writer has had the experience of being more involved in a set of data collected by himself personally, than in a set of data that were more important but collected by others. One of the bases for the exhortation to scientists-administrators to spend some time in the laboratory is to guarantee that some involvement is maintained so that the value of laboratory work does not diminish below a certain threshold. A positive relation between effort expended at task-mastery and value placed upon the task is intuitively reasonable. Moreover, interesting experiments being performed in various laboratories tend to support this assumption. In the discovery approach, the child is likely to attach more value to the task because he has to exert more effort. This conclusion might be regarded as a deduction from Festinger's (1957) dissonance theory, although this theory is not necessary for this assumption.

The inferential or discovery approach is likely to increase the child's expectancy that he is able to solve different problems autonomously. One of the most important beliefs the school must teach children is the self-descriptive statement, "I am able to think autonomously." The primary aims of education are not only to teach the child a set of cognitive skills, but also to teach him confidence in his ability to think creatively about intellectual problems. The method of discovery is more likely to accomplish this end, because it requires the child to infer a major principle without excessive guidance from an external agent.

The method of discovery learning helps those children who have a passive dependency conflict with respect to the teacher. Many boys have difficulty in a traditional school setting because they have strong conflict over assuming a dependent and passive orientation with the teacher. This conflict was discussed earlier. Young boys often resist working on an academic task because it is structured as a power play between teacher and child. This discovery approach gives the child more latitude and freedom and removes him from the submissive posture ordinarily maintained between teacher and child.

These are the four advantages of the discovery method. However, there are equally compelling arguments against this method of presentation, and we shall consider them immediately.

There are many children who do not have the initial motivation to exert the necessary effort required to make inferences. The method of discovery requires a period of five, 10, or 20 minutes during which the child is attempting to tease out a simplifying rule. For children who enter the task with high motivation, this delay is not of much import. But for children with lowered motivation and usually lower IQ, the requirement of even five minutes of involvement without immediate reward is too burdensome and these children are apt to withdraw involvement from the task if some success is not immediate. Thus, the method of discovery is minimally appropriate for children who begin a problem situation with low motivation.

Young children five to seven years of age do not have a sufficient appreciation of what a problem is or what a solution is, and, therefore, the incentive value attached to discovery is fragile. I refer here to an important developmental difference in the attractiveness of making inferences. Preadolescent children have learned the joy of discovery, and for them there is an inherent incentive in the discovery method. Seven-year-olds are still in the process of acquiring this refined source of joy, and many have not even learned to appreciate what a problem is. For example, eight-year-old children usually do not remain within the constraints of a problem. Margaret Donaldson's recent book, *A Study of Children's Thinking*, illustrates this problem beautifully (Donaldson, 1964). For example, an eight-year old child is given a matching problem of the following type: There are three girls, Mary, Paula and Jean, and there are three schools, the North School, the South School and the East School. Mary goes to the North School and Jean does not go to the East School; can you tell me which school Paula goes to? The child is likely to reply that Paula goes to the East School because her girl friend Paula goes there. Or, she might say the East School is the biggest school, and Mary goes there because she is the biggest girl. The young child intrudes personal information extraneous to the problem. We first have to teach the child the meaning of a problem and what it means to solve one before we initiate discovery procedures. The tendency to confuse reality with the artificial restraints of a problem is serious when one is trying to teach principles by the discovery method.

Impulsive children are apt to settle on the wrong conclusion in the inferential method and become vulnerable to developing feelings of intellectual importance. Our research during the last four years has been concerned with an individual difference variable which is called reflection-impulsivity (Kagan et al., 1964). This variable refers to the tendency to reflect for a long time (in contrast to responding impulsively) over the differential validity of a solution hypothesis. Some children offer answers impulsively without considering their differential validity, while others tend to reflect a long time offering an answer. It is to be noted that this variable is only relevant for problem situations with response uncertainty. Decision times to questions with low response uncertainty, such as, What is an envelope? or, Who discovered Tunisia? reflect avaliability of knowledge and are not a function of the child's tendency to reflect over multiple answer possibilities. Most of the tasks used in our research involve perceptual discrimination problems in which the child is shown a standard stimulus (either a design or a familiar picture) and six highly similar variants. The child is told to pick out the one variant that is exactly like the standard. This is a problem with high response uncertainty. Some children decide very quickly, are usually wrong, and are called impulsive. Other children take a long time to decide on their first hypothesis, are usually correct, and are called reflective. There is remarkable generality for this tendency across tasks, and moderate intra-individual stability over time. As might be expected, impulsive children make more errors in learning to read and are more likely to make errors of commission.

Finally, impulsive children make more errors of inductive reasoning than reflectives. In a recently completed experiment, children matched on verbal ability and previously classified as impulsive or reflective were given reasoning items in which the child was shown three pictures that told part of a sequence and then had to select which of four alternatives was logically the next step or event. Impulsive children made significantly more errors on these items. In the classroom the impulsive child is more likely to offer the wrong answer and suffer the humiliation that so often accompanies the incorrect response. This individual-difference variable is relevant for the discovery method because discovery procedures place the impulsive child at a disadvantage. The impulsive child is likely to choose the wrong inference, experience a negative reinforcement and, over time, become discouraged about his ability to extract insightful principles.

In sum, the method of discovery is best for highly motivated, older children who might have high dependency conflict and who are prone to a reflective strategy. The method is least appropriate for younger children, especially below the age of nine, who do not have high motivation to master intellectual tasks or who are prone to be impulsive. Some aspects of these recommendations have research support, others must be tested in the laboratory. But until they are refuted by empirical test, they are reasonable propositions to defend.

SUMMARY

Educators and psychologists must begin to acknowledge the multiple interactions among content, child, and developmental level, for learning in the child is a complex phenomenon. We must begin to develop a patience for elegant answers—and a skeptical irritation toward quick and easy solutions that appear to be a panacea but derive from fragile rational grounds. The task is awesome. But excitement is high and the potential implications unlimited.

Chapter XII

Psychological Inquiry and Educational Practice

IN THE COURSE OF HIS PAPER, GAGNÉ ASSERTED THAT THE LEARNING of concepts did not generally entail a process of discovery. Students learn concepts through the use of verbal instructions while, on the other hand, young children probably acquire new concepts through discovery. The group was now led to ask for a clarification of the terms. What is an example of a new concept? Learning of a concept does not necessarily involve attaching a verbal label. It is only necessary for the learner to identify a wide variety of instances of the concept.

Another participant suggested that there is more to concepts than words. A concept is a theoretical construct, an abstraction created by the psychologist. It exists neither in imagery nor in words. A word is a package of concepts, and so is an image. There must be some way in which a perceptual input can communicate with an inner system of concepts. Some packages of concepts have phonetic things attached to them which make them pronounceable. However, any attempt to reduce conceptual thinking to the mere manipulation of words, necessarily leaves out many conceivable concepts. This is totally in keeping with our knowledge of the psychology of language.

In clarifying his use of the word *concept*, Gagné supplied the following illustration: If I teach you, as an adult, a new concept, for example, *caliche*, a term used by President Johnson in his State of the Union address, and give you a formal definition of it, as the crust of calcium carbonate that forms on top of the stony soil of arid regions, have you acquired a concept? One reply was that you have attached semantic markers to that name. It is now a bundle of concepts. You may have had the bundle of concepts before, but simply without a name. You may not be able to identify it without error even with the name, but you probably can do better than five minutes before. The problem here is one of 'coding-in' the perceptual input to that particular package of concepts which you have now acquired.

Why is this called a bundle of concepts rather than a single concept? It is a single bundle! When one looks for a bundle, he looks for it in the same way that some look at the characteristics of a phoneme. The number of words in a language is finite, but the number of possible names is infinite. We put these bundles together as they are needed in referential distinctions in any particular time. We need this freedom in order to speak the language. The notion that all useful packages are preassembled and entered into the lexicon is simply unthinkable.

Gagné took the position that discovery must be regarded as an intervening process. If a student is not told an answer and finds it for himself, the intervening process must have been one of discovery. There are degrees of discovery which are probably inversely related to degrees of guidance. Guidance might take the form of supplying a large number of similar problems, all solvable by the same formula. Here you are giving a tremendous amount of guidance with the result that the amount of discovery involved in finding the formula is not large.

The topic now shifted to a consideration of what Kagan had called the paracognitive variables in the issue of learning by discovery. For example, has a child learned something different when he learns a rule inductively from what he learns by being told the rule first and then applying it? It was suggested that by allowing him to make mistakes in formulating the principle, he acquires the notion of a rule as something which is provisional, subject to later modification by experience. The rule-example method cannot lead, except by accident, to these outcomes. When the inductive method is adopted, the educational objective may be to teach children to modify and even throw away useless rules. Furthermore, when children learn by discovery, they are able to generalize their skills to solve problems that exist outside the classroom. This is similar to Cronbach's goal of intellectual independence. The teaching methods we have been calling discovery can most readily foster this kind of autonomy.

In his paper, Kagan had taken the position that for most children in the primary grades, learning is primarily a socially motivated enterprise; for many academic tasks are intrinsically boring. Social motivation is essential even though it is extrinsic to the school tasks. The discussion which followed dealt with the issue of whether the act of discovery was intrinsically motivating. Time and again, Bruner and others have maintained that there is a self-generating power to discovery. The question raised at this point was to what extent the intrinsic motivation of tasks might be fostered and used by teachers in the classroom. The answer appears related to individual differences; for any given child there must be some tasks which are intrinsically motivating. Using Kagan's categories, it appears that reflective children find tasks more intrinsically motivating than do impulsive children.

Through the course of the conference attempts were made to solve the problems of discovery in the reflected light of psychological theory. Both Gagné and Kagan attempted to generalize from their own bodies of psychological investigation to the instructional question of teaching and learning by discovery. How valid are such attempts? Can the gap between psychological and educational research be bridged? The deliberations of the discussants now centered about the following issues:

What kinds of research strategies are most likely to generate findings relevant to the problems of developing curricula and appropriate teaching procedures?

What is the status of psychological theory relative to problems of instruction?

The suggestion was made that some of the bi-fold or multi-fold methods that have been developed for looking at things like traffic flow patterns may serve as useful starting-points for a 'new look' in educational research. The traffic analyst maps out what happens and uses this map when trying to improve subsequent traffic flow. This may be a good analogy to what must be done in the field of education. This kind of approach, which one of the participants called classroom ecology, essentially suggests a modification in our over-all research strategy. We do not begin with experimental research. We try first to understand good examples of teaching and then use these as the input into subsequent experiments. Here was a position that was reiterated a number of times in the course of the conference deliberations.

How is it possible to carry out studies of sufficient complexity to meet the criteria outlined by Cronbach? Currently, in the field of psychology, there are a number of research strategies operating which show promise of converging on the basic issues at hand. These range on a continuum from the rather well-controlled studies in mathematical learning theory, computer simulation and programmed instruction, to direct observations of the classroom under grossly uncontrolled conditions. More important is the recognition that the naively simple question of discovery versus didactic teaching *per se* is really not very fruitful. Much more important are experiments to deal with such functional problems as, When do you verbalize in learning? or, How much does the instructor monitor, and how much is left for the student to check out his own verbalization? Hence, what is needed is a refurbishing of the basic paradigms utilized in curriculum research.

Further support was expressed for a practical orientation in teaching research. For example, we must attend to the structure of various pedagogical devices such as what constitute the criteria or characteristics of an effective lecture. A lecture, for example, generally provides no direct feedback for the teacher and rarely allows students to ask for clarification when they do not understand the presented material. What are the consequences of allowing questions during or after a lecture? What is the cognitive process of listening to, attending to, and understanding a lecture presentation? What really happens to the participants in a discussion class? Can subjects be trained to participate actively in the on-going process of discussion? Only with research of this practical kind can we in fact offer suggestions that have immediate pedagogical implications. We can do this only by using research strategies to better our knowledge of and appreciation for the structure of the educational system.

One member of the group raised the issue that, as a psychologist, he was much more concerned with special cases than he was with some of the more general problems being discussed by the group. He felt that the special problems were themselves already incredibly complex, and to expand the scope of our interests to these larger problems would quickly exceed the limits of our capabilities. He gave the example of an optimization scheme for paired-associate learning with which he was working. He does not really have a theory, except in the sense that meteorology has a theory. Meteorology has developed a set of useful statements for prediction purposes without any implication that these are parts of a systematic underlying theory with explanatory value. For example, we may know that certain configurations of high and low pressure areas are associated with certain weather phenomena to a high degree of probability, without suggesting that some theory of the upper atmosphere explains why this occurs. Psychology need not feel guilty about what it can only apply, but not necessarily explain. What we need is a theory on the same level as meteorology, not necessarily fitting the model of traditional psychological theories of learning.

A number of participants maintained that there was no problem of inadequate theory. Given a problem of instruction and classroom learning, it would be possible to analyze the stimuli which were input to the system of any child and the responses that constituted the output. Next, we could examine the relationships between groups of stimuli and responses. Present psychological theory was quite adequate to handle a problem of this form.

This position was opposed by another participant who felt that, although the essential problem may begin with the study of input and output, its adequate resolution goes well beyond that stage. There must be some understanding of the intervening system within the learner that transforms input into output. We must try to identify, in whatever terms will suffice, what these systems might be. Subsequently, we may try to decompose the system into components which make psychological sense. These components might be laws of association, i.e., ways of connecting Ss and Rs. In the more complex behavior studied by Piaget, what transforms the input into output is not far from statements of logic or mathematics. In fact, it appears that, for Piaget, there is not much psychology inside the child. There is really much more mathematics and logic. This participant took the position that the reason Piaget is so attractive to us today is that he is not really constructing a psychology of the child, but an epistemology instead. In terms of psychological theory, he maintained, we are bankrupt. Psychological theory as presently constituted is not built to measure these kinds of behavior. We simply do not have a psychology suitable for the teaching of a structured subject.

This position, which maintained the bankruptcy of psychological theory to handle the problem of the conference, now reiterated an earlier suggestion. The brilliant teacher is still the best instructional model available, far better than any theory. Here is where we ought to begin our research, not with theory, but with practice.

A participant now asserted that the issue had been put into either-or terms that were inappropriate and unrealistic. Since our theories are probably in bad shape for handling the more complex problems of education, we must get to work improving them as soon as possible. Meanwhile, however, we must continue to do empirical research in the classroom, even without better theories. The problem is simply too pressing to allow for any further delay. We must continue to engage in practical research without pause. A second discussant disagreed. He felt that refining our theories had priority over empirical research, for without better theories we will either find ourselves in the position of not knowing where to look for the relevant data, or of gathering quite a bit of data that will ultimately be useless.

One participant now suggested that the reason our theories were bankrupt was that psychologists, unlike meteorologists, had, throughout the history of the discipline, taken the easy way out. That is, instead of asking which questions were most critical to society and then developing techniques for dealing with these problems, psychology has preferred to remain tied to those problems which were most amenable to the safe, clean laboratory techniques that had been perfected. We turned our back on the questions that were pressing, but difficult, and instead did what we already knew how to do. Psychology has very successfully insulated itself from those essential problems of human behavior to which society has constantly been seeking answers.

Those who bemoan the sorry state of psychological theory tend to operate in a manner quite different than might be inferred from their declarations alone. We find they are still out in the classroom, engineering excitely, and gleaning all the insights they can from that very body of psychological theory whose puniness they are so quick to point out. Although they imply that education and psychology ought somehow to go their separate ways for the time-being, with psychological theories staying in the laboratory while educational research focuses on the classroom, they are surely not practicing this suggestion.

Is the issue really one of theory? We have not heretofore been in a position to gather the kinds of data in the classroom which are necessary to evaluate the relevant problems of complex human learning processes. It is this lack of a means for observing and analyzing these processes that has stymied us heretofore. However, we now have a growing computer-based technology with which we can go into classrooms and look at the problems of learning in greater detail. New techniques for teaching and studying the reading process are exemplary of this trend. As this research develops, it will have a much greater impact on the problems of education. With this observation, the discussion was brought to a close.

PART FIVE

THE CONFERENCE: RETROSPECT AND PROSPECT

Chapter XIII

Reflections on the Conference

HOWARD H. KENDLER

IF NOTHING ELSE, THIS CONFERENCE HAS DEMONSTRATED THAT DIF-
FERENT linguistic communities, each with a different style of talking
and thinking, exist within both psychology and education. Perhaps the
intellectual distances between these communities have been exagger-
ated by all of the possible meanings that can be, and have been,
assigned to the concept of discovery, but there is no doubt that the
communities do, in fact, exist.

I will try to summarize the ideas put forth at this conference in
terms of the questions they raised. I am not completely confident that
I can report what happened, so I will protect myself by insisting that
I will report only what I think happened. This, hopefully, will be done
in a detached way without offering any value judgments—at least not
too many. Initially some remarks about the concept of discovery will
be made, then research strategy and theory will be discussed, and
finally some conclusions will be offered.

There is no disagreement that we failed to agree about the meaning of the concept of discovery. To say the least, the concept is
ambiguous. People have referred to it in a variety of ways, ranging
from phenomenal experience to a particular arrangement of a classroom situation. Perhaps most commonly discovery was equated with
some theoretical cognitive process, but the theory in which the
concept was embedded was not always crystal clear. This lack of
agreement about the meaning of discovery, although hampering communication, did not block it. When difficulties arose the participants
gracefully slipped back into common-language meanings of the term.
Although ordinary language is not the perfect vehicle for scientific
communication, it nevertheless possesses some capacity to transmit
ideas.

It was recognized that discovery cannot, and should not, be

equated with a laissez-faire educational philosophy. Students can be encouraged, prodded, and shaped to discover. In short, learning by discovery implies controlling the behavior of the student just as does the old-fashioned drill method. The only difference is the pattern of control.

One thing that I felt should have been emphasized more, although it was mentioned, is the relationship between discovery and language behavior. One of my own intuitions is that when a person discovers something, he is able to formulate it in his own language so that it fits in—that is, meshes—with his linguistic network. This allows him to retain and apply the idea he has discovered more effectively because it becomes part of a well-practiced and highly integrated habit system. On the other hand, if he is given the principle in somebody else's words, his own language system very often cannot absorb it. The idea does not really become a part of him. I know of very little research of this sort in the field of education, but I certainly think this kind of analysis might be useful.

Gagné desires to extend the concept of discovery to motor skills, a suggestion that probably surprised some participants since we think of discovery in relation to intellectual tasks that can be represented symbolically. But Gagné's idea is an interesting one, if only to focus attention upon what seems to be an apparent difference in discovering a mathematical principle and the correct way of hitting a golf ball.

Glaser offered a useful distinction between learning by discovery and learning to discover. This should help us break down the global concept of discovery into manageable components. Perhaps the distinction between discovery as assimilation and discovery as accommodation, to use Piaget's terms, will also prove useful.

The major focus of this conference was on what might be referred to as research strategy. Every scientist is, or should be, aware that every decision he makes cannot be justified by facts or logic. This is particularly true when one has to guess what kind of research problem will lead to fruitful results. If one does not want to be immobilized by doubts and fears, one must prejudge the potentialities of a research strategy in the absence of any convincing information of its ultimate worth. Differences in prejudgments is often at the root of controversy. In order to convince themselves that their prejudgments are correct, psychologists and educators often decide that only their prejudgments are appropriate; all others are misleading, sterile, and trivial. Such prejudice is unfortunate. If this conference has any positive value, some sort of tolerance and understanding of the different research strategies should develop. After this brief homily, let me now try to identify some of the different orienting attitudes that were expressed at this conference.

Differences existed about the need for operational definitions. At one end we have Hawkins, who emphasized the need to use concepts before one can actually define them. At the other extreme was the strong operational attitude of Glaser and, to the lesser extent, that of Gagné.

The participants disagreed about the relevance of experimental psychology to educational problems. Hawkins implied that it had little value as evidenced by the fact that he failed to mention any ideas or information from the traditional literature of the experimental psychology of learning except for one; the California latent-learning studies. As a person who was actively engaged in the latent-learning controversy, my advice to the philosopher Hawkins is to find a better model. The latent-learning model has a shaky empirical foundation. It is neither a clear-cut nor reliable phenomenon. It is influenced by a host of variables (e.g. swinging instead of guillotine doors in the maze) that are apparently of no relevance to learning by discovery.

Bruner also bemoaned the horrible state of experimental psychology and its inability to contribute anything of value to the classroom teacher. This has led him to get into the classroom and try to discover what, among different educational techniques, will work. Then, hopefully, the successful technique can be analyzed and its important factors can be uncovered. Bruner and Hawkins can be grouped together in their belief that the significant educational research will come from the classroom. I doubt whether Bruner accepts this principle as enthusiastically as does Hawkins, since this would mean turning his back on some of his own past efforts. At the other extreme, we find Glaser, Gagné, and Wittrock quoting data from the experimental psychology laboratory. The conflict between the Hawkins-Bruner axis and the Glaser-Gagné-Wittrock entente represents, upon analysis, a difference of opinion about the kind of behavior we should try to predict. Should we stick out our necks and try to predict 'real live' classroom behavior, or should we investigate more circumscribed educational situations and try to find the principles that govern behavior within them, and then on the basis of sophisticated intuition extend the principles to the classroom situation? I prefer the latter approach. With simple mathematical, physical, or social-science problems, the behavior of large groups of subjects in well controlled situations can be measured and analyzed, and theoretical principles formulated. But my preference is a prejudice, a prejudgment that cannot be demonstrated to be true, or even to be the most strategic.

Another basic problem raised was that of assessing educational techniques. All educational practices sooner or later should be assessed. No disagreement exists here. The problem is when and how the assessment should take place. A novel educational technique cannot get off the ground if it is obsessed initially with problems of assessment. The problem is when assessment procedures should be incorporated within an educational research program.

How should we assess educational techniques? That is, what outcome variables should we select? The discussion can begin by referring to Cronbach's list of twelve outcome variables—all of which represent to varying degrees value judgments about different forms of behavior. Kagan agreed that value judgments were involved but concluded that we educators and psychologists should make the decision. I do not disagree with him completely, but I would like *society* to play a larger role in the decision-making process. When psychologists are involved in establishing social values in a democracy, they should be very cautious and not confuse personal prejudices with scientific truths. I resonate to Cronbach's list but it can be used insensitively. For example, how would the final item in Cronbach's list, 'creative urge', be applied to the education of the mental retardate and the low normal. Should we try to instill in them a creative urge? Should we try to build intellectual ambitions in people who have not got the ability to achieve these goals?

Assessing educational procedures became more complicated when other factors were brought into the picture. Glaser emphasized cognitive characteristics of the student, represented in terms of stimulus-response associations, while Kagan discussed the interaction between personality variables and educational techniques. It seems that whenever an educational problem is analyzed its complexity increases.

The goals of education were also discussed. Hawkins, representing one extreme, more or less felt we should ignore them. Educate the child and the goals will be achieved. Cronbach insisted we *had* to be concerned with goals. As a psychologist, I think we can say with some degree of confidence, that our discipline has been successful in controlling behavior only when we know the kind of behavior we want to encourage. To put it in terms of specific examples, when we train people to be effective pilots or efficient radio code operators, we can develop techniques to select and train them. When we try to train people to be adjusted, we run into difficulty because we are uncertain what adjusted behavior is. Psychology often seems ineffective only because we are uncertain about what kind of behavior we want to encourage. Once we are sure what behavior we want to encourage, the chances of developing techniques to get people to behave in this manner improves tremendously. The effectiveness of psychology in solving educational problems will be proportional to the precision with which our educational goals are stated.

An interesting point about evaluating different educational programs was raised by Cronbach. What constitutes a control group in such assessment studies? I have become convinced that there is no such thing as a simple control group in any experimental situation. Control groups are generated by theories, and one control group is relevant to some theoretical assumptions and not to others. However, Cronbach, the pragmatist, suggests a rather interesting way of handling the problem of control groups: Limit different educational programs to the same time allotment and then see which is better. Now this seems to be a solution, but quite obviously you can have two programs which have a different effect with one time limit and have an entirely opposite effect with another time limit. How would you discover this if the two programs were compared under only one time limit? An educator can be fooled about the potential of an educational program if he limits his assessment to one arbitrary time unit.

What kind of a theory do we want? The participants differed about this issue. Bruner has a global theory. I resonate to it in spirit but not in content. I believe that everything that Bruner said could be translated into language involving habits, drives, mediational processes, and response-produced cues. He emphasized contrast effects; there are data from discrimination learning which would agree with his analysis. Gagné offers a systematic analysis within the S-R tradition, but it is obvious that it would not be acceptable to all participants. The qualities of Bruner's global theory and Gagné's theory are different, and personal preference of one over the other reflects an individual's predilection, to some extent, in favor of certain concepts and theoretical structures.

Wittrock structured the problem in terms of a theoretical formulation which distinguished independent, intervening, and dependent variables. Although I have some sympathy with this, I would like to point out that this is a model for a theory, but not necessarily the pattern for discovering the theory. I do not know what the pattern is, but I think we tend too frequently to confuse philosophy of science, or the principle of some philosophers of science, with the techniques of achieving the theory.

To me, the major theoretical problem of education is one of understanding language behavior and controlling it. I was disappointed by the limited references to language behavior at the conference. Cronbach cited the quotation that we learn not by doing, but by thinking about what we do. I interpret this to reflect the importance of language behavior on educational processes.

There is certainly no agreement about what strategy we should pursue, and to some extent this is good. In some ways it would be unfortunate if we were all doing the same thing, even though we might then have greater agreement. Can anyone have complete confidence that his research strategy will be productive? Cronbach concluded that we should be hospitable to new ideas, be skeptical, do good research, and be willing to advise the schools. Of course, quite unconsciously, no doubt, he was describing himself. Perhaps there should be some division of labor. Perhaps in addition to the solid, socially sensitive researcher we need the messiah who stirs things up, causes confusion, but nevertheless gets people to test out new ideas.

Kagan emphasized areas that are too often ignored by specialists in learning and cognitive processes. These areas are motivation and personality. Some discussion revolved about the problem of whether scholarly motives were generated in the student by other people (e.g., teacher) or by problems and ideas themselves. To me, it seems obvious that motives can emerge from both sources.

Let me conclude by making two brief points. If we emphasize the importance of identifying the behavior we wish to predict then perhaps we must get involved more in social planning. If we encourage certain kinds of behavior in schools we should be sure that these forms of behavior will be reinforced in the outside world. Otherwise we may find ourselves encouraging maladaptive responses.

No great desire was expressed among the participants to preserve the term 'discovery.' I would like to vote for its elimination. This is not a criticism of the concept of discovery. In the history of science, often concepts are extremely important until you analyze them and discover that they can be broken down into more fundamental components. I believe, with Morrisett, that this is the case here. Even though at various times Maier and others have had tremendous justification to use this term, it has become a nine-letter dirty word and we ought to eliminate it. Let us start with new words emphasizing more analytical approaches as we continue to attack the problems of education.

Chapter XIV

Further Reflections

LLOYD N. MORRISETT

HOWARD KENDLER HAS GIVEN US AN EXCELLENT REVIEW OF THE CON-ference. He accepted the responsibility to be rational and detached. As a result, I am able to be a bit irresponsible and offer some personal conclusions without necessarily being able to justify them fully.

My first conclusion is that the idea of discovery is useful for teachers and for people who are building curricula. Conversely, I doubt very much that the term has great utility for people doing research in psychology and education.

Teachers and curriculum builders may find the concept of discovery useful as a guide in the presentation of classroom materials, in the kinds of materials that they choose, and in the ways in which curriculum materials are sequenced. Discovery may thus have a place in a theory of instruction, if you conceive of a theory of instruction being useful in classroom practice.

However, even here, I think there are limits. Applying Bruner's dictum that we should sometimes push ideas to the limit to see how far they can go, I am sure we can all imagine situations in classes and curricula where discovery can be dysfunctional for learning. For example, this can happen when the discovery becomes punishing, either because the student discovers punishing information about himself or because he is led to discover something that he later finds is trivial or could have been learned more easily. In the first case the student may discover that he is slow while others are quick, or that a respected teacher's values are different from his own and his family's. It may be argued that this information can be used constructively, but to do so something must be added to discovery teaching. In the second case, a student can easily be given too little information or asked the wrong questions so that discovery becomes drudgery. This may still be called discovery, but I doubt that we would call it good teaching.

The use of discovery in teaching to build the student's confidence in his own ability to think and solve problems is certainly a highly desirable goal. As Hawkins pointed out, it may well be that in the year 1965 this is the direction in which education should be pushed, because it has been very badly overbalanced in other directions. However, other virtues that we would like to encourage through education are intellectual humility and the ability to accept the work of others. I am not sure that intellectual humility will necessarily be produced through the discovery technique. Complete reliance on discovery refutes culture.

A final comment along this line concerns the importance of knowing when to stop a line of fruitless thought or investigation. If you sort out highly creative people from those who are less creative, it is my impression that the creative person frequently stops early in an unproductive train of thought, while the less creative person takes longer to stop. How do you teach this? I do not know of any relevant studies, but I think it is important to consider the value of terminating unproductive thought sequences at the same time that we are trying to give people confidence in their intellectual abilities through the use of discovery techniques in teaching. Discovery is important, but so is knowing when to stop.

One contrast that I am trying to draw is between the usefulness of a concept in a theory of instruction, in curriculum building, and in teaching on the one hand, and in psychological and educational research on the other. So far, I think, the problem of defining the unit of behavior that is germane to a theory has not been considered at all effectively except at the level of psychological research. Here the work of Atkinson and others interested in mathematical modeling is impressive in the degree to which they have tried to specify the units of behavior to which their models will apply. A theory of instruction must also face this issue. What is to be discovered—stimuli, responses, concepts, relations, theories, or something else? Is discovery teaching equally relevant to all these goals? I think we have relatively little feeling about the definition and size of the units of behavior we are talking about when we refer to learning by discovery.

The concept of discovery is not very helpful in psychological and educational research because there is little evidence that it is useful in pointing to classes of variables that cannot be better designated by theoretically relevant names. Several papers have illustrated this. While both Glaser and Gagné were willing to talk about discovery, their papers could have been given without using the term 'discovery' at all. Glaser took somewhat of a relativistic position and said that if you wanted to call it discovery, this is the way he would talk about it. Gagné said that he would talk about some things that involve discovery, but if you leave discovery out we can still talk about those same things.

The concept of discovery seems to refer, at different times, to motivational effects, reinforcing effects, and heuristic or mediating effects of sequences of behavior. The first two, need little comment. The process of discovery can be highly involving and sustain task-relevant behavior. A discovery can also, quite obviously, be personally satisfying and tend to increase the probability that similar behavior will recur. In some areas of intellective performance, useful problem solving heuristics are known and can be taught. In other areas, however, teachable heuristics are not well known. Several speakers have made the point that discovery teaching may allow students to invent their own heuristics when recognized teachable heuristics are not available. Intuition and other important but poorly defined abilities may well involve the use of indiosyncratic heuristics, and these modes of thought may be encouraged by discovery teaching.

The second main conclusion that I have drawn as I listened to the discussion, is that research on the topic of discovery, as judged by both Wittrock's review and our discussions, is relatively impoverished. It is impoverished first in the range of variables that have been considered. Cronbach's, Kagan's, and Bruner's papers all pointed toward the conclusion that the main things we know about learning by discovery have also been found important in other areas of psychological research. This may be because the range of variables being studied has been restricted and that attention to the interaction of learning by discovery with personality variables, previous experience, and teacher behavior will reveal new knowledge. If not, this becomes further justification for discarding learning by discovery as a research topic.

A second kind of impoverishment in this research is the impoverishment of the subject matters that have been studied. We talk as if learning by discovery was a generally interesting phenomena, but the work is almost entirely in mathematics and the sciences. This is a serious deficit both to educational research and to the utility of discovery in teaching. I wonder if learning by discovery, as we have been discussing it, is thought to be useful in building curricula in the humanities and arts. Perhaps so, but the meaning of learning by discovery will probably change when we move from mathematics, through the sciences, to the humanities and arts.

I conclude with a very general comment on the kinds of statements that have been made throughout the conference regarding values and educational philosophy. One of the beliefs most commonly shared by scientists is that application of rational thought will lead to human progress. This theme has been a *leitmotif* in our conference. This is very natural, for, as research scientists and psychologists, this is a necessary part of our value system—necessary in order that we engage ourselves in research effectively. As we have talked about learning by discovery, we have implied that this method of learning will necessarily lead people to rational decisions and better lives. Is this, however, any more of a panacea than any other educational method? Educational statistics show higher percentages of age groups in high-school and college. More people than ever before are being exposed to education. Good, bad, or indifferent, I suspect that increased education increases rationality, the ability to be critical, and the ability to learn by discovery. I wonder, however, if this education is inclining people to build a better society. Do people make the right choices? As Kagan asked, Have we made the value commitments that lead students to the right choices? Do they learn about the good and the beautiful and things of enduring value, or do they discover things of less worth? No education is value-free, and a commitment to rational discovery as a method of learning may ignore issues that we cannot afford to turn aside.

Chapter XV

The Problem of Discovery: Conference in Retrospect

EVAN R. KEISLAR
LEE S. SHULMAN

THE CONTROVERSY OVER LEARNING BY DISCOVERY EXISTS SIMULTANEOUS-ly at a number of levels. These levels include those of classroom instruction, curriculum development, psychological studies of learning, and research strategy. Hence, in order to deal with this issue in some meaningful fashion, it becomes necessary to distinguish among these levels of discourse and to specify at which level we are operating at any given moment.

At the level of classroom instruction, the question to be studied is, As I teach Johnny, should I give him a wide variety of examples and expect him to infer the underlying rule, or should I tell him what the rule is while he applies it to examples?

At the level of curriculum development, the question involves something like the following: To what extent ought the order of subjects into which the students inquire be determined by us, and to what extent should this order be determined by the students themselves?

At the level of psychological investigations of learning, the question becomes, What is the transfer value of statements of principles given to a subject, as contrasted with individually-derived principles?

At the level of research strategy, the issue takes on a very different, yet parallel form: What is the most fruitful way to investigate the nature of instruction?

It is the purpose of this chapter to reexamine the contributions of the conference members within the framework just described. One of the difficulties is that the participants tended to shift back and forth among levels. We will thus distinguish among the levels of discourse implicity or explicitly utilized by contributors, and will examine the extent to which consensus or disagreement resulted. We will also attempt to outline the important questions, as we see them, remaining at each of these levels. Thus, though this chapter is, in fact, a view of the conference in retrospect, it might also be seen as a prospectus for further dialogues.

THE LEVEL OF CLASSROOM INSTRUCTION

When we explore the meaning of the learning-by-discovery issue for classroom teachers, we need to ask what the statements on this question will lead teachers to do. Sentences which are worded in the form of clear specific suggestions are likely to elicit greater uniformity in teacher practice than statements where the referents are unclear. However, since teachers relate to their pupils in a highly complex fashion, even phrases which have vague denotations may have profound and varied effects on teaching styles. Instructions such as Help the child to discover the solutions by himself, might lead some teachers to undertake a most productive lesson; conversely, this same statement might lead other teachers, with the best of intentions, to let many pupils flounder entirely too long.

When the assertion was made at the conference that research studies had not yet produced evidence to support the hypothesis of learning by discovery, concern was expressed that the publication of this statement could have ill effects on teacher behavior. It was hinted that some teachers might go back to a learning-by-rote approach to teaching if it were implied that learning by discovery had been discredited. While no one at the conference perceived the issue in terms of this dichotomy, the importance of examining the kind of statements made to teachers cannot be ignored.

One way of posing the issue, therefore, is in terms of teacher behavior: How much and what kind of guidance should the teacher provide? Attempts to offer answers to this question have usually been expressed at a common-sense level, such as that found in the following selections from *Theory and Practice of Teaching*:

> It is always a very difficult question for the teacher to settle, 'How far shall I help the pupil and how far shall the pupil be required to help himself?' . . . That the pupil should be taught mainly to depend on his own resources . . . is the teaching of common sense. Whatever is learned, should be so thoroughly learned, that the next and higher step may be comparatively easy. And the teacher should always inquire, when he is about to dismiss one subject, whether the class understands it so well that they can go on to the next. He may, indeed, sometimes give a word of suggestion during the preparation of a lesson, and by a

seasonable hint, save the scholar the needless loss of much time. But it is a very greater evil if the pupils acquire the habit of running to the teacher as soon as a slight difficulty presents itself, to request him to remove it. . . . The inquirer should never be frowned upon; this will diminish his self-reliance without enlightening him; for whatever is done for a scholar without his having studied closely upon it himself, makes but a feeble impression upon him, and is soon forgotten. The true way is, neither to discourage inquiry nor answer the question. Converse with the scholar a little as to the principles involved in the question; refer him to principles which he has before learned, or has now lost sight of; perhaps call his attention to some rule or explanation before given to the class; go just so far as to enlighten him a little and *put him on the scent,* then leave him to achieve the victory himself (Page, 1885).

This excerpt, first written in 1847, dramatizes how little what is said to the average classroom teacher has changed over the past century. The quotation might easily have been taken from an article written for teachers today.

How did the conference deal with this problem of specifying the nature and amount of guidance to be supplied by the classroom teacher? There was general agreement among the conference participants that the degree of guidance by the teacher varies from time to time along a continuum, with almost complete direction of what the pupil must do at one extreme to practically no direction at the other. This was illustrated in both of the examples of teaching presented by Cronbach and Davis. We may here add a third illustration. A teacher introduces a group of students to a totally new subject-matter area, for example, surveying, simply by arranging a wide variety of materials such as instruments, maps, and so forth, across the classroom. There is no overt guidance here from the teacher in the form of clear-cut distinctions between correct and incorrect student responses. Hence, there is little probability of behavior that could be called 'error' on the part of the students.

Subsequently, the teacher might shift to a second phase wherein she provides almost full guidance for the students. They are given very careful practice in using the surveying instruments and in recording their observations. After they have acquired some of the basic skills, the teacher might demonstrate how certain kinds of problems are handled in surveying flat land. When the students have understood some of these possible applications, she then poses the question of surveying other types of terrain. Students would be expected to arrive at a number

EVAN R. KEISLAR—LEE S. SHULMAN

of possible solutions to these general questions with little guidance from the teacher.

As the class progresses, the teacher may thus provide sometimes more and sometimes less guidance, depending on her objectives and the performance of the students. Here, in a period of a few days, a teacher may have manifested behavior that ranged from little guidance to full guidance and it would seem patently absurd in this context to ask the question of which degree of guidance was best. This question can only be asked in terms of the specific situation in which a decision about guidance must be made. Clearly, it is more relevant to ask, specifically, Given the subject matter, the kind of students in the class, the objectives to be attained, and what the students have previously learned, what kind and how much guidance is best?

The conference brought out the distinction between what the teacher might do during a given lesson when she, for example, is helping the students to induce a rule, and what she might do during the days and weeks and months prior to that event to prepare the students to profit from this learning experience. The period of preparation, for Hawkins, would involve experiences of exploration during which a student learned the lay of the land for the subject to be mastered. It would require teacher planning, selection, and arrangement of materials, so that related objects could be seen together and compared by the learner. This form of guidance does differ from guided instruction with respect to the scope of sequential decisions left to the students and to the student's perception of the extent to which he is being directed. For example, the student makes his own decisions on such questions as, What should I look at first?

While this period of antecedent criss-crossing of a field may be considered as undirected by the teacher, it depends upon careful teacher planning and is as profound in its effects as directed instruction. For example, the teacher should thoughtfully arrange the materials in a classroom so that the exploration is likely to be most profitable. What the student will look at first may be determined, for example, by placing the object to be noted in an eye-catching location. While the student is clearly making his own decisions in these explorations, the range of alternatives available to him has been somewhat constrained and directed by the teacher's preparation of the situation.

In his paper, Bruner suggested six ways in which teachers may prepare pupils for discovery. He would include such devices as having pupils learn strategies and heuristics for attacking problems, teaching them to select and use information, helping them make full use of their own self-cues, and cultivating appropriate motives. So prepared, children would not have to resort to blind trial-and-error in order to discover. Teachers' guidance would also involve helping children locate and master the essential information they need; no one suggests that children should discover all facts anew.

Is it possible to *prepare* a student to learn by discovery, using a direct program of guidance? A sequence of learning activities, based on an hierarchical analysis of the task, might be highly effective by assuring competency in the prerequisite abilities for the inductive experience. Gagné reported one study to support such a possibility but the evidence still is fragmentary.

What can be said about the particular lesson in which a teacher expects her pupils to learn inductively? The guidance she provides at this point can take many different forms. She may set the stage for the desired behavior by posing a problem, revealing a paradox, or directing the learner's attention to a problem-filled situation. She may need to supply broad general instructions to direct the learner's attention somewhat more appropriately. She will, presumably, have structured the environment so that the student will obtain relevant information as a consequence of his own efforts. She may even provide general hints or indirect clues affording further guidance; but she does not, of course, provide the solution directly. It is thus clear that there are many dimensions along which the amount of guidance may be considered.

The conference also examined the dilemma of meeting individual differences when the inductive teaching method is used with a group. If the questions are posed for group discussion, the most competent pupils in the class are likely to make all of the discoveries. It was pointed out that in such a class situation there is heightened activity on the part of all members because of competition, demand for social approval, and so forth. A critical question involves what is learned by that large portion of the class which does not participate actively but simply listens to the few discoverers. Is their learning indistinguishable from that of students who have been taught the same material didactically? Is there some additional advantage to having been a participant, albeit vicariously, in an inductive learning experience? These are pivotal questions in the learning-by-discovery controversy which appear quite amenable to empirical study.

How can the teacher tell whether she has provided the right amount and kind of guidance during a lesson? One alternative is to ask herself, Has the student discovered? and proceed to get evidence as to whether or not the act of discovery has occurred. On the other hand, she may turn her attention directly to the outcomes of the experience and ask whether students demonstrate new abilities and values without reference to the hidden act of discovery. In either case, she must ultimately see if the learner is now able to deal effectively with a broader class of problems as a consequence of her instruction. The teacher may or may not find it helpful to use the language of discovery for this purpose.

Whether one chooses to talk about the effects of guidance in terms of an inferred internal act or its observable consequences is a reflection of one's point-of-view about instructional goals. In the former case, it is assumed that the inferred, covert event of 'discovery' is to be sought, in and of itself, as a major objective. In the second case, the observable outcomes are the primary criteria; less attention is paid to the intervening events. Which way is best? This question is a reflection of the issue of 'process' versus 'product,' and will be examined in the following section.

In any event, two conclusions for classroom instruction are clear: (1) There is no useful way of posing a broad question regarding how much and what kind of guidance the teacher should supply. The question should always be formulated for a specific context including the type of subject, the maturity of the pupils, prior learning experiences and so on. (2) Regardless of which way of talking about learning by discovery is adopted, no single teaching method is likely to accomplish the wide range of cognitive and affective objectives discussed at the conference.

THE LEVEL OF CURRICULUM DEVELOPMENT

At the level of curriculum, two kinds of decisions are made. One deals with the 'oughts' of education: What objectives do we choose as the goals of our teaching? The other decision reflects the general organization and patterning of subject areas and topics, 'scope and sequence,' in the language of the curriculum-writers: How do we organize a subject matter and identify the order in which it is taught?

At the conference, the questions which dealt with the identification of goals for education took two forms: (1) What is the role of the psychologist in making value judgments which influence the activity of educational institutions? (2) What form is most appropriate for the statement of educational objectives?

The first of these two questions created more consternation than possibly any other raised at the conference. It was generally agreed that psychology is a science which deals with the description, prediction, and, ultimately, control of human behavior. Does this then provide the psychologist with uniquely relevant insights concerning the most fruitful directions in which to modify that behavior? Participants seemed to divide into three camps. Some felt that, as scientists of human behavior, they are obliged to extrapolate their understanding into objectives for education. Others felt that, considerations of psychology aside, they have this obligation as individual private citizens who happen to be psychologists. A third group reflected the position that psychologists must actively avoid involving themselves in such controversies, because of the necessity for continually emphasizing that science deals with the description of nature and not with the manner in which it ought to be modified. This was a deep-seated disagreement for which no hint of resolution was forthcoming at the conference.

On the second question, the form in which objectives must be stated, discussions were somewhat more fruitful. Concerning the topic, the arguments pivoted around the question of whether statements of educational objectives ought to be made in operational terms which identify in detail the behaviors to be acquired. On those occasions when clear-cut descriptions of desired behaviors have been employed, psychologists have often been successful in producing the desired outcomes. Yet, to some participants, the notion of discovery in learning connoted the very antithesis of such behavioral control. Discovery implies diversity; teaching for specified objectives suggests conformity to a model. Discovery implies novelty and unpredictability; instruction for predetermined goals suggests imitation and constraint. At times, these participants seemed to be defining themselves out of business. They implied that true discovery behavior cannot be defined a priori, or it is not discovery. Their goal was to 'open up' the pupil, and they maintained that attempts to define this outcome behaviorally constrain the young scholar. Yet, the dual function of stated objectives is to suggest courses of action on the one hand, and, on the other, to provide a set of standards for evaluating the consequences of action. If one's goal statements are not specific and subject to subsequent evaluation, how do they differ from a vague poetic set of pious pronouncements?

As we read between the lines of controversy, one possible interpretation emerges. A good deal of what semanticists call 'bypassing' was occurring in these dialogues. Participants disagreed to a great extent because they were focusing on different aspects of learning behavior. Those favoring goal-directed teaching were concerned with 'what' questions—What is to be learned, and What methods are most appropriate to that end? Those favoring open-ended teaching were also concerned

187

with what is to be learned, but they give a higher priority to the question, of How is it to be learned? In many ways, the old distinction between process and product in psychology is reflected in these disagreements. At present, and for the foreseeable future, psychologists can make far more precise and communicable statements about product variables and their control than they can about the more ephemeral range of intervening process variables. We simply lack a reliable language for discussing processes, and the ambiguity of the term discovery as a process-referent is a case in point. Does open-endedness deny the importance of clear-cut objectives? We doubt it. On the other hand, does goal-directedness imply that openness and autonomy are unacceptable human goals? Probably not. The emphasis is simply upon the present inaccessibility of such constructs to scientific explication and investigation.

Those supporting open-ended teaching correctly insist that psychologists attend to the multi-level complexity of the learning process, i.e., that the child who learns a new concept is simultaneously, if incidentally, learning ways to understand future concepts, ideas about the stability or tentativeness of concepts in general, as well as some perceptions about himself as a conceiver. Yet, in focusing upon these important processes, they too often ignore or pay too little attention to the specific learning task from which the others are derived. We not only wish students to discover as an end in itself; we wish them to discover something which will contribute to their further growth, and thus serve as a basis for new learning.

Participants favoring goal-directed teaching were accused of saying, If you can't measure it, don't try to teach it. It appears likely that some participants, while rejecting such a statement, in practice reflect the narrowness implied by the comment; they give little attention to broadening the range of outcomes measured in education. While progress in bringing 'fuzzy' goals within the purview of measurement will not alter the basic issue, at the practical level it can alter the importance given to it.

We may now move briefly to the questions of scope and sequence in the curriculum. By overemphasis upon the process of discovery, one group of participants tended to denigrate the engineering of learning, i.e., the careful planning of sequences of activities through which students will attain desired objectives. Hawkins called attention to Tolman's finding that rats presumably benefit from unreinforced and, hence, undirected, exploration. In contrast, those who speak in terms of the careful planning or programming of learning sequences seem to ignore the possible educative consequences of relatively unguided exploratory activity.

We would direct both groups to the wisdom of Dewey's *Experience and Education*. The first position reflects the folly of Progressive Education (as distinct from progressive) which sacrificed necessary experience to momentary experiencing. The second position resembles Traditional Education (again in Dewey's sense) which used the subject-matter to be learned as the starting point and too often treated the pupil as a learning machine.

The different emphases on process and product may be seen in another light. Those who favored stressing the act of discovery did not regard such events necessarily to be beyond the scope of evaluation in terms of outcomes. They objected to the premature application of external criteria to such a method. This point of view essentially was saying, Let us focus our attention on how to teach children to discover more effectively as a way of learning; later on we can find out the relationship between this process of learning and overall outcomes. To some extent, but probably not entirely, the disagreement reflected a difference in strategy, rather than a fundamental divergence in value systems.

Another way in which the curriculum problem has been posed is whether the activities of students studying a subject matter ought to parallel the activities of the practitioners of the discipline themselves or whether the learning of a subject content, e.g., physics, demands a structure quite different from that of the discipline qua object of inquiry. The implication is that the activity of scientists is discovery, in contrast to the traditional activity of students, reception learning. This, however, is much too facile, and resembles a verbalism more than a viable distinction.

Quite clearly, scientists do not spend all their time discovering. They exhibit a broad range of activities, from hypothesis-generation and model-building to listening to lectures and reading journal articles reporting someone else's research. Hence, justification of curriculum development which stresses inductive teaching on the grounds that induction is the *sine qua non* of scientific behavior is a half-truth, at best. Scientists do discover, it is true. That they also engage in a wealth of additional activities is also true. That many of these are didactic or receptive in nature is apparent. It is further clear that whether a scientist induces, deduces, plays hunches, or looks up answers in trade books, is contingent not upon the values of those processes in themselves, but on what he intends to accomplish in a given situation. If one wishes to emphasize the analogy of the scientist to the student, one cannot ignore that in science, decisions about means are dictated by goals.

What then can be said about the issue of learning by discovery and the area of curriculum development? First, unless some consensus can be reached about the statement of objectives, there is little reason to continue dialogues regarding methods of teaching. The question of the superiority of one curriculum over another is moot if the objectives of each are stated in mutually incompatible terms. One approach would be the extension of present efforts in educational measurement to develop procedures which assess far more complex behaviors than has been done up to now. We need more adequate measures of the kinds of outcomes in Cronbach's list, such as 'creative urge,' and 'openness.' As long as our present objective criteria are deemed utterly inadequate, debate concerning the general question of process versus product will remain clouded.

Second, process and product variables are not inexorably labeled as such, but are definable only in terms of the other variables to which they are referred. Thus, problem-solving can be a process variable in one context and a product variable in another.

Third, the activities of scientists vary too greatly from day to day and man to man to be used as the model justifying any single curricular strategy based on discovery.

Fourth, a curriculum refers to the organization and sequence of a subject matter in which statements about that subject, methods of teaching, and the activities of the learners are intricately interrelated to form a single entity. Research at this level, as distinct from the level of specific acts of instruction or general psychological processes, should include the study of the consequences of the curriculum as a whole. The effects of a particular segment of a curriculum may be quite different *in vivo* than they are when studied in isolation from the rest of that curriculum. If research is to be relevant to curriculum development and evaluation, the research must be conducted at the same level of abstraction as are the decision-alternatives which confront the curriculum workers. This does not exclude the possibility of using such overall evaluation in a diagnostic sense, to throw light, for example, on those aspects of the curriculum which need improvement. But the issue of learning by discovery will not be adequately assessed until we can obtain a broad evaluative base to assess the effectiveness of the curriculum.

THE LEVEL OF PSYCHOLOGICAL INVESTIGATIONS OF LEARNING

One of the major questions posed for this conference was the following: What conclusions can be drawn from the research evidence to date regarding the effectiveness of the method of learning by discovery?

Examination of both the exhaustive reviews of the literature and deliberations of the conference lead to an inescapable conclusion: The question as stated is not amenable to research solutions because the implied experimental treatment, the discovery method, is far too ambiguous and imprecise to be used meaningfully in an experimental investigation. Where investigators have spelled out learning by discovery in terms of a set of educational procedures, the results have been equivocal. For example, there is no evidence that supports the proposition that having students encounter a series of examples of a generalization and then requiring them to induce the rule is superior to teaching the rule first and asking the students to apply it to a wide variety of examples.

Wittrock's review indicated that research has not yet done justice to the magnitude and complexity of the problem. One basic difficulty is that of precise description of procedures. Studies purportedly designed to assess this question have used the same term to apply to a wide variety of instructional activities. In some experiments the name 'rote learning' is applied to a treatment which other investigations call 'discovery.' Unfortunately, not enough information is supplied to enable the reader to identify the precise procedures under either label.

Instead of debating whether or not to call a treatment by the label 'discovery,' we should insist that published reports include a clear description of the events which comprise the treatment or lesson, as well as a few typical examples of each of the instructional procedures being contrasted. In some studies, a complete record might be made available in the form of a program, a tapescript, a film, or a typed record which would be available on request. When such details are available to experimenters, reanalysis and replication of studies is possible. For example, the conference members generally agreed that the filmed demonstration lesson shown by Davis was excellent group teaching, even though the interpretations of what was happening in those filmed lessons differed widely.

A fundamental question from which much of this disagreement derived was related to the nature and the role of unobservable mediating events in learning. The participants who treated discovery as an internal event considered it to be different from the processes that characterize reception or didactic learning. How can one know when such a covert act of discovery has occurred? This hidden event is always an inference based on several kinds of evidence, among which the following are minimal criteria:

1) Although the learner may have access to a good deal of information prior to solving a problem, the identification of the solutions themselves must never be part of the information he is given.

2) The learner must be able to generalize the solution to other situations. If no such transfer is evident, the successful first solution is considered an accident and not a discovery.

There were four different approaches represented at the conference, differing with respect to the value of internal events, the use of the word 'discovery' to apply to these events, and the importance of the act of discovery as a goal.

The first group of participants discarded the whole issue of covert mediational mechanisms as having no practical relevance. They maintained the researcher should focus directly on the relationship between the environmental changes a teacher introduces (the input variable) and what a student consequently learns to do (the output variable); the language of mediation is excess baggage.

Most of the participants in the conference, however, took the position that a discussion of mediating mechanisms is necessary for any fruitful investigation of learning by discovery. Of this number, a second group felt that the mediating mechanisms of language play a central role in the educational process. In his reflections on the conference, Kendler regretted that greater attention had not been given to a discussion of language. He felt that investigators should study the ways in which students can be helped to incorporate new experiences into preexisting linguistic structures so as to produce optimal learning in subsequent situations. Thus, the second group recognized the value of talking about internal events, but felt that this could be done more efficiently if the centrality of language for these mediating processes were emphasized.

A third group, represented by Gagné, used the term, 'discovery', in an exceedingly broad sense. Gagné maintained that a learner is discovering if he is engaged in any process involving search and selection. This would include the acquisition of many motor skills (such as learning to hit a golf ball), simple verbal learning (such as paired-associates, for which appropriate mediators might be found), as well as more complex verbal learning (such as concept formation, or the derivation of rules for solving various classes of problems).

A fourth group of participants limited the use of the word discovery to cognitive areas of learning. Some members of this group saw the critical process as one wherein the student by himself sought a match between models he had stored in his own head and objects, sets of objects, or events experienced about him. This process could be seen as operating at different levels of discovery. Finding a stored model to fit the problem event exactly, e.g., seeing that all words in an anagram task were coded by being written backwards, was an example of a little-d discovery. On the other hand, big-D discoveries were involved in cases where the stored models themselves had to be restructured or recombined in order to make a fit, as might be the case when a student constructs a general principle under which he can subsume and integrate a series of isolated rules previously learned in a somewhat mechanical fashion.

For this last group, the internal process of search and selection, this act of discovery, was seen as the essence of what the student is learning. Bruner, for example, was more concerned with devising procedures to foster this act of discovery than he was with evaluating the valuable consequences of the act itself. Such evaluation, he felt, could come later. It is this emphasis on the act of discovery, per se, which distinguishes the fourth group from the other three. For the rest of the participants, regardless of how they differed concerning the value of talking about mediating mechanisms, there was greater interest in measurable progress with respect to educational outcomes.

The conference gave some attention to the frameworks within which research on this topic might proceed. There was disagreement, however, regarding the usefulness of psychological theory as a basis for deriving questions and launching new studies. Several participants felt that psychological concepts and tools were ill-suited for the complexities of classroom endeavors, and Hawkins suggested that the practitioner's common-sense way of talking might be more valuable than scientific language. On the other hand, as we noted earlier, Kendler and others emphasized that more precise terms are exactly what we need.

A large number of promising suggestions for future research were presented during the conference. The previous papers have described in detail these proposed directions. In particular, both the critical reviews of Wittrock and Cronbach offered specific as well as general suggestions for the improvement of research investigations concerning this problem. Cronbach, for example, advocated focusing on a narrow problem under limited circumstances with a well-defined population rather than attempting definitive tests of the overall hypothesis of learning by discovery. Other suggestions involved important features of experimental design such as the use of multiple criteria as dependent variables, the handling of the problem of time differences in instructional treatments, and the disposition of subjects who fail to discover. Research studies were generally criticized for failing to pose questions relevant to education. It was suggested that investigators should pay greater attention to tasks growing out of classroom learning situations.

Participants suggested other possible approaches to this research area such as the application of information theory, mathematical models, and computer simulation. Research in education might also be seen as an engineering task, involving, tryout, revision, and evaluation, until an adequate educational program has been developed.

Another promising approach, with implications for the issues of the conference, is the development of computer-based instruction. Because of the flexibility continuously afforded during instruction, the use of such a research program permits the presentation of task and guidance in almost any way desired. It is possible, therefore, to study, under controlled situations, a wide diversity of sequences to answer questions involving instructional decisions concerning the amount and kind of help teachers should offer.

At the level of psychological investigations of learning, the discussions of the conference reflected an underlying parallel between statements made about the process of education and pronouncements by the same individuals about the process of scientific inquiry. It appeared that often the image of what constitutes the most fruitful approach to teaching was a reflection of the same participants' position concerning the best kind of research strategy for scientific investigation. Quite clearly, adjective pairs such as controlled-open, precise-global and logical-intuitive are equally applicable within the domains of both research and instruction. Hence, the two questions of, How should the teaching of a given subject be conducted? and How should research on teaching be conducted? were inexorably interwoven.

Those who took the position that the best kind of teaching opened up the child and insisted that the demand for operational statements of objectives was instructionally constricting, took a similar position with reference to the practice of research. They advocated the discarding, or at least the temporary suspension, of the classical hypothesis-testing model of experimental psychology and recommended in its place a more general exploratory approach to the problems. They have usually found their research approaches most fruitful when applied to forms of human behavior that are difficult to identify reliably and measure accurately, and their formulations concerning education have tended to reflect the degree of precision that is typical of their objects of research.

In contrast, those who maintained that the best instruction occurs when objectives are carefully specified also felt that systematic experimental studies with precisely stated goals and procedures showed the most promise leading to knowledge about teaching. Those with this goal-directed research orientation have been most successful in dealing with situations where the individual parameters can be reliably identified and systematically varied. Hence, in studying educational problems, they too have been drawn to those situations which best fit their own model. As Dewey observed repeatedly, the processes of education and of scientific inquiry are remarkably similar. It should be no surprise that men are found to hold parallel positions about the 'best' form of each activity. It is to a consideration of these strategies of inquiry that we now turn.

THE LEVEL OF RESEARCH STRATEGY

There is an oft-related story of the drunk who was crawling on his hands and knees under a lamppost when he was accosted by a policeman. The policeman asked the drunk what he was doing. "Looking for my wallet," was the drunk's reply. The policeman offered to help him find his wallet and asked him where he had lost it. The drunk thought for a moment and answered "About half a block down, in the alley." The policeman asked, with a mixture of curiosity and sarcasm, "Why in the world don't you look for your wallet where you lost it?" The drunk quickly responded, "It's much too dark to look for it there."

Controversies over research strategies reflect much of this drunk's dilemma. Do we look where the visibility is good, but where the probability of finding what we seek is low; or do we venture forth into the dark where the answers frequently lie, but probably in some form so obscured by their surroundings that they will not be visible to us?

The problem of strategy may be posed in the following fashion: Is it better to begin a research program by asking highly limited questions in an area where precise answers are possible, and then gradually extend the scope of inquiry so that ultimately precise answers are possible to broad questions? Or is it better to start by posing general questions which, although loosely formulated, deal with a large section of the field, and subsequently to attempt to increase the precision of the statements made?

195

It is unfortunate that precision and generality, both important research goals, are usually incompatible. If a line of research deals with a series of closely related but precise experiments, inevitably the scope must be restricted. The experimenter's findings, although precise, may well be irrelevant with respect to many interesting problems. Hopefully, of course, the researcher will gradually, in a small-step program of development, extend his sphere of precise description and control to include more and more general questions.

On the other hand, a research strategy which deals broadly and comprehensively with issues in a, field may produce statements which appear to be relevant to important issues; however, these generalizations are so lacking in definition that they are of no greater value than the gross over-extrapolations obtained under the first strategy. Here the need is to make the vague formulations more precise so that statements made about a large class of phenomena are more meaningful.

Thus, the dilemma remains. The strategy of beginning with narrowly focused and well controlled studies may not yield the expected base for broadening the scope. Yet, the findings of the global approach may be so inadequate to cope with the problems posed that the researcher finds himself able to state only tenuous formulations which he offers hopefully to others as a general guide.

But there is another alternative. Cronbach has suggested that perhaps an intermediate strategy is desirable. First, the tasks used for the experiments would represent the mastery of some phase of the subjects actually being taught in the school. Second, the duration of the instructional treatment would be long enough to produce cumulative learnings, without becoming so long as to be unwieldy and undefinable; experiments lasting two to twenty weeks might provide an appropriate compromise. As has been previously suggested (Keislar and Mace, 1965), generalizing from a two-month experiment to a two-year curriculum may involve over-extrapolation but at least it seems more reasonable than to base one's judgment on data collected from a 50 minute laboratory session on the same problem.

Third, with an experimental treatment a few weeks in length, it is possible to use standardized instruction, carefully prepared lessons which are manageable in terms of time and money. Under such controlled conditions, the problems of teacher variability and adequate monitoring of instructional events are minimized. Fourth, where instructional treatments last for many weeks, the total testing time can be increased to permit the assessment of a wide diversity of outcomes which may take several sessions for testing alone.

It is always satisfying to recommend a golden mean as the solution to a confrontation of opposites. The middle way has time and again demonstrated its durability in a wide range of circumstances and over a broad array of controversies. There is yet another form of middle way, which can be identified by using Schwab's (1960) term, the "grand strategy."

Since different approaches to research in themselves can highlight only parts of a total object of inquiry, a possibility could be, in Schwab's ords, "that some particular order of different strategies, constituting a grand strategy, may be better than all other orders." That is, instead of committing himself to a single orientation, whether polar or intermediate in our framework, the investigator would shift among strategies as he reformulated his questions and refocussed his inquiry. Thus, for example, it is not uncommon for psychologists to combine correlational, descriptive, and experimental designs into the same program of research. Similarly, the investigator might pose his research questions in a sequence of different ways, very much like the teacher who utilizes different instructional procedures.

The grand strategy is probably best reflected in the history of psychological studies of learning. Individual investigations, growing out of contrasting or conflicting orientations, reflect a long-term dialectic of strategies. As one set of approaches has asserted its superiority for dealing with some psychological issue, some other group has inevitably proposed an alternative to it. Frequently, these confrontations have fostered productive restatements of important issues. Yet, the resulting rhetoric of claim and counter-claim has too often led to an unfortunate overemphasis upon differences in theory, leading to research involving the examination of otherwise trivial problems. The advantage of a grand strategy for an individual worker is that he may be able to retain the flexibility of alternating among strategies while avoiding the pitfalls of conflict among them.[1]

However, such a broad approach may require the coordinated efforts of a group of specialists; few individual investigators are likely to possess the temperament and the diversity of high-level skills required. The currently rapid growth of centers of research in education

---

[1] The authors of this chapter are fully aware that the positing of these intermediate and grand strategies does not exhaust the range of alternatives available. As participants in the conference themselves, they can lay no greater claim to omniscience than any other participants. It was, in fact, with some amusement that they simultaneously recognized that the two solution strategies outlined above represented extensions of their respective research styles.

may foster the development of research programs which reflect such grand strategies. Yet, the frequent emphasis upon *inter*disciplinary research in these settings, though clearly not objectionable in themselves, may obscure an important alternative. There is great value in gathering together members of the same discipline who reflect highly contrasting investigatory styles, thus constituting an *intradisciplinary* research approach. In this way, the development of centers of research may encourage a continuing dialogue among advocates of various strategies and thus permit a fruitful restatement of a question in the early stages of a research enterprise before conflicting points of view become vested interests.

THE STATE OF THE ISSUE

This volume has attempted, from many vantage points, to deal with a major issue in education and psychology. We have described the past history of the issue and its present status. What lies ahead for the controversy over learning by discovery?

John Dewey (1910a), in his essay on "The Influence of Darwinism on Philosophy," wrote:

> . . . the conviction persists—though history shows it to be a hallucination— that all the questions that the human mind has asked are questions that can be answered in terms of the alternatives that the questions themselves present. But in fact, intellectual progress usually occurs through sheer abandonment of questions together with both of the alternatives they assume—an abandonment that results from their decreasing vitality and a change of urgent interest. We do not solve them: We get over them. Old questions are solved by disappearing, evaporating, while new questions corresponding to the changed attitude of endeavor and preference take their place.

Dewey maintained that controversies are resolved through redefinition and reformulation, rather than through victory of one side over another. We have seen in this volume a recurrent call for this very kind of reformulation of the present issue. Throughout the history of psychology, similar issues have arisen and, though not resolved in the same terms in which they were set, have nevertheless disappeared. Such questions have included nature versus nurture, insight versus trial-and-error and imageless versus image-full thinking; in not too many years, we will probably add to that list such burning questions as incremental versus all-or-none learning and learning by discovery versus guided learning.

Dewey has observed that "old ideas give way slowly, for they are more than abstract logical forms and categories. They are habits, predispositions, deeply engrained attitudes of aversion and preference." This is particularly true of the terms in which we couch those compelling controversies of which this volume is characteristic. These terms have become part of the 'familiar furniture of the mind,' and the resolution of the issue lies not in the moving of this furniture about, but in refurnishing with new terms, and perhaps, coming up with new oppositions.

It is the hope of the authors of this chapter that a highlighting of the terms of the controversy will hasten the process of reformulation rather than impede it.

Bibliography

Numbers in square brackets refer to pages in this volume where reference is cited. A number of references which were not cited directly have been included because of their general relevance to the topic.

Adams, J. K. Laboratory studies of behavior without awareness. *Psychol. Bull.*, 1957, 54, 383–405. [67]

Anderson, G. L. Quantitative thinking as developed under connectionist and field theories of learning. In Swenson, Esther J. et al, *Learning theory in school situations.* Minneapolis: University of Minnesota Press, 1949. Pp. 40–73. [48–49, 145]

Atkin, J. M., and Karplus, R. Discovery or invention? *Sci. Teacher,* 1962, 29 (5), 45–51.

Ausubel, D. P. In defense of verbal learning. *Educ. Theor.*, 1961a, 11, (1), 15–25.

Ausubel, D. P. Learning by discovery: rationale and mystique. *Bull. nat. Assoc. sec. sch. Princ.*, 1961b, 45, 18–58. [145, 149]

Ausubel, D. P. *The psychology of meaningful verbal learning.* New York: Grune and Stratton, 1963. [45, 145]

Baddeley, A. D. A Zeigarnik-like effect in the recall of anagram solutions. *Quart. J. exp. Psychol.*, 1963, 15, 63–64. [83–84]

Barnes, J. M., and Underwood, B. J. "Fate" of first-list associations in transfer theory. *J. exp. Psychol.*, 1959, 58, 97–105. [139]

Beberman, M. An emerging program of secondary school mathematics. In R. W. Heath (Ed.), *New curricula.* New York: Harper and Row, 1964. Pp. 9–34. [38]

Boole, M. E. *The preparation of the child for science.* Oxford: Clarendon Press, 1904.

Bower, G. H. An association model for response and training variables in paired-associate learning. *Psychol. Rev.,* 1962, *69,* 34–53. [20]

Breland, K., and Breland, M. The misbehavior of organisms. *Amer. Psychologist,* 1961, *16,* 681–684. [137]

Brown, R., and Fraser, C. The acquisition of syntax. In C. N. Cofer and Barbara S. Musgrave (Eds.), *Verbal behavior and learning.* New York: McGraw-Hill, 1963. Pp. 158–197. [144]

Bruner, J. S. Learning and thinking. *Harvard educ. Rev.,* 1959, *29,* 184–192. [34–35]

Bruner, J. S. *The process of education.* Cambridge: Harvard University Press, 1960.

Bruner, J. S. The act of discovery. *Harvard educ. Rev.,* 1961, *31,* 21–32. [33–34, 54, 140, 148]

Bruner, J. S. The course of cognitive growth. *Amer. Psychologist,* 1964a, *19,* 1–15.

Bruner, J. S. Some theorems on instruction illustrated with reference to mathematics. In *Sixty-third yearb. nat. Soc. Stud. Educ.,* 1964b, 306–335, Part 1. [55]

Bruner, J. S., Goodnow, Jacqueline J., and Austin, G. A. *A study of thinking.* New York: Wiley, 1956. [148]

Bugelski, B. R., and Scharlock, D. P. An experimental demonstration of unconscious mediated association. *J. exp. Psychol.,* 1952, *44,* 334–338. [67]

Burke, C. J., Estes, W. K., and Hellyer, S. Rate of verbal conditioning in relation to stimulus variability. *J. exp. Psychol.,* 1954, *48,* 153–161. [20]

Campbell, J. A. CHEM Study—an approach to chemistry based on experiments. In R. W. Heath (Ed.), *New curricula,* New York: Harper and Row, 1964. Pp. 82–93. [39]

Carroll, J. B. A model of school learning. *Teachers Coll. Rec.,* 1963, *64,* 723–733. [86, 89]

Clarkson, D. M. Taxicab geometry, rabbits, and Pascal's triangle—discoveries in a sixth-grade classroom. *The Arithmetic Teacher,* 1962, *9,* 308–313.

Corman, B. R. The effect of varying amounts and kinds of information as guidance in problem solving. *Psychol. Monogr.,* 1957, *71,* No. 2 (Whole No. 431). [59–61, 85, 88]

Craig, R. C. *The transfer value of guided learning.* New York: Teacher's College, Columbia University, 1953. [57–58, 61–62, 146]

Craig, R. C. Directed versus independent discovery of established relations. *J. Educ. Psychol.*, 1956, 47, 223–234. [57–59, 61–62, 145]

Cronbach, L. J. *Educational psychology*, 2nd edition. New York: Harcourt, Brace and World, Inc., 1963. [76]

Cronbach, L. J. Evaluation for course improvement. In R. W. Heath (Ed.), *New curricula.* New York: Harper and Row, 1964. Pp. 231–248.

Croobach, L. J. Issues current in educational psychology. In Morrisett, L. N., and Vinsonhaler, J. F. Mathematical learning. *Monog. Soc. Res. Child Develpm.*, (Serial No. 99), 1965. Pp. 109–126.

Crutchfield, R. S., and Covington, M. V. Facilitation of creative thinking and problem solving in school children. Paper presented in Symposium on Learning Research Pertinent to Educational Improvement, American Association for the Advancement of Science, Cleveland, 1963.

Davis, R. B. Mathematical thought and the nature of learning: The Madison project view. *Frontiers of education.* Report of the Twenty-Seventh Educational Conference Sponsored by the Educational Records Bureau. American Council on Education, Educational Records Bureau. 21 Audubon Ave., New York 32, New York. 1963. Pp. 79–83.

Davis, R. B. *Discovery in mathematics: A text for teachers.* Reading, Massachusetts: Addison-Wesley Publishing Co., 1964.

Davis, R. B. The Madison project's approach to a theory of instruction. *J. res. sci. Teaching*, 1964, 2, 146–162.

de Charms, R., Carpenter, Virginia, and Kuperman, A. The 'origin-pawn' variable in person perception. *Sociometry.* In press. [126]

Deese, J. From the isolated verbal unit to connected discourse. In C. N. Cofer (Ed.), *Verbal learning and verbal behavior.* New York: McGraw-Hill, 1961. PP. 11–31. [140]

Della-Piana, G., and Eldredge, G. M. Discovery learning in programmed instruction. Paper read at the Second Annual Convention of the National Society for Programmed Instruction, San Antonio, Texas, 1964. [54, 70, 72]

Dewey, J. *How we think.* Boston: Heath, 1910. [41–42]

Dewey, J. The influence of Darwinism on philosophy. In *The influence of Darwinism on philosophy and other essays in contemporary thought*. New York: Henry Holt and Co., 1901a. [198]

Dienes, Z. P. *The power of mathematics*. London: Hutchinson Educational Lte., 1964.

Dietze, Doris. The facilitating effect of words on discrimination and generalization. *J. exp. Psychol.*, 1955, 50, 255–260.

Donaldson, Margaret. *A study of children's thinking*. New York: Humanities Press, 1964. [160]

Duncan, C. P. Recent research on human problem solving. *Psychol. Bull.*, 1959, 56, 397–429. [71]

Duncan, C. P. Effect of instructions and information on problem solving. *J. exp. Psychol.*, 1963, 65, 321–327.

Duncan. C. P. Learning to learn in response-discovery and in paired-associate lists. *Amer. J. Psychol.*, 1964, 77, 367–379. [79, 86]

Elliott, R. Physiological activity and performance: A comparison of kindergarten children with young adults. *Psychol. Monogr.*, 1964, 78, No. 10 (Whole No. 587). [153]

Ervin, Susan M. Transfer effects of learning a verbal generalization. *Child Develpm.*, 1960, 31, 537–554.

Estes, W. K. The statistical approach to learning theory. In S. Koch (Ed.), *Psychology: A study of a science; Vol. 2., General systematic formulations, learning, and special processes*. New York: McGraw-Hill, 1959. Pp. 380–491. [137]

Evans, J. L., Homme, L. E., and Glaser, R. The ruleg system for the construction of programmed verbal learning sequences. *J. educ. Res.*, 1962, 55, 513–518. [15–16]

Ewert, P. H., and Lambert, J. F. Part II: The effect of verbal instructions upon the formation of a concept. *J. gen. Psychol.*, 1932, 6, 400–413. [66, 67]

Farber, I. E. The things people say to themselves. *Amer. Psychologist*, 1963, 18, 185–197.

Festinger, L. *A theory of cognitive dissonance*. Evanston, Ill.: Row, Peterson, 1957. [159]

Finlay, G. C. Secondary school physics: The physical science study committee, *American J. Physics*, 1960, 28, 286–293.

Forgus, R. H., and Schwartz, R. J. Efficient retention and transfer as affected by learning method. *J. Psychol.*, 1957, 43, 135–139. [49, 82]

Fowler, H. *Curiosity and exploratory behavior.* New York: Macmillan, 1965. [25–26]

Gagné, R. M. The acquisition of knowledge. *Psychol. Rev.*, 1962, 69, 355–365. [55, 68–69]

Gagné, R. M. Problem solving. In A. W. Melton (Ed.), *Categories of human learning.* New York: Academic Press, 1964. Pp. 293–317. [56]

Gagné, R. M. *The conditions of learning.* New York: Holt, Rinehart and Winston, Inc., 1965. [139, 143]

Gagné, R. M., and Brown, L. T. Some factors in the programming of conceptual learning. *J. exp. Psychol.*, 1961. 62, 313–321. [52–54, 71, 79–81, 84–85, 88–89, 146–148]

Gagné, R. M., and Paradise, N.E. Abilities and learning sets in knowledge acquisition. *Psychol. Monogr.*, 1961, 75, No. 14 (Whole No. 518). [69]

Gagné, R. M., and Smith, E. C., Jr. A study of the effects of verbalization on problem solving. *J. exp. Psychol.*, 1962, 63, 12–18. [67, 85]

Gagné, R. M., Foster, Harriet, and Crowley, Miriam E. The measurement of transfer of training. *Psychol. Bull.*, 1948, 45, 97–130. [72]

Gagné, R. M., Mayor, J. R., Garstens, H. L., and Paradise, N. E. Factors in acquiring knowledge of a mathematical task. *Psychol. Monogr.*, 1962. 76, No. 7 (Whole No. 526).

Gibson, J. J. A critical review of the concepts of set in contemporary experimental psychology. *Psychol. Bull.*, 1941, 38, 781–817. [135–136]

Gilbert, T. F. An approximation to principles of programming continuous discourse, self-instructional materials. A report to the Bell Telephone Laboratories, September, 1958. (Unpublished paper, mimeo). Abstracted in Lumsdaine, A. A. and Glaser, R. (Eds.) *Teaching machines and programmed learning.* Washington: National Education Association, 1960. Pp. 630–635. [22–23]

Glaser, R. Instructional technology and the measurement of learning outcomes: Some questions. *Amer. Psychologist*, 1963, 18, 519–521. [72]

Glaser, R., Klaus, D. J., and Egerman, K. Increasing team proficiency through training. II. The acquisition and extinction of a team response. Pittsburgh: American Inst. for Res., 1962. [86]

Glass, B. Renascent biology: A report on the AIBS biological sciences curriculum study. In R. W. Heath (Ed.), *New curricula*. New York: Harper and Row, 1964. Pp. 94–119.

Goldstein, M., and Weber, R. J. Contingent discrimination in humans. *Percept. and Mot. Skills*, 1965, 21, 171–176. [142]

Grote, C. N. A comparison of the relative effectiveness of direct-detailed and directed discovery methods of teaching selected principles of mechanics in the area of physics. Unpublished doctoral dissertation. Urbana, Ill., University of Illinois, 1960. [63]

Hanson, N. R. *Patterns of discovery*. New York: Cambridge University Press, 1958. [78]

Harlow, H. F. The formation of learning sets. *Psychol. Rev.*, 1949, 56, 51–65. [140–142]

Harlow, H. F. Learning set and error factor theory. In Sigmund Koch (Ed.), *Psychology: A study of science*. Vol. 2. New York: McGraw-Hill. 1959. Pp. 492–537. [20]

Haslerud, G. M., and Meyers, Shirley. The transfer value of given and individually derived principles. *J. educ. Psychol.*, 1958, 49, 293–298. [62, 67, 79, 82–83]

Hawkins. D. On living in trees. Karl Muenzinger Memorial Lecture, University of Colorado, 1964.

Hendrix, Gertrude. A new clue to transfer of training. *Elem. sch. J.*, 1947, 48, 197–208. [44–45, 49–50]

Hendrix, Gertrude. Prerequisite to meaning. *Math. Teacher*, 1950, 43, 334–339. [49]

Hendrix, Gertrude. Learning by discovery. *Math. Teacher*, 1961, 54, 290–299. [49]

Hilgard, E. R., Edgren, R. D., and Irvine, R. P. Errors in transfer following learning with understanding: Further studies with Katona's card-trick experiments. *J. exp. Psychol.*, 1954, 47, 457–464. [85]

Hilgard, E. R., Irvine, R. P., and Whipple, J. E. Rote memorization, understanding, and transfer: An extension of Katona's card-trick experiments. *J. exp. Psychol.*, 1953, 46, 288–292. [80–81, 89]

Hunter, W. S. The delayed reaction in animals and children. *Behav. Monogr.*, 1913, 2, No. 1. [141]

Jeffrey, W. E. The effects of verbal and nonverbal responses in mediating an instrumental act. *J. exp. Psychol.*, 1953, 45, 327–333.

Jenkins, J. J. Mediated associations: Paradigms and situations. In C. N. Cofer and Barbara S. Musgrave (Eds.), *Verbal behavior and learning.* New York: McGraw-Hill, 1963. Pp. 210–245. [139–140]

Judd, C. H. The relation of special training to general intelligence. *Edu. Rev.,* 1908, 36, 28–42. [57]

Judson, A. J., and Cofer, C. N. A study of direction in problem solution. *Amer. Psychologist,* 1950, 5, 274. (abstract)

Kagan, J. The child's sex role classification of school objects. *Child Develpm.,* 1964, 35, 1051–1056. [156]

Kagan, J., Rosman, Bernice L., Day, D., Albert, J., and Phillips, W. Information processing in the child: Significance of analytic and reflective attitudes. *Psychol. Monogr.,* 1964, 78, No. 1 (Whole No. 578). [160]

Katona, G. *Organizing and memorizing.* New York: Columbia University Press, 1940. [67, 147–148]

Keislar, E. R., and Mace, L. Sequence of speaking and listening training in beginning French. In J. Krumboltz (Ed.) *Learning and the educational process.* Chicago: Rand McNally & Co., 1965. [196]

Keller, F. S., and Schoenfeld, W. N. *Principles of psychology.* New York: Appleton-Century-Crofts, 1950. [19]

Kendler, Tracy S., and Kendler, H. H. Reversal and nonreversal shifts in kindergarten children. *J. exp. Psychol.,* 1959, 58, 56–60.

Kendler, H. H., and Kendler, Tracy S. Effect of verbalization on reversal shifts in children. *Science,* 1961, 134, (3490), 1619–1620. (abstract) [141–143]

Kendler, H. H., and Kendler, Tracy S. Vertical and horizontal processes in problem solving. *Psychol. Rev.,* 1962, 69, 1–16.

Kersh, B. Y. The adequacy of "meaning" as an explanation for superiority of learning by independent discovery. *J. educ. Psychol.,* 1958, 49, 282–292. [50–51, 71, 84, 87–89, 146]

Kersh, B. Y. The motivating effect of learning by directed discovery. *J. educ. Psychol.,* 1962, 53, 65–71. [50–52, 88]

Kersh, B. Y. Directed discovery vs. programmed instruction, a test of a theoretical position involving educational technology. Final Report, NDEA Title VII. Project Number 907, Grant Number 7-47-0000-165, Oregon State System of Higher Education, 1964. [86, 88–89]

Kersh, B. Y. Learning by discovery: what is learned? *The Arithmetic Teacher*, 1964, 11, 226–232. [86, 88–89]

Kersh, B. Y., and Wittrock, M. C. Learning by discovery: An interpretation of recent research. *J. teacher Educ.*, 1962, 13, 461–468. [45]

Kittle, J. E. An experimental study of the effect of external direction during learning on transfer and retention of principles. *J. educ. Psychol.*, 1957, 48, 391–405. [57–58, 61–62, 146]

Kuenne, Margaret. Experimental investigation of the relation of language to transposition behavior in young children. *J. exp. Psychol.*, 1946, 36, 471–490. [141]

Lawrence, D. H. The evaluation of training and transfer programs in terms of efficiency measures. *J. Psychol.*, 1954, 38, 367–382. [84]

Lewis, B. N., and Pask, G. The theory and practice of adaptive teaching systems. In R. Glaser (Ed.), *Teaching machines and programmed learning. II: Data and directions.* Washington: National Educational Association. 1965. [20–21]

Lorge, I., Fox, D., Davitz, J., and Brenner, M. A survey of studies contrasting the quality of group performance and individual performance, 1920–1957. *Psychol. Bull.*, 1958, 55, 337–372. [86]

Luchins, A. S. Mechanization in problem solving: The effect of Einstellung. *Psychol. Monogr.*, 1942, 54, No. 6 (Whole No. 248). [66]

Luria, A. R. *The role of speech in the regulation of normal and abnormal behavior.* New York: Liveright Publishing Corporation, 1961.

McConnell, T. R. Discovery vs. authoritative identification in the learning of children. *Stud. Educ.*, 1934, 9, (5), 13–60. [81–82, 86, 89, 145]

MacKinnon, D. W. Personality and the realization of creative potential. *Amer. Psychologist*, 1965, 20, 273–81. [155]

Mackworth, N. H. Originality. *Amer. Psychologist*, 1965, 20, 51–66. [78]

Maier, N. R. F. Reasoning in humans I: On direction. *J. comp. Psychol.*, 1930, 10, 115–143. [65–66, 147–148]

Mandler, G. From association to structure. *Psychol. Rev.*, 1962, 69, 415–427. [55]

Mechner, F. *Programming for automated instruction.* New York: Basic Systems, 1961. (Mimeo) [16–18]

Mechner, F. Science education and behavioral technology. In R. Glaser (Ed.), *Teaching machines and programmed learning. II: Data and directions.* Washington: National Educational Association, 1965. [23–24]

Melton, A. W. Learning. In W. S. Monroe (Ed.), *Encyclopedia of educational research.* (rev. ed.). New York: Macmillan Company, 1950. Pp. 668–690. [138, 149]

Montessori, Maria. *The Montessori method.* New York: Frederick A. Stokes Company, 1912. [40]

Montessori, Maria. *The advanced Montessori method: Spontaneous activity in education.* New York: Frederick A. Stokes Co., 1917. [40–41]

Moss, J., Jr. An experimental study of the relative effectiveness of the direct-detailed and the directed discovery methods of teaching letterpress imposition. Unpublished doctoral dissertation. Urbana, Ill.: University of Illinois, 1960. [63]

Mowrer, O. H. *Learning theory and behavior.* New York: Wiley and Sons, Inc., 1960. [136]

Noble, C. E. Meaningfulness and familiarity. In C. N. Cofer and Barbara S. Musgrave (Eds.), *Verbal behavior and learning.* New York: McGraw-Hill, 1963. Pp. 76–119. [139]

Olson, D. R. Note on Haslerud and Meyers' transfer-of-principles experiment. *J. educ. Psychol.,* 1965, 56, 107–108. [82–83]

Orata, P. T. Recent research studies on transfer of training with implications for the curriculum, guidance, and personnel work. *J. educ. Res.,* 1941, 35, 81–101.

Osgood, C. E. *Method and theory in experimental psychology.* New York: Oxford University Press, 1953. [55]

Osgood, C. E., Suci, G. J., and Tannenbaum, P. H. *The measurement of meaning.* Urbana, Illinois: University of Illinois Press, 1957. [55]

Osler, Sonia F., and Fivel, Myrna W. Concept attainment: I. The role of age and intelligence in concept attainment by induction. *J. exp. Psychol.,* 1961, 62, 1–8. [90]

Osler, Sonia F., and Trautman, Grace. Concept attainment: II. Effect of stimulus complexity upon concept attainment at two levels of intelligence. *J. exp. Psychol.,* 1961, 62, 9–13. [90]

Page, D. P. *Theory and practice of teaching.* New York: A. S. Barnes and Company, 1885. [183]

Pincus, M. An adventure in discovery. *The Arithmetic Teacher,* 1964, 11, 28–29.

Postman, L. The present status of interference theory. In C. N. Cofer (Ed.), *Verbal learning and verbal behavior.* New York: McGraw-Hill, 1961. Pp. 152–179. [139]

Postman, L. Short-term memory and incidental learning. In A. W. Melton (Ed.), *Categories of human learning.* New York: Academic Press, 1964. Pp. 145–201. [67]

Postman, L., and Sassenrath, J. The automatic action of verbal rewards and punishments. *J. gen. Psychol.,* 1961, 65, 109–136. [67]

Ray, W. E. Pupil discovery vs. direct instruction. *J. exp. Educ.,* 1961, 29, 271–280. [63, 88]

Reed, H. B. The learning and retention of concepts: II. The influence of length of series: III. The origin of concepts. *J. exp. Psychol.,* 1946a, 36, 166–179. [66]

Reed, H. B. The learning and retention of concepts. IV. The influence of the complexity of the stimuli. *J. exp. Psychol.,* 1946b, 36, 252–261.

Ripple, R. E., and Rockcastle, V. N. (Eds.), Piaget rediscovered. *J. res. sci. teaching,* 1964, 2, (3). And as a separate, Cornell University, 1964. [79]

Rowlett, J. D. An experimental comparison of direct-detailed and directed discovery methods of teaching orthographic projection principles and skills. Unpublished doctoral dissertation. Urbana, Ill.: University of Illinois, 1960. [63]

Russell, W. A. Purpose and the problem of associative selectivity. In C. N. Cofer and Barbara S. Musgrave (Eds.), *Verbal behavior and learning.* New York: McGraw-Hill, 1963. Pp. 258–271. [139]

Sassenrath, J. M. Transfer of learning without awareness. *Psychol. Rep.,* 1962, 10, 411–420. [67]

Saugstad, P. Problem-solving as dependent on availability of functions. *Brit. J. Psychol.,* 1955, 46, 191–198. [66]

Saugstad, P., and Raaheim, K. Problem-solving, past experience and availability of functions. *Brit. J. Psychol.,* 1960, 51, 97–104.

Schlosberg, H., and Solomon, R. L. Latency of response in a choice discrimination. *J. exp. Psychol.,* 1943, 33, 22–39. [19]

Schultz, R. W. Problem solving behavior and transfer. *Harvard educ. Rev.*, 1960, 30, (1), 61–77. [71]

Schwab, J. J. What do scientists do? *Behavorial Sci.*, 1960, 5, 1–27. [197]

Schwab, J. J., and Brandwein, P. F. *The Teaching of Science*. Cambridge: Harvard University Press, 1962.

Simon, H. A., and Newell, A. Information processing in computer and man. *Amer. Scientist*, 1964, 52, 281–300. [24]

Simon, H. A., and Simon, P. A. Trial and error search in solving difficult problems: Evidence from the game of chess. *Behavioral Sci.*, 1962, 7, 425–429. [24–25]

Smedslund, Jan. The acquisition of conservation of substance and weight in children. III. Extinction of conservation of weight acquired 'normally' and by means of empirical controls on a balance. *Scand. J. Psychol.*, 1961, 2, 85–87. [89]

Snyder, H. D. An impromptu discovery lesson in algebra. *The mathematics teacher*, 1964, 57, 415–416.

Spence, K. W. The differential response in animals to stimuli varying within a single dimension. *Psychol. Rev.*, 1937, 44, 430–444. [141]

Staats, A. W., and Staats, Carolyn K. *Complex human behavior*. New York: Holt, Rinehart and Winston, 1963. [139]

Stacey, C. L. The law of effect in retained situation with meaningful material. In Swenson, Esther J. et al, *Learning theory in school situations*. University of Minnesota Studies in Education. Minneapolis: University of Minnesota Press, 1949. Pp. 74–103. [57–58, 79]

Stanley, J. C., Jr. The role of instruction, discovery, and revision in early learning. *Elem. sch. J.*, 1949, 49, 455–458.

Stolurow, L. M., and Bergum, B. Learning diagnostic information-effects of direction of association and of prose versus paired-associate presentation. Air Force Personnel and Training Research Center, Technical Documentary Report Series, AFPTRC-TN57-12, ASTIA Document Number 113052, 1957. [69–70]

Suchman, J. R. Inquiry training in the elementary school. *Sci. Teacher*, 1960, 27, (7), 42–47.

Suchman, J. R. Inquiry training: Building skills for autonomous discovery. *Merrill-Palmer Quart. Behav. Develpm.*, 1961, 7, 147–169. [37–38]

Suchman, J. R. The child and the inquiry process. In A. H. Passow (Ed.), *Intellectual development: Another Look*. Washington, D. C.: Association for Supervision and Curriculum Development, 1964. [124]

Suppes, P., and Ginsberg, Rose. Application of a stimulus sampling model to children's concept formation with and without overt correction responses. *J. exp. Psychol.*, 1962, 63, 330–336. [20]

Swenson, Esther J. Organization and generalization as factors in learning, transfer, and retroactive inhibition. In Swenson, Esther J. et al, *Learning theory in school situations*. Minneapolis: University of Minnesota Press, 1949. Pp. 9–39. [46–48, 145]

Taba, Hilda. Learning by discovery: Psychological and educational rationale. Paper presented to the American Educational Research Association, Atlantic City, N. J., February, 1962.

Terrace, H. S. Discrimination learning with and without "errors." *J. exp. anal. Behav.*, 1963a, 6, (1), 1–27. [19]

Terrace, H. S. Errorless transfer of a discrimination across two continua. *J. exp. anal. Behav.*, 1963b, 6, (2), 223–232. [19]

Thiele, C. L. *The contribution of generalization to the learning of addition facts*. New York: Teachers College, Columbia University, 1938. [49, 81–82, 145]

Thorndike, E. L. Animal intelligence. An experimental study of the associative processes in animals. *Psychol. rev. monogr. Suppl.*, 1898, 2, No. 4 (Whole No. 8). [137]

Thorndike, E. L. *The psychology of wants, interests, and attitudes*. New York: Appleton-Century, 1935. [46]

Tolman, E. C. Cognitive maps in rats and men. *Psychol. Rev.*, 1948, 55, 189–208. [11, 97, 173]

Tomlinson, R. M. A comparison of four methods of presentation for teaching complex technical material. Unpublished doctoral dissertation. Urbana, Ill.: University of Illinois, 1962. [63]

Toulmin, S. *The philosophy of science*. London: Hutchison's University Library, 1953. [9–10]

Travers, R. M. W. *An introduction to educational research* (2nd ed.), New York: Macmillan, 1964. [83]

Underwood, B. J., and Richardson, J. Verbal concept learning as a function of instructions and dominance level. *J. exp. Psychol.*, 1956, 51, 229–238. [66–67]

Underwood, B. J., and Schulz, R. W. *Meaningfulness and verbal learning*. Chicago: Lippincott, 1960. [56, 139]

Underwood, B. J. Stimulus selection in verbal learning. In C. N. Cofer and Barbara S. Musgrave (Eds.), *Verbal behavior and learning*. New York: McGraw-Hill, 1963. Pp. 33–48. [139]

Underwood, B. J. The representativeness of rote verbal learning. In A. W. Melton (Ed.), *Categories of human learning*. New York: Academic Press, 1964. Pp. 47–78. [139]

White, R. W. Motivation reconsidered: The concept of competence. *Psychol. Rev.*, 1959, 66, 297–333. [53, 107]

Wickelgren, W. A. Cues that elicit analytic-deductive methods in concept attainment. *Brit. J. Psychol.*, 1964, 55, 143–154. [85]

Wittrock, M. C. Set applied to student teaching. *J. educ. Psychol.*, 1962, 53, 175–180. [66]

Wittrock, M. C. Effect of certain sets upon complex verbal learning. *J. educ. Psychol.*, 1963a, 54, 85–88. [62–63, 66]

Wittrock, M. C. Set to learn and proactive inhibition. *J. educ. Res.*, 1963b, 57, 72–75. [66]

Wittrock, M. C. Verbal stimuli in concept formation: Learning by discovery. *J. educ. Psychol.*, 1963c, 54, 183–190. [45]

Wittrock, M. C., Keislar, E. R., and Stern, Carolyn. Verbal cues in concept identification. *J. educ. Psychol.*, 1964, 55, 195–200. [63–65, 79]

Wittrock, M. C., and Keislar, E. R. Verbal cues in the transfer of concepts. *J. educ. Psychol.*, 1965, 56, 16–21. [64–65]

Wooten, W. The history and status of the school mathematics study group. In R. W. Heath (Ed.), *New curricula*. New York: Harper and Row, 1964. Pp. 35–53. [39]

Index

Accommodation and assimilation:
(see Assimilation and accommodation)
Activation, 103, 107
(see also Motivation)
Adaptive teaching systems
(see Teaching systems, adaptive)
Advice to schools, 91, 176, 182
AIBS (American Institute of Biological Sciences), 39
Algorithm, 85
for subtraction, 120–121
Analysis, rational:
contrasted with "educated intuition," 127
Answers:
separation of right from wrong, 128
Antecedent learning, 13
Anxiety, 90, 153–155
distinguished from expectancy of failure, 155
over competition, 157
Assimilation and accommodation, 118, 172
as types of discovery, 29–30
Association:
(see Learning, associative; Learning, verbal associate)
Attention, 151–153, 157–158
problems of, in young children, 152–153, 157
role in learning, 152–153
Attitude:
established by making discoveries, 87
of reflection on the habitual, 103–104, 107, 112
Authority:
independence of, in discovery learning, 90, 122
Autonomy, 12, 115, 121–122, 159, 163

Baboons, 106, 112
Behavior:
experimental analysis of, 13–14, 83
identification and prediction, 173–176
Behavioral repertoires, 13, 23
Behavioral objectives, 15
(see also Objectives, educational)
Bushmen, 105–106

CHEM (Chemical Education Material Study), 39
Classroom observation:
as research strategy, 164
Cognitive dissonance:
(see Dissonance theory)
Cognitive psychology:
(see Psychology, cognitive)
Cognitive skills:
and motivation, 151–152

Cognitive structures, 93
"Commando teaching":
distinguished from didactic, 129–130
distinguished from "messing around," 129–130
Committee on Learning and Educational Process, iii
Compatibility:
of new learning with some structured body of knowledge, 103, 107–109
Competence, 107
in educational design, 13–14
increased by contracting performance criteria, 22
as outcome variable, 13–14
standard of, 13
Competition:
anxiety over, 157
in group situation, 115, 131, 157
Computer-based instruction, 24–25, 67, 194
facilitation of data gathering, 167
Computer simulation, 164, 194
of chess playing, 24–25
of information processing, 24–25
Concept:
learning of *caliche*, 162
practice in using, 108–109
relation to name, 9, 162–163
significant, can be learned but not taught, 9
as theoretical construct, 162
as tool, 107–109
Concept acquisition:
and amount of information given, 142–143
(see also Concept learning)
Concept availability:
and principle learning, 146
Concept formation:
and negative instances, 113, 143
for Wittgenstein, 108–109
(see also Concept learning)
Concept learning, 140–143, 149, 162–163
definition, 140
differences between animal and human subjects, 142–143
differences between younger and older children, 162
as discovery process, 140–143
distinguished from associative learning, 141
effect of negative and positive exemplars, 18, 113, 143
examples, 140–143
guidance in, 142–143
by induction, 17–18
as internal symbolic cue, 141

213

PRINTED IN U.S.A.